Poverty in Plenty

A Human Development Report for the UK

Edited by
Jane Seymour
for UNED-UK

EARTHSCAN

Earthscan Publications Ltd, London and Sterling, VA

NATIONAL
LOTTERY
CHARITIES
BOARD

Poverty in Plenty is funded by
the National Lottery Charities Board
and Oxfam GB

First published in the UK and USA in 2000
by Earthscan Publications Ltd

A catalogue record for this book is available from the British Library

ISBN: 1 85383 707 5

Typesetting by JS Typesetting, Wellingborough, Northamptonshire
Printed and bound in the UK by Bell & Bain Ltd, Glasgow
Cover design by Declan Buckley
Cover photo by Jon Walter, Third Avenue

For a full list of publications please contact:

Earthscan Publications Ltd
120 Pentonville Road, London, N1 9JN, UK
Tel: +44 (0)20 7278 0433
Fax: +44 (0)20 7278 1142
Email: earthinfo@earthscan.co.uk
http://www.earthscan.co.uk

22883 Quicksilver Drive, Sterling, VA 20166-2012, USA

Earthscan is an editorially independent subsidiary of Kogan Page Ltd and publishes in association
with WWF-UK and the International Institute for Environment and Development

This book is printed on elemental chlorine-free paper

Contents

Part I: Issues and Context

Part II: Key Elements and the UK Policy Agenda

Part III: The Way Forward

Part IV: Reference Section – HDR-UK Report Statistics at Regional Level

List of Figures, Boxes and Tables

Figures

Boxes

Tables

List of Main Contributors

Chapter 1

Jane Seymour, Editor, *Human Development Report*, UNED-UK
David Gordon, Head of the Centre for the Study of Social Exclusion and Social Justice, and
  Director of the Townsend Centre for International Poverty Research, University of Bristol
Sanjiv Lingayah, Centre for Participation, New Economics Foundation

Chapter 2

Chris Church, Community Development Foundation
Simon Bullock, Friends of the Earth (Environmental Justice, pp12–18)
Carolyn Stephens, London School of Hygiene and Tropical Medicine

Chapter 3

Sanjiv Lingayah
David Gordon*
Sakiko Fukuda-Parr, Director, Human Development Report Office, UNDP (Making
  Comparisons, pp33–36)
Carolyn Stephens
Rebecca Tunstall, Department of Social Policy and Centre for the Analysis of Social Exclusion,
  London School of Economics (The Social Exclusion Unit, pp49–53)
Alison Gilchrist, Community Development Foundation (In the Regions, pp53–4)

Chapter 4

Damian Killeen, Director of the Poverty Alliance

Chapter 5

Sally Hall, on behalf of the Association for Environment-Conscious Building
Jane Seymour

---

* Some of this work received funding from an ESRC seminar series grant for 'Developing Poverty Measures:
Research in Europe'

Chapter 6

Katherine Duffy, Principal Lecturer at the Business School, De Montfort University, and Director of Research for the Council of Europe Initiative in Human Dignity and Social Exclusion

Chapter 7

Simon Bullock (An Equitable Environment, pp97–9)
Gabriel Chanan, Director of Research and Dissemination, Community Development Foundation
Chris Church
Sanjiv Lingayah
Carolyn Stephens

Appendix 1

David Gordon and Danny Dorling,* University of Bristol

Editorial Group

Peter Beresford/Fran Branfield, Centre for Citizen Participation, Brunel University
Fran Bennett, Oxfam GB
Simon Bullock, Friends of the Earth
Tony Colman, MP
Karen Dugdale, Communities Against Poverty
Nick Robins, International Institute of Environment and Development
Peter Bargh, Preston Borough Council

Project Coordinator

Tom Bigg, UNED-UK

Funders

National Lottery Charities Board
Oxfam GB

---

* Danny Dorling is now at the University of Leeds.

UNED-UK

The United Nations Environment and Development – UK Committee (UNED-UK) was set up in the wake of the United Nations Conference on Environment and Development (known as the Earth Summit) to promote environmental protection and sustainable development at the global, national and local levels. We are a membership organisation, providing organisations and individuals in the UK and other countries with up-to-the-minute information on the broad range of activities in the UK and the UN which are designed to realise the objectives established at the Earth Summit in Rio in 1992.

We also encourage the active involvement of all sectors of society in making progress towards the key elements of sustainable development, emphasising the importance of integrating the environmental, social and economic elements in a coherent, comprehensive policy framework. UNED-UK now functions within the host organisation of UNED Forum which is working to build momentum among a wide range of actors in preparation for the Rio +10 Earth Summit in 2002.

For more information, visit our website at: http://**www.earthsummit2002.org**.

Foreword

The annual UNDP *Human Development Report* (HDR) is unapologetically independent and provocative. This has enabled us to present clear messages which identify the societal and economic elements necessary for all human beings to achieve productive and fulfilling lives, and the barriers to progress. In recent years the HDR has focused on issues of poverty, production and consumption, globalisation and human rights. In addition, each year we produce indices that aggregate statistics and allow comparisons between countries on broad themes, including human development, gender empowerment and human poverty. To complement these global efforts we have developed a programme of national HDRs which assess levels of human development within countries, and help create a policy environment for achieving human development goals.

UNED-UK's report *Poverty in Plenty* breaks new ground in two ways. It is the first national HDR to focus on an industrialised country and it is the first to be produced by a non-governmental organisation (NGO). At all levels of development it is essential that people are able to lead long and healthy lives, to have access to knowledge and information and to receive the resources necessary for a decent standard of living. This book explores the degree to which these basic requirements are met in the UK. It considers the barriers and incentives which currently exist, and puts forward ways in which improvements could be made.

There are two further elements of this report that I welcome. The first is the use of UNDP's Human Poverty Index (HPI), which has been calculated here at local level and clearly shows the gap between the areas of the UK with the best and the worst human development. The second is the strong emphasis on the need for greater consistency between work intended to tackle poverty and deprivation on the one hand, and initiatives focusing on sustainable development and the environment on the other.

While problems of poverty and deprivation are less extreme in countries such as the UK than in some other parts of the world, the human development message is still highly relevant. There are many people who suffer through inadequate housing, insufficient means to guarantee a nutritious diet and the absence of secure, rewarding and remunerative employment. Access to positions of influence for women remains low, and the gap between the richest and the poorest continues to rise. Yet *Poverty in Plenty* also demonstrates that there are positive messages from a wealth of initiatives taken by NGOs and by official bodies, and increasing evidence that these issues are moving to the heart of UK policy in a range of important areas.

Sakiko Fukuda-Parr
Director, Human Development Report Office
UNDP
New York

Preface

Poverty diminishes people. It condemns them to a continuous struggle to find the means for a basic existence. It constricts their ability to acquire skills and resources and to make the most of any opportunities. The vicious circle of poverty perpetuating itself over years and from one generation to the next is all too familiar within families, wider communities and even whole countries. This report looks at how poverty undermines human development in the UK.

The United Nations Development Programme (UNDP) produces an annual *Human Development Report* (HDR) on the state of development throughout the world. This provides a regular and comprehensive picture of the trends in human development, including health and life expectancy, literacy and educational attainment, access to resources and the prevalence of inequality and poverty.

Over the years, the successive reports record the progress which the world has made in reducing the impact of some of the major diseases and in spreading literacy. They chart the gradual improvement in the availability of food and the emergence of new businesses. At the same time, however, they underline how much remains to be done to set the world on a path of more sustainable development.

The HDR highlights the differences in life expectancy in different countries and the prevalence of disease. It shows progress in education, and the large areas of ignorance that remain. It draws attention to the great variations in access to resources in the world, both between and within countries, and the very unequal shares of wealth and opportunity available to different groups and individuals.

The HDR is frequently used to focus attention on the problems – and successes – of the developing world. But it contains much that is relevant and important to the developed world. Poverty may be harsher and more widespread in the developing world but it also persists as a blight, a reproach and a challenge in parts of many developed countries, including our own.

Poverty in Plenty therefore analyses the lessons of the UN's HDR for the UK. The results are disturbing: they reveal clearly and explicitly the disparities between one area of the country and another. Problems reinforce one another, and it is no surprise that the most deprived areas experience multiple problems including below average health and life expectancy, low attainment levels and poor job prospects, poor environments and lack of access to facilities.

This volume exposes the extent of these disparities and the depth of the poverty within plenty which our society displays. There is more inequality in Britain than in most other developed countries, and this accentuates the problems of the most deprived groups and individuals.

The analysis presented here should be read and taken to heart by all those concerned with issues of deprivation and social exclusion. We need to reinforce the message that these problems are strongly correlated with bad environments and poor access to opportunities. The challenge of sustainable development is to ensure that economic, social and environmental objectives are pursued in an integrated way. *Poverty in Plenty* shows how far we are from achieving that in some parts of the country, and how much we need integrated approaches to tackle the problems.

It is not enough to develop environmental policies that ignore or even exacerbate their impacts on vulnerable groups or communities. But it is equally not sufficient to tackle problems of poverty and social exclusion simply by promoting the creation of new jobs or social measures that do nothing to improve the poor environments and lack of access which hold people back in some of the most deprived communities.

The work of the Social Exclusion Unit and many other recent government initiatives are beginning to make an impact on the problems. This book seeks to build on those enterprises and offers suggestions for further action in the UK. Above all, it emphasises the importance of a well-rounded integrated approach which puts together social, economic and environmental measures in a way that will achieve true sustainable development and eliminate poverty.

The new integrated community strategies for sustainable development which local authorities in England and Wales are to develop following the current Local Government Bill should help local communities to develop more rounded approaches to this whole complex of issues. But such communities will need help and support from government and other agencies if they are really to break out of the cycle of deprivation which *Poverty in Plenty* reveals. Community-based, nationally supported partnerships for change could be the way forward.

It is true that no country has yet found an ideal path to achieving sustainable development. All should be able to learn from the experience of others. This book is a valuable contribution to that learning process.

Derek Osborn
Chairman, UNED Forum
London

Editor's Acknowledgements

A large number of organisations and individuals have taken time to comment on and contribute to this report, many at extremely short notice. I'd like to thank particularly the contributors and members of the editorial team whose hard work, continual support and good humour made the task of editing this report possible.

I'd also like to thank the staff in the UNDP Human Development Report office, especially Sakiko Fukuda-Parr and Richard Jolly, for their encouragement, and those in the UNED-UK office – especially Tom Bigg, Claire Nugent and Amy Cruse – for being there when the going got tough.

The Poverty in Plenty Project was made possible by funding from the National Lottery Charities Board and Oxfam GB.

Jane Seymour
London
June 2000

List of Acronyms and Abbreviations

BPCV	Bath Place Community Venture
CFC	chlorofluorocarbon
CFSP	European Common Foreign and Security Policy
CITES	Convention on International Trade in Endangered Species of Wild Fauna and Flora
CSA	Child Support Agency
CSD	UN Commission on Sustainable Development
DETR	Department of the Environment, Transport and the Regions
DSS	Department of Social Security
DTI	Department of Trade and Industry
EU	European Union
FAO	Food and Agriculture Organization (of the UN)
FES	Family Expenditure Survey
GATS	General Agreement on Trade in Services
GATT	General Agreement on Tariffs and Trade
GDI	Gender Development Index
GDP	gross domestic product
GEM	gender empowerment measure
GNP	gross national product
HBAI	*Households Below Average Income* series
HDI	Human Development Index
HDR	*Human Development Report*
HEES	Home Energy Efficiency Scheme
HPI	Human Poverty Index
HPI-1	Human Poverty Index for Developing Countries
HPI-2	Human Poverty Index for Industrial Countries
IALS	International Adult Literacy Survey
ILO	International Labour Organization
IMF	International Monetary Fund
JSA	Jobseeker's Allowance
LA21	Local Agenda 21
LETS	Local Exchange and Trading Scheme
LTU	long-term unemployed
MAI	Multilateral Agreement on Investment
NACAB	National Association of Citizens' Advice Bureaux
NAFTA	North American Free Trade Agreement
NDC	New Deal for Communities
NDYU	New Deal for the Young Unemployed

NHS	National Health Service
NGO	non-governmental organisation
NIESR	National Institute for Economic and Social Research
NSNR	National Strategy for Neighbourhood Renewal
OECD	Organisation for Economic Co-operation and Development
ONS	Office for National Statistics
ORB	Opinion Research Business
OT	other training
PAT	policy action teams
PCB	polychlorinated biphenyl
PIC	prior informed consent
PSE	poverty and social exclusion (survey)
RDA	regional development agencies
RPI	retail price index
SERPLAN	South East Regional Planning Conference
SEU	Social Exclusion Unit
SMR	standardised mortality ratio
SPS	sanitary and phytosanitary
TBT	technical barriers to trade
TfW	Training for Work
TRIPS	trade-related intellectual property rights
UAE	United Arab Emirates
UN	United Nations
UNCED	United Nations Conference on Environment and Development
UNCTAD	United Nations Conference on Trade and Development
UNDP	United Nations Development Programme
UNED-UK	United Nations Environment and Development–UK Committee
WCED	World Commission on Environment and Development
WFTC	working families tax credit
WHO	World Health Organization
WTO	World Trade Organization

Part I

Issues and Context

Chapter 1

Why a UK Human Development Report?

Introduction

When the term 'sustainable development' was defined by the World Commission on Environment and Development (WCED), its head, Gro Harlem Brundtland, made it clear that the concept included an assurance that those who lived in poverty should receive a fair share of the resources they needed to ensure their own development. Writing that sustainable development ensures development 'meets the needs of the present without compromising the ability of future generations to meet their own needs', she didn't mean that only some sections of the world's populations had a right to have their needs met.

The WCED's report *Our Common Future* (1987) underlined the fact that sustainable development contained two key concepts:

1 *'the concept of "needs", in particular the essential needs of the world's poor, to which overriding priority should be given';* and

2 *'the idea of limitations imposed by the state of technology and social organization on the environment's ability to meet present and future needs'.*

But at the United Nations Conference on Environment and Development (UNCED), or what came to be known as the Earth Summit, in Rio in 1992, the media concentration on the environmental aspects of sustainable development drowned out that first key element: tackling poverty. Except for some notable exceptions, until very recently there has been a distinct lack of enthusiasm among people working on anti-poverty and environmental issues for taking on board each other's agenda. This is reflected in the tension between policies designed to tackle poverty and those which focus on protecting the environment, from global down to local levels. These problems are explored further in Chapter 2 and ways of resolving them are considered throughout the rest of this book.

What is a Human Development Report?

Each year the United Nations Development Programme (UNDP) publishes a *Human Development Report* (HDR) that provides an assessment of how the countries of the world are doing in human development terms. Human development is about putting people at the heart of development, emphasising their needs, aspirations and capabilities. It is defined as:

'. . . a process of enlarging people's choices. In principle, these choices can be infinite and can change over time.

But at all levels of development, the three essential ones are for people to lead a long and healthy life, to acquire knowledge and to have access to the resources needed for a decent standard of living. If these essential choices are not available, many other opportunities remain inaccessible.

But human development does not end there. Additional choices, highly valued by many people, range from political, economic and social freedom to opportunities for being creative and productive and enjoying personal self-respect and guaranteed human rights.

Human development thus has two sides. One is the formation of human capabilities – such as improved health, knowledge and skills. The other is the use people make of their acquired capabilities – for productive purposes, for leisure or for being active in cultural, social and political affairs. If the scales of human development do not finely balance the two sides, much human frustration can result.

According to the concept of human development, income clearly is only one option that people would like to have, though certainly an important one. But it is not the sum-total of their lives. The purpose of development is to enlarge all human choices, not just income.

The concept of human development is much broader than the conventional theories of economic development. Economic growth models deal with expanding GNP [gross national product] rather than enhancing the quality of human lives. Human resource development treats human beings primarily as an input in the production process – a means rather than an end. Welfare approaches look at human beings as beneficiaries and not as agents of change in the development process.

The basic needs approach focuses on providing material goods and services to deprived population groups rather than on enlarging human choices. Human development, by contrast, brings together the production and distribution of commodities and the expansion and use of human capabilities. [Whilst] encompassing these earlier concerns, human development goes beyond them. It analyses all issues in society whether economic growth, trade, employment, political freedom or cultural values, from the perspective of people. It thus focuses on enlarging human choices – and it applies equally to developing and industrialised countries.' (UNDP, 1995)

In other words, human development is a process of enlarging people's choices by ensuring they have the capacity to lead long and healthy lives, and that they enjoy access to knowledge and the resources needed for a decent standard of living. These elements are contained in the Human Development Index (HDI) which the HDRs calculate for each country. However, the conditions required for human development also include a sense of community, opportunities to be creative and productive, self-respect and human rights. The process of achieving them needs to be equitable, participatory, productive – and sustainable. HDRs also include a whole range of indicators that measure these elements of a country's progress. They do not present new research but pull together a wide range of statistics to focus on human development.

HDRs reveal some interesting perspectives. For example, a country such as the United Arab Emirates (UAE), which has a high gross domestic product (GDP) per capita of US$19,115, fails to make the top 40 countries in human development terms while Sweden, with a comparable US$19,790 GDP per capita, ranks in sixth position. Conversely, Costa Rica, which has a GDP per capita of only US$6,650, is just a couple of couple of places behind the UAE in human development terms, in 45th position (UNDP, 1999).

Each UNDP report takes a different theme, analysing that particular issue in terms of human development and suggesting a policy agenda. The 1997 report marked the United Nations International Year for the Eradication of Poverty by focusing on poverty and high-lighted its theme by generating a Human Poverty Index (HPI) for developing countries (UNDP, 1997). This enabled it to focus on inequalities and deprivation rather than the average achievement that the HDI measures. The following year the report also contained a revised HPI for industrialised countries (HPI-2). It is this index which will be used to make comparisons within the UK in Chapter 3.

The Definitions We Have Used

There is, currently, no official definition of poverty in the UK. However, during the past 25 years, the government has signed various international treaties and agreements which have incorporated definitions of poverty. In 1975, for example, the Council of Europe adopted a relative definition of poverty as 'Individuals or families whose resources are so small as to exclude them from the minimum acceptable way of life of the Member State in which they live' (EEC, 1977). The concept of 'resources' was defined as 'goods, cash income, plus services from public and private resources' (ibid).

On 19 December 1984, the European Commission extended the definition: 'the poor shall be taken to mean persons, families and groups of persons whose resources (material, cultural and social) are so limited as to exclude them from the minimum acceptable way of life in the Member State in which they live' (EEC, 1985).

Poverty has been defined differently in many contexts, and by academics, policy makers and people who consider themselves to be living in poverty. The definitions tend to fall into two areas: relative measures that define a person as poor within a particular population, whether income-based or more widely oriented, and poverty lines that set an absolute standard and so enable comparison between populations. After the UN World Summit for Social Development in Copenhagen in 1995, 117 countries, including the UK, agreed a programme of action which included com-mitments to eradicate 'absolute' and reduce 'overall' poverty, and made the drawing up of national poverty-alleviation plans a priority.

Absolute poverty is defined by the UN as 'A condition characterised by severe deprivation of basic human needs, including food, safe drinking water, sanitation facilities, health, shelter, education and information. It depends not only on income but also on access to services' (United Nations, 1995). Overall poverty has many elements, including 'lack of income and productive measures to ensure sustainable livelihoods . . . inadequate housing; unsafe environments and social discrimination and exclusion' (ibid). Since 1997 the Bristol Poverty Line Survey has attempted to use the UN definitions of absolute and overall poverty to measure levels of poverty in Britain. The latest results of using these definitions to measure poverty in this country are revealed in Box 3.1, p30.

This desire to determine a realistic income that would keep households out of poverty and give them an acceptable standard of living fuelled the Low Cost But Acceptable project of the Family Budget Unit based at King's College in London. Although the whole remit of this project is to determine sufficient income levels for households – and thereby suggest realistic benefit levels – the comprehensive nature of its work covers an approach which accepts that people should live rather than merely survive. The Department of Social Security approach, conversely, measures poverty by considering the income households have rather than what they need, taking as their basis for measuring living standards their 'Households Below Average Income' surveys. Although lack of income is the traditional way of identifying who is 'poor', considering poverty in human development terms allows policy makers to focus on what creates poverty and therefore tackle its causes. These issues are explored further in Chapter 3.

The focus on social exclusion in UK policy circles reflects this recognition that eradicating poverty is not simply a matter of income or, indeed, the economic growth of a country. Although economic growth can reduce poverty, the trickle-down effect is largely discredited. Instead, economic growth that is not 'pro-poor' produces a widening gap between rich and poor. This process and its effects are discussed further in Chapter 2.

Other aspects of poverty, such as lack of access to a healthy diet and not having a warm, safe home, are introduced in the relevant chapters of this report. However, when the term 'poverty' is used without qualification, the human development concept of poverty is being referred to.

There has also been much debate over the precise meaning of sustainable development. In this book we take the original definition in *Our Common Future* (WCED, 1987) as our reference point and explore some of the many ways in which it has meaning for all the aspects of our lives. We therefore take sustainable development to include an assurance of equitable access to resources.

However, the practice of measuring progress towards sustainable development is not long out of its infancy; the government only published a set of indicators that included this element late in 1999. The government indicators are discussed in Chapter 3. All the discussions of how sustainable development should be measured reflect the notion that it has many different aspects and the development to which it refers means much more than merely economic growth.

Social Capital: Making the Connection to Poverty

In saying that sustainable development means more than simply economic growth one has to take on different notions of wealth as well as poverty. The idea of social capital reflects this and emphasises the community rather than individuals' personal wealth. Social capital is the 'skills and knowledge, health, self-esteem and social networks of communities' (DETR, 1999), and links are increasingly being made between the creation of social capital at local level, and national quality of life. Some academics argue that strong social capital leads to benefits such as better health, lower crime, faster economic growth and greater support

for government. It is also relevant to poor communities in that it is a useful notion in evaluating the resources to be found in those communities (Smith, 1998). Unfortunately, it is those with the fewest resources who are often least able to generate and tap into social capital.

There is evidence that those who are economically poor are excluded from an active community life that could allow them access to a wealth of social capital. The most recent British Social Attitudes Report comments that 'those who probably have the most to gain from a vibrant community life – such as poorer communities with their higher turnover and lower resources – are in fact the least likely in practice to benefit from it' (Jowell et al, 1999). If this pattern of access to social capital could somehow be altered, then social and economic benefits could be redistributed as a result.

Because of the potential benefits that can accrue from social capital, it is part and parcel of a community-based anti-poverty strategy. Fortunately, some of the ways of changing patterns of access are well known, and they are highlighted in Chapter 7.

The Process

The United Nations Environment and Development UK committee (UNED-UK) was set up in the wake of the Earth Summit to promote environmental protection and sustainable development at global, national and local levels. As part of its programme it has set up round tables to bring together government, non-governmental organisations (NGOs) and other participants to address issues that are being tackled by the UN Commission on Sustainable Development (CSD). One of these addressed poverty and the idea came out of that round table to take a closer look at poverty in the UK in the form of a human development report. It was suggested that although the HDRs contain excellent data, their global approach means that the data on the UK are embedded within a mass of statistics. A report that focuses on the UK would make it easier to see how the UK compares with other countries, especially those elsewhere in Europe.

Subsequent to the round table on poverty, a wide range of organisations involved in analysing and tackling poverty were consulted on what a UK HDR should contain. A scoping report was produced in late 1998 which summed up the existing work on poverty and sustainable development and drew on the results of the consultation to provide a focus for considering the key elements of the UK HDR. A subsequent steering group meeting in Preston, which included participants from a wide range of different organisations, set up the parameters for the HDR which forms the

basis of this book. As a result its contents include:

- data on human development in the UK, including the HPI-2 at the level of British parliamentary constituencies;
- an analysis of how sustainable development is happening at local, regional and national levels and of anti-poverty initiatives in the current political context; and
- policy proposals on combining environmental initiatives with lifting people out of poverty.

A number of other countries, especially in eastern Europe, Africa and Asia, have also produced their own HDRs, but this is the first from an industrialised nation and the first to be put together by an NGO. UNED-UK's aim in producing this report is to build on the data and policy proposals of the UNDP's HDRs and show how these international issues are linked to our national debates. It also provides a bridge between sustainable development work and anti-poverty work in the UK.

Overall, this report is intended to go some way to redressing the balance between the environmental issues that have been uppermost in consideration of sustainable development in the UK and the importance the WCED, or Brundtland Commission as it became known, originally gave to tackling poverty. It looks at how developing sustainably can help tackle poverty but also at the tensions that are particularly likely to ensue if one element is considered without thought to how it impacts on the other. It does this within the context of human development, allowing us to not only look at the UK's performance against other countries but also to compare the different regions within the UK.

Structure of the Book

Care has been taken to present the information in this book in clear, non-technical language, supported throughout by useful graphics, tables and boxes. For quick reference, the main messages discussed in Chapters 2–7 are summarised at the end of each chapter.

Part I introduces the main issues and provides a quantitative evaluation of human development in the UK. Chapter 2 describes the context in which this book should be read and expands on the links made between environmental issues and tackling poverty. These are illustrated by looking at the issues surrounding environmental justice. It also describes the range of driving forces, from the global to the local level, that undermine different aspects of human development and consequently the policies which try to lift people out of poverty and create a more sustainable society. It goes on to show how the government is meeting its commitments in international trade treaties compared with its progress in responding to social and environmental agreements, in order to highlight these tensions. Chapter 3 looks at how we can measure our progress towards human development. It discusses different types of indicators, how different regions in the UK fare and how the UK compares with its counterparts in the industrialised world. It then looks at how the government is tackling some of the issues raised by analysing the work of the Social Exclusion Unit.

Part II considers three key elements of human development – food, shelter and material means – in the light of current government policy and how the policy agenda can be designed to deliver sustainability and tackle poverty. Chapter 4 looks at the issues of food poverty and developing food security. It shows that food security is essential to human development and discusses ways of creating it, using the Scottish experience as its focus. Chapter 5 looks at how the government can contribute to a sustainable housing policy in terms of planning and construction. It refers particularly to the issue of heat-efficient homes to illustrate how sustainable housing can prevent fuel poverty. Chapter 6 focuses on the government's efforts to combat poverty and social exclusion by increasing access to employment for those on a low income or who are otherwise less advantaged. As this book is focusing on linking poverty and sustainability policy, the framework of sustainable livelihoods is employed to review the extent to which the government's labour-market approach enables participants to escape and stay out of poverty.

Part III brings together the central themes of the book and looks at ways of pursuing human development through policy changes at all levels, and Part IV contains a range of statistics which reflect the many elements of human development in the UK, and the HPI-2 calculated for Britain's parliamentary constituencies.

Chapter 2

Human Development in Context

Setting the scene

Although the media's emphasis at Rio in 1992 was on the environment, the links between poverty and sustainable development were spelt out in Chapter 3 of Agenda 21, the conference's blueprint for the 21st century: 'A specific anti-poverty strategy is one of the basic conditions for ensuring sustainable development.' So, tackling poverty – within rich countries, as well as poorer ones – is an essential element of sustainable development. This is recognised in the UK sustainable development strategy's commitment to 'social progress which meets the needs of everyone' (DETR, 1999). Yet so far there has been little action within the UK to link this basic condition with other sustainability issues. There are still few visions of sustainable communities where poverty has been reduced or eradicated, for example, and few local authority Local Agenda 21 plans integrate their anti-poverty work with environmental issues. Poverty and environmental issues also remain inadequately integrated at a national policy level.

In the UK the relationship between environmental and social issues is complex. In inner cities poverty can degrade both the physical and social environment, making the area less attractive and drawing more people in the neighbourhood into the poverty trap – in other words, they suffer the consequences of being identified with a poor neighbourhood and from the lack of facilities in it. It can also reduce the opportunities for community-based action, by undermining people's confidence, their willingness and ability to participate, and the time they have available in which to take action. It can also lead to alienation, which can manifest itself destructively in anti-social behaviour.

Even though the poorest communities tend to be burdened with the worst environments, over the past three decades environmental action in the UK has overwhelmingly been led and dominated by the better-off, to the point where environmental concern has been described by some as a leisure activity for the middle classes. It is to be hoped that the emerging focus on environmental justice, a subject explored later in this chapter, will translate into more effective action to benefit the most deprived communities.

As we saw in the previous chapter, poverty itself has become a word of many meanings. Debates on poverty have moved to take on wider needs and rights arguments, moving towards an emphasis on social exclusion. However, all these developments include a key message: that improving the local environment is not an 'add-on' but is an essential part of rebuilding community spirit, which encourages those people benefiting from training and development programmes to stay in the area and help it improve.

Yet it is not surprising that it is taking time for these messages to be absorbed and acted on. At all levels – global, national and local – there are driving forces created by the economic and administrative structures of society. These often act against the human development that is at the heart of this book, and pit environmental and social aims against each other. For the rest of this chapter we explore these forces and tensions, and describe the context in which the rest of the book is set.

Thinking globally

Although there is increasing understanding that actions to protect the environment must also be 'pro-poor', we need to recognise that there are also driving forces originating in the international economic system that feed into the processes in this country. These forces are reflected, for example, in the way we are increasingly dependent on international corporations for employment in a world where changes in manufacturing processes and society have left the rich with a decreasing need for the labour power of the poor. An increasing reliance on technology reinforces this split: people with the 'right' skills are rewarded while those without those skills are excluded. These conditions are part of the broader phenomenon known as globalisation. Unless we understand and take account of how these forces shape our national systems we will not manage to put sustainable development on a sound basis.

Globalisation is partly responsible for the continued problems of inequality between and within countries. This is happening worldwide, as the latest World Bank data illustrate:

- World inequality is mainly driven by differences between countries; both have risen sharply over the long haul.
- The ratio of income per capita in the richest countries to that in the poorest countries has increased from 11:1 in 1870, to 38:1 in 1960 and 52:1 in 1985. The gap in the world distribution of income appears to have continued to widen over the recent decade, mainly due to an increase in differences between countries.
- The ratio between the average income of the richest 5 per cent of the world's countries and poorest 5 per cent increased from 78:1 in 1988 to 123:1 in 1993. (World Bank, 1999.)

The impact of these inequalities on human development is explored further in Chapter 3. Nevertheless, the driving forces for international inequalities are economic and social, and many analysts see direct links between these trends in inequality and globalisation. Globalisation is weakening the power of the nation state to regulate while it increases economic and social fragmentation, particularly of peripheral communities. It is also a strong counterweight to any attempts to reduce inequalities or environmental injustices. Also, the continuing actions of organisations such as the World Trade Organization (WTO) appear to be exacerbating rather then reducing inequalities by prioritising trade and economic concerns over environmental or social issues. (We explore this topic further in the final section of this chapter, but see Box 2.1 for more on the international monetary organisations.)

The links between inequality and globalisation are particularly well illustrated in those countries with large populations and a history of industrial development. The UK, for example, has relied historically on manufacturing industry, and has been hit particularly hard by technological changes. All countries in Europe have also been hit by shifts in employment opportunities towards countries with lower labour standards and costs. Un- and under-employment has become a major issue throughout the world and affects Europe and the UK badly. Europe's population of 872 million faced rising rates of unemployment until the mid-90s: rates rose from 7.8 per cent to 10.2 per cent between 1990 and 1995

Box 2.1 *The multilateral economic organisations*

Early in 2000 the International Monetary Fund (IMF) questioned the UK government's public spending plans, and old fears of inflation were raised. The relatively wealthy UK was facing an intrusion into its domestic economic management from an international financial institution – something that is the daily reality for most very poor countries around the world. Officially, the IMF should not interfere in the politics of nation states. In reality, the line between acting to preserve global financial stability and direct involvement in the domestic politics of sovereign states is frequently crossed. The World Bank too has been criticised from sometimes surprising sources.

The Economist magazine wrote in 1999 that 'The Fund and Bank have been hijacked by their major shareholders for overtly political ends. Whether in Mexico in 1994, Asia in 1997 or Russia throughout the 1990s, the institutions have become a more explicit tool of western, and particularly American, foreign policy.'

There is also a fear among developing countries about what might happen when all the major multilateral economic organisations – the IMF and World Bank together with the WTO – begin to coordinate their pursuit of particular economic ideas. Speaking at the first international conference on trade to follow the controversial Seattle meeting of the WTO in 1999, India's Minister of Commerce warned, 'We should be careful that in the name of coherence we do not create a networking behemoth which puts pressure on developing countries.'

At the same conference Michel Camdessus, the retiring head of the IMF, appeared to announce a startling U-turn in the IMF's approach. Poverty issues were rarely if ever discussed by the Fund. This time Camdessus described poverty as the 'ultimate threat' to society and 'morally outrageous'. Widening gaps between rich and poor, he said, would undermine our societies through 'confrontation, violence and civil disorder'.

Bank and Fund policies, distilled into structural adjustment programmes, traditionally promote economic deregulation as the best way for countries to develop and meet their social and environmental needs. But the United Nations Conference on Trade and Development (UNCTAD) said in 1999 that this approach had led to the 20th century closing on a note of crisis. It said that 'after more than a decade of liberal reforms in developing countries' their problems remained 'as acute as ever'. Conventional approaches had failed to tackle 'the deep rooted problems of poverty and underdevelopment'.

The IMF's recognition of poverty is welcome. But many will be worried that attached to this new awareness is a determination to continue with mostly unchanged policy proposals. A reinvigorated international effort to tackle poverty should be based, according to the IMF, on further liberalisation of trade and capital flows, in spite of the fact that these same policies have overseen the 'widening gaps between rich and poor within nations, and the gulf between the most affluent and most impoverished nations'.

The resistance to changing policy was further underlined by the publication of a World Bank research paper (2000) arguing the case for a focus on economic growth. It both asserted the need for economic liberalisation and attacked much of the development policy subscribed to by organisations such as the UNDP.

Bank, Fund and WTO policies represent the type of globalisation we have seen in the past few decades. But while some of the technologies that accompany and fuel these changes may be an unavoidable fact, according to Juan Somavia, the director general of the International Labour Organisation, the policies that go with them 'have been made by policy-makers and they can be changed by policy-makers' to expand the benefits of globalisation. Nothing is inevitable. The future of the global economy depends entirely on our efforts to shape it.

Source: Andrew Simms, New Economics Foundation

(UNECE, 1996). Unemployment is a major factor in the creation and perpetuation of social exclusion, while health inequalities result from social and economic inequalities between groups in most European states (Wilkinson, 1996).

Unemployment trends are linked closely to inequalities within countries, reflecting changes in demand for different types of labour. It has been suggested that the trends of the past couple of decades mean that within the global economic system the labour of more and more people is becoming permanently superfluous or even hinders its functioning – the price of inclusion in the globalised system being intensified exploitation and insecurity (Wolfe, 1995). The most disadvantaged groups in society are particularly vulnerable. In the UK, this theme is illustrated by the fact that youth employment is higher now than it was in 1991 and employment rates are higher among unskilled workers than among professional groups. The lack of skills within these two groups leaves them open to exploitation as they are less able to defend their working conditions, or indeed their jobs as they are replaced by other workers.

By driving employment trends, globalis-ation is contributing to inequality, poverty and social exclusion both globally and within the UK. These factors, in turn, encourage poor human development opportunities and gross health inequalities within the UK. In a rich country such as the UK, human development is linked strongly to equal access to the theoretically universal benefits of economic growth, including education, housing, transport and employment. However, this country's population does not have access to the benefits of economic growth on equal terms.

Economic inequalities impact profoundly on human development. They affect all opportunities throughout lifecycles and across generations. Children are most profoundly hit by inequalities in access to human development opportunities. Children of poorer countries, and of poorer families within wealthier countries, experience less healthy living and learning environments. They go on to experience reinforcement of this cycle in their adult lives, with their poor educational opportunities leading to less access to well-remunerated, secure and rewarding employment. The cycle then repeats itself in the next generation.

Environmental justice

This chapter argues that protecting the environment and social progress, including poverty alleviation and ensuring a decent quality of life for all, are the key aims of sustainable development. The complexities and interactions within these aims may be seen by considering first that a healthy, clean, safe environment is in fact a key element of social progress, and second that in some types of economic development, gains for one group of people can be made at the expense of both the environment and quality of life of others (see Box 2.2). An examination of environmental justice highlights these issues.

Ensuring that people have equitable access to environmental resources and do not suffer disproportionate environmental impacts is known as environmental justice. More specifically, the US Environmental Protection Agency defines it as:

'The fair treatment and meaningful involvement of all people, regardless of race, ethnicity, income, national origin or educational level with respect to the development, implementation and enforcement of environmental laws, regulation and policies. Fair treatment means that no population, due to policy or economic disempowerment, is forced to bear a disproportionate burden of the negative human health or environmental

---

Box 2.2 *Unsustainable growth*

The UNDP argues that all countries should pay much more attention to the quality rather than the quantity of growth. It identifies 'five damaging forms of growth:

1   jobless   growth which does not translate into jobs
2   voiceless   growth which is not matched by the spread of democracy
3   rootless   growth which snuffs out separate cultural identity
4   futureless   growth which despoils the environment
5   ruthless   growth where most of the benefits are seized by the rich.'

They call these types of growth 'neither sustainable nor worth sustaining'.

Source: UNDP, 1996

impacts of pollution or other environmental consequences resulting from industrial, municipal and commercial operations or the execution of federal, state, local and tribal programs and policies.' (EPA, 1999)

Environmental justice in the UK can be usefully thought of in two ways: first, as the effects of the UK's actions on people in other countries and generations; and, second, as the way effects of the UK's actions on people in the UK are distributed now.

A global imbalance

One country or one generation can impose environmental injustices upon another by taking more environmental resources than they are proportionately entitled to and leaving other countries to get by on very little – take for example the appropriation of developing countries' land for the cultivation of the industrialised world's food supply, or by imposing an environmental burden, such as an ozone hole, which has major effects on developing countries. The impacts of climatic change are already being seen to be greater in poorer countries, which are more vulnerable to extreme weather events and lack the financial

resources to respond – Hurricane Mitch in Central America, for example, or the recent flooding in Venezuela and Mozambique. Yet, the UK produces 2.5 per cent of the world's carbon dioxide emissions, but has only 1 per cent of the world's population (World Resources Institute, 1999).

Developing countries also suffer from the appropriation of environmental resources by richer countries. The UK is one of the richest 20 per cent of countries that use 80 per cent of global environmental resources (McLaren, 1998): the developing world's wood, land, minerals and metals are still being used predominantly for western development and raw commodity prices are low. Poorer people outside Europe are not the main beneficiaries of their own country's resources, a fact which is driven by a development model dominated and run by countries in the northern hemisphere. As the United Nations warned in 1996: 'The imbalances in economic growth, if allowed to continue, will produce a world gargantuan in its excesses and grotesque in its human and economic inequalities' (WHO, 1997).

Both of these issues are growing in importance as environmental problems become global and are viewed on a longer timescale. For example, current levels of greenhouse gas emissions are higher than the planet can tolerate. The majority of these gases are produced by industrialised countries. This is in itself an unequal appropriation of what should be held in common by the Earth's whole population, but to compound the injustice the majority of the negative impacts will be felt by future generations, and people in developing countries. The UK needs to reduce its consumption of environmental resources to an equitable share of what is globally available.

We can see the same pattern when we look at issues such as nuclear waste, consumption of environmental resources – rainforest timber, for instance – and the production of chemicals that accumulate and persist in the environment.

Environmental justice in the UK

Even in rich countries like the UK, there are major environmental problems which have profound impacts on people. These impacts are borne disproportionately. There is a lack of information, and more research is needed, but the available evidence strongly suggests that poor people suffer from the worst environmental conditions (see Box 2.3).

Policies as well as impacts can be deeply unjust. Substantive injustices are caused, in part, by the way policies are developed. For example, waste disposal policies are not designed to hurt poorer communities, but can do so through the decision-making process if wealthier groups can affect decisions more easily and avoid any risk of harm. In 1998, residents of Greengairs, a relatively poor community in Scotland, found that a local landfill operator was accepting toxic PCB (polychlorinated biphenyl) waste from Hertfordshire in England, a much richer area. Dumping of this waste is illegal in England, but regulations are less strict in Scotland. Community campaigning brought an end to the dumping and also secured other environmental and safety improvements (Scandrett et al, 2000), but inadequate enforcement of regulations, derisory fines and poor ident-

ification of pollution levels are still major problems (McBride, 1999).

An analysis of current UK performance shows a lot remains to be done. The UK has major environmental injustices, with poorer people in the UK suffering worse environmental impacts and having less access to basic resources than their richer counterparts. Environmental injustice is a component of poverty and inequality in the UK. The UK is also imposing major environmental injustices on other countries and future generations.

Friends of the Earth Scotland summarised these links in this way:

'Our conception of environmental justice therefore brings together the need for global and intergenerational equity in resource consumption and ecological health, with a priority to act with those who are the victims of that inequality in the present. No less than a decent environment for all, no more than our fair share of the Earth's resources' (Scandrett et al, 2000).

The extent of environmental injustice in the UK effectively demolishes the argument that the poor have less reason to care about the environment, because poorer people live in the worst environments and their quality of life is reduced as a direct result. Poor communities may be less concerned about 'traditional' environmental issues, such as tropical rainforests, but surveys have shown they care more than rich people about their local environment – on issues such as public transport and litter. 'Environment' to most people means 'where I live'. This highlights the point that environment is a key factor in people's quality of life, and that a poor environment is an indicator of poverty. It is also worth noting that traditional environmental issues such as rainforest destruction also have major social and poverty dimensions and, again, it is usually the poorest people in those localities who suffer most from environmental damage.

Box 2.3 *Examples of environmental injustice in the UK*

Pollution

Factories emitting toxic pollutants are located with disproportionate frequency in poor communities. Research that compares the government's data on factories that pollute the environment with the income data for particular areas shows that:

- There are 662 polluting factories in the UK in areas with an average household income of less than £15,000, and only 5 in postcode areas where the average household income is £30,000 or more.
- The more factories there are in an area, the lower the average income. In Teesside, one area has 17 large factories. The average income in the area is £6,200, 64 per cent less than the national average.
- The poorest families (defined as households with incomes of less than £5,000) are twice as likely to have a polluting factory in their immediate area as families with an income of £60,000 or more.
- In London, more than 90 per cent of polluting factories are in areas with below average income, and in the North East the figure is over 80 per cent.

Polluting factories concentrated in low income areas around Merseyside

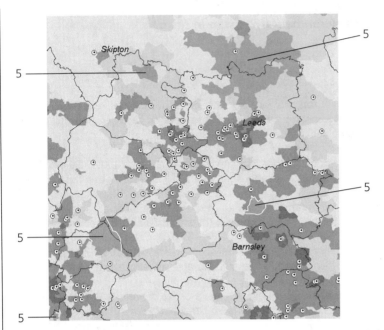

Polluting factories concentrated in low income areas in West Yorkshire

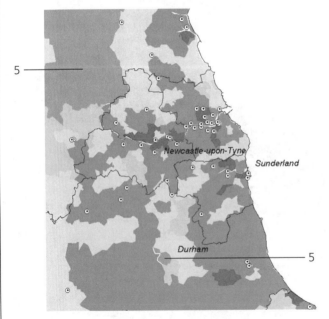

Polluting factories concentrated in low income areas around Tyneside

Source: Friends of the Earth, April 1999, from mapping data supplied by Kingswood Ltd and income data supplied by Business Geographics Ltd

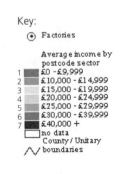

Key:

⊙ Factories

Average income by postcode sector

1	£0 -£9,999
2	£10,000 - £14,999
3	£15,000 - £19,999
4	£20,000 - £24,999
5	£25,000 - £29,999
6	£30,000 - £39,999
7	£40,000 +
☐	no data

⋀ County / Unitary boundaries

Note: In order to distinguish income areas of £0–£9,999 (1) and £10,000–£14,999 (2) from areas of £30,000–£39,999 (6) and £25,000–£24,995 (5) respectively, areas 5 and 6 are annotated. There are no areas of average income >£40,000 (7).

POVERTY IN PLENTY

Transport

A recent government inquiry into inequalities in health noted that 'The burden of air pollution tends to fall on people experiencing disadvantage, who do not enjoy the benefits of the private motorised transport which causes the pollution' (Acheson, 1998). As with pollution, road accidents affect the poorest people worst. Children in social class 5 are five times more likely to be killed in road accidents than children in social class 1.

In the following maps of south-east England, deprivation and pollution from vehicles can be seen concentrated in central London while car ownership is higher outside the city itself.

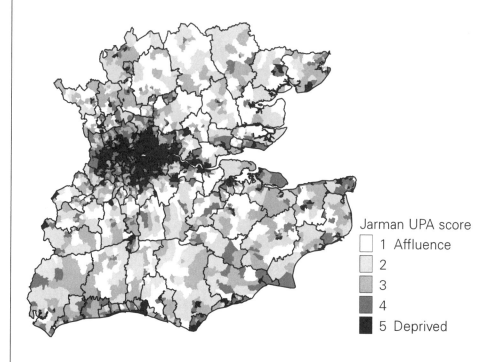

Jarman UPA score

☐ 1 Affluence
☐ 2
▨ 3
▨ 4
■ 5 Deprived

Deprivation (ward)

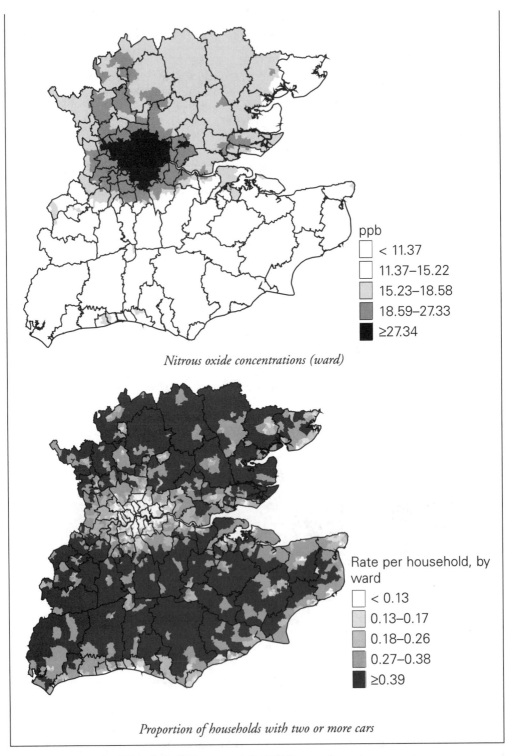

Nitrous oxide concentrations (ward)

ppb
☐ < 11.37
☐ 11.37–15.22
▨ 15.23–18.58
▨ 18.59–27.33
■ ≥27.34

Proportion of households with two or more cars

Rate per household, by ward
☐ < 0.13
☐ 0.13–0.17
▨ 0.18–0.26
▨ 0.27–0.38
■ ≥0.39

Source: McLaren et al, 1999 (pollution); Stevenson et al, 1998 (transport)

A National View

The national policy agenda has highlighted the tension between those tackling poverty and those focusing on the environment. For example, green taxes were widely discussed in the early 1990s and the first such tax, VAT on fuel, was clearly going to have a disproportionate impact on the poor, who spend a much higher percentage of their disposable income on fuel costs. The initial support of some environmental groups for this measure led to disputes with social sector groups and finally an agreement that such taxes would only be acceptable if they did not penalise the poor.

Other tensions have emerged: building homes in the countryside has been an issue over which there has been much dispute, for instance. These disputes have been characterised by a split between those seeking to maintain their rural communities by providing more homes for local people, and those environmental campaigners who have been perceived and portrayed as wishing to preserve the countryside unchanged. This split has increasingly been seen as misguided: in many cases the new homes planned are far too expensive for the local people who need them. The real argument about how to preserve and strengthen rural communities while protecting the countryside is more complex.

These tensions are the inevitable result of considering issues in isolation. Yet the UK government's sustainable development strategy's key objective is 'social progress for all'. This and other commitments, such as the eradication of child poverty, means that ensuring the basic minima of a healthy home, a livelihood, access to a healthy, affordable diet and a healthy environment for all people should be a fundamental priority for the government. Addressing unequal distribution of environmental impacts and securing universal access to resources is a key element in achieving this goal. In the next chapter we consider one way in which the government has tried to resolve these conflicts by looking at the work of the Social Exclusion Unit (SEU). First, however, we illustrate how these tensions surface by comparing how the UK meets its commitments in social and environmental agreements with those in trade agreements.

The UK's Treaty Commitments

Since the end of the Second World War and the creation of the UN, the UK has signed up to many conventions, treaties and international laws. These, in theory and practice, affect policies within the UK, but also underline the UK's commitment to international policy. At the end of the 20th century there was a series of UN summits that drew up treaties and agreements to safeguard human development and environmental sustainability. In 1992 at the UN Conference on Environment and Development in Rio, the UK was among the many governments that signed up to the Conference's key proposals to move the world towards sustainable development. It acknowledged the role of the UK population's consumption patterns in producing climate change, the necessity for strong action on poverty and the need to reduce consumption of natural resources. Specific policies were proposed on reducing carbon emissions, developing global support for sustainable development in less developed countries, and managing the reduction of overconsumption in industrialised countries, such as the UK. A key mechanism for implementation of the recommendations was the unwieldy but important Agenda 21, the plan for sustainable development for the 21st century to be implemented at local, national and international level.

Three years later, in 1995, Beijing hosted the Fourth World Conference on Women, at which representatives from 189 countries adopted a 'platform for action' for the advancement of women that reflected international commitment to goals of development, equality and peace. This included action on: poverty; education and training; healthcare; violence against women; armed conflict; inequality in economic structures and policies, power and decision making; institutional mechanisms; the human rights of women; communication systems; environment and natural resources; and the rights of the girl child. The platform focused on improving gender equity throughout the world. In the same year, the Copenhagen UN World Summit on Social Development focused on three core problems: poverty, unemployment and social exclusion. This summit adopted an extensive array of ambitious commitments with an emphasis on creating political, economic and legal environments that promote social development. Occurring at the high point of global pressures for economic liberalisation, these conferences articulated some of the drawbacks in reducing regulation and relying on global market forces to generate stable, properous societies.

However, these gender, environment and social treaties of the 1990s must be put in historical context and must be discussed in terms of their weight and force in comparison to other treaties. The UK is a signatory to many other international and regional treaties that could be used to reinforce the progressive agreements emerging in the 1990s. However, the UK commitment to these agreements has always been matched by a parallel commitment to liberal market processes. Therefore, running alongside the commitments to human rights, equity and justice are agreements put in place since the 1940s that do not emphasise the rights of women, the poor, or future generations. In fact, the UK has often been signatory

to agreements, principally on trade and economics, that appear to undermine concerns of sustainable development, equity and rights.

Trade agreements and human development

The UK has long been part of a global trading system that sees liberal macro-economic development as a key tool for improving human development. This process was balanced by a strong welfare system, based on entitlement to healthcare and social benefits. Thus, in the postwar years, the UK government set up systems such as the National Health Service based on principles of universal coverage and equal access to care according to need. But, at the same time, the UK government has been a key player in the international trade system which has come to have such influence over national and international human development. The UK government was a key signatory to the original General Agreement on Tariffs and Trade (GATT) of 1947.

In the past five years there has been much debate and dissent over the world's trade agreements. These are numerous and complex, but the essential elements of the trade agenda are described in the core GATT articles outlined in Box 2.4. Created by international treaty in 1995, the WTO evolved out of the original body formed to develop GATT. GATT focused mainly on repealing tariffs – that is, the taxes that protect domestic producers against foreign competition. The original GATT agreement still provides the foundation of the WTO, but the WTO now has an extended mandate that also aims to repeal 'non-tariff barriers to trade'. These include environmental standards, food safety standards, investment policies and public health legislation. Indeed, it is within the context of 'trade barriers' that human wellbeing, labour rights, or gender, are discussed by the WTO. In relation to health, 'To the more excessive free trading economist, any

---

Box 2.4 *The interface of treaties for human development and those for trade*

There are several international trade agreements supported by the UK at present; four will have crucial impacts on human development and environmental sustainability. They are:

1   The agreement on the trade-related aspects of intellectual property rights (TRIPS): this sets minimum standards of protection for intellectual property rights, such as patents and industrial designs.
2   The agreement on the application of sanitary and phytosanitary (SPS) measures: this has an impact on national policies for food safety, including pesticide regulation and biotechnology. The SPS precludes the use of the 'precautionary principle' as a basis upon which to establish regulatory controls with regard to new pesticides or foods. In other words, for countries to restrict trade in these substances, they need to show scientific evidence of risks to health.
3   The agreement on technical barriers to trade (TBT): this stipulates that products must be compared with 'like' products regardless of production methods or practices. The agreement has implications for the production, labelling, packaging and quality standards of drugs and foods, and for environmental standards.
4   The general agreement on trade in services (GATS): under GATS rules, countries will be expected to open up their public and private services, including health and social services, to foreign investment, with potentially far-reaching implications for health and welfare worldwide.

Source: Drager, 1999; Shrybman, 1999; Arblaster et al, 1999; Bertrand and Kalafatides, 1999.

mention of health is a fig leaf for protectionism, whereas for public health, protection and prevention carry positive rather than negative connotations' (Lang, 1999). The UK government has supported the extension of international trade agreements to include issues such as intellectual property rights and services, including health services. This indicates that a large number of areas of policy and law formerly the responsibility of governments, and with little to do with trade per se, will now fall under the jurisdiction of the WTO (Shrybman, 1999).

Many fear that institutions such as the World Health Organization (WHO) or UNDP, which have developed global public health and anti-poverty programmes in the second half of the 20th century, are now being marginalised in favour of less accountable institutions such as the WTO and the World Bank. The trade agreements that have been negotiated in the late 1990s and early 2000 will have wide-reaching effects on the UK's systems of public health, social security and environmental protection.

It is not clear how the UK government, or any other, will be able to ensure that commercial interests do not override those of health and social welfare. Primarily, this is because, unlike the many other agreements on the environment, health, human rights and social welfare that we have highlighted above, the WTO agreements are enforceable, and enforced. Cases of violations of WTO rules are heard and decided in camera by a tribunal consisting of three trade bureaucrats. Documentation of the hearings is not available to the public. To date, WTO dispute settlements have placed trade issues above public health as well as environmental and social considerations (Koivusalo, 1999). In addition, the trade negotiations are conducted in secret with no input from, or accountability to, civil society. Generally, little information is available until the agreements have been concluded (Shrybman, 1999). Therefore, while the latest WTO negotiations may 'provide the public health community with an opportunity to ensure that trade agreements improve access to good quality health services, particularly for poorer populations' (Drager, 1999), past experience does not give cause for optimism.

Despite growing criticism of free trade, the UK government sees it as a way towards better economic development; it assumes that this development is equally shared and will benefit human development and environmental sustainability. It is not clear, however, just how

the government will ensure that human development and sustainability goals are met, given the power of the free trade agreements.

The most important aspect of these agreements on environmental and social issues is their strength in relation to the global trade treaties which the UK government has signed. The original GATT functions were already powerful and were partly responsible for the fact that there has been limited progress made on the Beijing and Copenhagen commitments. The UK government's mixed response to the Copenhagen commitments is summed up in Box 2.5.

Box 2.5 *UK activity since the Copenhagen Summit commitments*

Commitment 1: We commit ourselves to creating an economic, political, social, cultural and legal environment that will enable people to achieve social development.

Reformed legislation on civil and political rights and access to information, democratic processes, and ways of working within government. The Human Rights Act to be implemented in October 2000; already in force in Scotland and Wales. A Freedom of Information Bill under debate, while equivalent measures in Scotland give greater public access. The UK has signed but not yet ratified the Council of Europe's revised Social Charter. Widespread devolution; House of Lords being reformed. More emphasis on value for money in legal aid, and on alternative methods of resolving disputes. Powers to issue antisocial behaviour orders and impose child curfews introduced, but not widely used. Proposal to abolish many defendants' right to trial by jury.

Commitment 2: We commit ourselves to the goal of eradicating poverty in the world, through decisive national actions and international cooperation, as an ethical, social, political and economic imperative of humankind.

The 1999 UN Human Development Report identifies the UK as third worst out of 17 industrialised nations for its record on poverty and for combining high levels of poverty and inequality (UNDP, 1999). Government says tackling poverty is a high priority, and new official measures of quality of life include poverty indicators. Government committed to eliminating child poverty within 20 years, and halving it within 10. Policies are not yet consistently 'poverty-proofed', and there are no formal mechanisms for involving people in poverty, or their organisations in developing an anti-poverty strategy. Budgets have been modestly redistributive. Social Exclusion Unit created to take a cross-departmental approach. Strategies in Scotland, Wales and Northern Ireland focus on creating an inclusive society (rather than combating social exclusion). The government's aims for welfare reform are modernisation, reorienting welfare around (paid) work, and reducing the bills for economic failure. Welfare claimants' responsibilities are emphasised more than their rights.

Commitment 3: We commit ourselves to promoting the goal of full employment as a basic priority of our economic and social policies, and to enabling all men and women to attain secure and sustainable livelihoods through freely chosen productive employment and work.

Government prioritises increasing employment opportunities for unemployed people and others in workless households, with the emphasis on improving employability and work incentives rather than direct job creation. There is concern over a geographical mismatch between workless people and available jobs, and about the quality and sustainability of many entry level jobs. Rights at work, including union recognition and employment protection, were improved in the Employment Relations Act. The government also signed the European Union Social Chapter.

Commitment 4: We commit ourselves to promoting social integration by fostering societies that are stable, safe and just and that are based on the promotion and protection of all human rights, as well as on non-discrimination, tolerance, respect for diversity, equality of opportunity, solidarity, security, and the participation of all people, including disadvantaged and vulnerable groups and persons.

Government ratified the International Labour Office convention on discrimination in employment, but rejected the Commission for Racial Equality's recommendations for stronger race relations legislation. A bill extends the Race Relations Act to cover more functions of public authorities, including law enforcement and immigration agencies. Asylum and immigration issues are increasingly decided at a European level but most asylum seekers will have to survive on inadequate support provided largely in the form of vouchers. Government is improving anti-discriminatory disability legislation, leading a campaign for positive images of disabled people, and creating a Disability Rights Commission; but many disabled employees will still be unprotected, due to small-company exemptions.

Commitment 5: We commit ourselves to promoting full respect for human dignity and to achieving equality and equity between women and men, and to recognising and enhancing the participation and leadership roles of women in political, civil, economic, social and cultural life and in development.

Government set up a women's unit (now in the Cabinet Office), appointed a minister for women and carried out a 'listening to women' exercise, but rejected the Equal Opportunities Commission's proposals for a 'superlaw' to update and improve gender equality legislation. Mainstreaming of gender issues was promised and guidance issued, but only one department routinely examines how its policies affect women. Targets were set for appointing women to civil service posts and public bodies. The gap between men's and women's full-time pay narrowed in 1998 by 1 per cent, to 19 per cent. The government developed a national childcare strategy (partly financed by the National Lottery), and a childcare tax credit covering registered childcare for low- and middle-income families. Maternity leave is being lengthened, and maternity allowance extended to low-paid women. Parental and family leave is being introduced, but parental leave will be unpaid, so many low-paid workers unlikely to take it. The UK signed an EU directive improving part-time workers' rights.

Commitment 6a: *We commit ourselves to promoting and attaining the goals of universal and equitable access to quality education.*

Education is a priority of the government; it wants primary schools to prioritise literacy and numeracy to improve educational standards. Truancy and school exclusions should be reduced; parents whose children persistently play truant will be fined more. Education action zones in deprived areas will experiment with different approaches. There is concern about selection and private sector involvement. A strategy for the training and education of post-16 year olds, including lifelong learning for adults, was published; the functional illiteracy rate is high, and innumeracy is also a serious problem. Tuition fees introduced for higher education in England and Wales.

Commitment 6b: *We commit ourselves to promoting the highest attainable standard of physical and mental health, and the access of all to primary healthcare, making particular efforts to rectify inequalities relating to social conditions and without distinction as to race, national origin, gender, age or disability.*

The health divide between rich and poor has widened. Health action zones aim to improve the health of the poorest, and healthy living centres will experiment with new approaches. The UK's teenage pregnancy rate is amongst the highest in Europe, and the Social Exclusion Unit proposed halving teenage pregnancies within ten years. The means-tested maternity grant was doubled but made conditional. Free eye tests were reintroduced for pensioners, and plans were announced to tackle problems of access to NHS dentists. Internal market in health care has been abolished.

Commitment 9: *We commit ourselves to increasing significantly and/or utilising more efficiently the resources allocated to social development in order to achieve the goals of the Summit through national action and regional and international cooperation.*

Government has committed an extra £40 billion over three years to education and health, but these figures are being challenged on the grounds that this sum is not composed of entirely 'new' money.

Commitment 10: *We commit ourselves to an improved and strengthened framework for international, regional and sub-regional cooperation for social development, in a spirit of partnership, through the UN and other multilateral institutions.*

Government has not publicised the Copenhagen commitments or organised monitoring with outside organisations, although the UK report includes domestic and development issues. The government agreed to mark October 17 (the UN day for the eradication of poverty) as a UK event in 2000.

Source: F Bennett of Oxfam GB, 'Marking five-year review of the Copenhagen Summit', *Social Watch*, no 4, 2000, Instituto del Tercer Mundo, Montevideo, Uruguay. With the kind permission of Social Watch.

This mixed outcome has not been the case for the commitments made at Rio in 1992. Indeed, the UK government now claims considerable success in meeting commitments made in several of the environmental agreements (Table 2.1). This may be because of the long history of UK concern for environmental resources, such as fisheries, with treaties going back to the 1950s. The UK has been a key advocate of the Convention on International Trade in Endangered Species of Wild Fauna and Flora (CITES), for example.

Although new money for the Rio commitments has been provided via the Global Environmental Facility, and private investment in developing countries has increased significantly, overall flows of official development aid have fallen since Rio. The UK is one of only a few countries where the proportion of expenditure on overseas development aid is increasing (Mabey, 2000), although the current figure of 0.25 per cent of GNP compares poorly with the UN target of 0.7 per cent.

However, there is no doubt that the UK is one of the key governments advocating the shifts in the trading system towards greater liberalisation. Papers commissioned by the Department for International Development in 1998 on the proposed Multilateral Agreement on Investment (MAI), for example, argued that more free trade would benefit developing and developed countries through higher levels of direct foreign investment (Fitzgerald, 1998), while critics of the MAI argued that it would undermine national sovereignty on social, environmental and health issues. Furthermore, the government played a key role in the trade negotiations at Seattle in 1999.

And although the UK hosted the 1999 WHO Environment and Health Ministers' Meeting in London, there was little discussion of the issues of conflict and convergence between the trade agreements being negotiated by the Department of Trade and Industry, and the multilateral environmental and health agreements. As WHO has put it, 'regrettably, business practices aimed at reducing costs and trade restrictions can result in a conflict of interest between business and environmental protection'. Indeed, the major problem is that the multilateral environmental and health agreements have little weight against the trade agreements under negotiation at the moment.

The new trade agreements may threaten health and wellbeing in a number of ways. First, trade provisions may roll back hard-won employment and public health legislation developed to ensure workplace standards or environmental protection. Under the agreements, transnational companies may be able to sue governments that ban dangerous pesticides or pollutants, try to protect their environment, or restrict the sale of tobacco. For example, under the provisions of the North American Free Trade Agreement (NAFTA), a Canadian ban on imports of the fuel additive MMT, which contains manganese, a suspected neurotoxin, was withdrawn after the additive's US manufacturer, Ethyl Corporation, sued the government of Canada for potential losses estimated at C$160 million. Canadian taxpayers now have a legal bill exceeding C$8 million. Second, the right to a safe work environment might be eroded as investors could claim that this is an 'unfair performance requirement'. Third, by forcing the opening of all economic sectors, including natural resources, to largely unaccountable foreign ownership, the trade agreements could worsen the already substantial negative effects of natural resource exploitation, particularly in developing countries. International evidence suggests that such ownership may impact adversely on the short- and long-term health of people and may threaten sustainable development in entire regions (Stephens et al, 2000). Finally, the new agreements may well have provisions that are stronger than national laws and more powerful than any of the global conventions set up by the UN to protect individual and collective health or the environment.

This evidence of the influence of trade agreements on human development gives yet another perspective when linked to the data

Table 2.1 *Objectives of selected multilateral environmental agreements and associated trade measures*

Objective	Trade measure
The Montreal Protocol	
Protect the stratospheric ozone layer from destruction by human-induced emissions of cholorofluorocarbons (CFCs)	Ban trade in the regulated substances, and in any products containing them, between parties of the protocol and between parties and non-parties
The Basel Convention	
Eliminate environmental risks arising from the transboundary movement of hazardous and other wastes	Follow prior informed consent (PIC) procedures before exporting any hazardous substances, or products containing them, that are banned in the exporting country
	Each party has the right to ban the import or export of hazardous or other wastes
	Ban on trade in such wastes with non-parties
The Convention on International Trade in Endangered Species (CITES)	
Protect endangered species from continued over-exploitation	Ban trade in those species of flora and fauna listed as endangered under the rules and procedures of the convention, and their products
Biodiversity Convention	
Conservation and the sustainable use of global biological diversity	Reversal of previous assumption of free access to genetic resources in developing countries
	Follow PIC procedures when access to genetic resources is requested by another party or non-party
Cartagena Protocol on Biosafety	
A legally binding agreement protecting the environment from risks posed by the transboundary movement of living modified organisms created by biotechnology	Addresses the safe transfer, handling and use of living modified organisms that may have an adverse effect on biodiversity. Establishes an advance informed agreement procedure for importation of such substances and emphasises the precautionary principle
Trade in Chemicals: London Guidelines and UN Food and Agriculture Organization (FAO) Code of Conduct	
Protection of countries from the import of chemical products banned or severely restricted in their country of origin	Follow non-legally-binding PIC procedures before exporting chemicals which are banned or severely restricted in the country of origin or the country of manufacture

Source: UNEP, 1999; CBD Secretariat, 2000

on inequality presented in other sections of this book. Data on growing inequality are gradually challenging the whole development paradigm, as the UN agencies shift their definitions to include critical issues such as gender inequality, poverty and consumption, and human, natural and social capital (United Nations Environment Programme, 1999).

Conclusion

Thoughout this chapter we have acknowledged that there are a range of forces that undermine sustainable development, and therefore human development in the UK. These are expressed in tensions between government departments, for example, or local groups with different interests. The conclusion, however, should not be that such forces inevitably prevent human development; we have described them to acknowledge the tensions they cause. The next chapter describes their impact on human development. This will illustrate, however, that they have a different degree of impact on different countries and regions. Therefore it follows that national and local policy and action can make a difference to the impact that these forces have.

Main Messages of this Chapter

- The links between poverty and the environment are many and complex, and the perspectives vary for different people and different organisations.
- The driving forces of globalisation threaten to undermine sustainable development.
- There are still few visions of sustainable communities where poverty has been reduced or eradicated, and few local authority Local Agenda 21 plans integrate their anti-poverty work with environmental issues.
- Effective local programmes are needed to address environments in poor communities and integrate Local Agenda 21 work with anti-poverty work.
- There is a need for environmental and social action groups to work together more effectively.
- Policy processes should be planned to improve participation and equity.
- There needs to be a more structured approach to achieving environmental justice by all agencies. The government needs to ensure that programmes to reduce the environmental impacts from industry prioritise the needs of groups of people suffering from multiple deprivations.
- All people have the right to live in a healthy environment; this is an essential requirement of social progress for all and of any anti-poverty strategy.
- Environmental justice must be achieved in the UK without compromising the rights of people in other countries or subsequent generations.
- International trade agreements are enforced more rigorously than social and environmental ones.
- Although the UK has made progress on some of its international environment and social commitments, these are in danger of being undermined by its willingness to support free trade principles.

Chapter 3

Getting the Measure of Human Development

Thinking About Poverty

In deciding to measure something we underline its value, and the regularity with which we measure it gives an idea of how we view its importance. All news programmes regularly mention the economy's financial measures: the various stockmarkets' indices such as the FTSE or the Dow Jones, and the GDP and GNP. Indeed the term 'the economy' is often used as though the economy has a life of its own. In reality, it is based on social relations and is meant to serve society, rather than the other way round. As a result of this narrow concentration on economics, many mainstream indicators of wealth and poverty have been wide of the mark; they have failed to capture what it means for individuals and societies to be rich or poor and so fail to contribute to monitoring or managing poverty effectively. Because of the way in which we measure its success, our growing economy hides a multitude of sins, from environmental degradation to social exclusion.

Until recently there has been relatively little dispute about the pre-eminence of GDP as an indicator of the health and vibrancy of our economy. GDP measures the economy's ability to generate cash, but it does not measure how productive that cash is nor does it measure national welfare. Indeed, it was not designed to do so. At the outset, Simon Kuznets, one of the architects of the notion of GDP, warned that: 'The welfare of a nation ... [can] ... scarcely be inferred from a measurement of national income' (quoted in New Economics Foundation, 1997). Nevertheless, all chancellors since then have used every opportunity to emphasise the importance of growth in GDP for the UK economy.

There are two main problems with GDP and this 'more is always better' approach:

1   What GDP counts. GDP includes all kinds of money-based economic activity, from car crashes to oil spills. In the case of the latter, for example, the company that clears up the spill can show they have made money in doing so. It all goes on the account and makes it look as if we are making progress.

2   What GDP does not count. If there isn't money in it then GDP cannot count it, even if the activity generates considerable welfare. So things that make us better off in a social sense, such as childcare, housework and community volunteering, get missed.

To counter this emphasis on purely financial measures, the past couple of decades have seen work by individuals and organisations to develop new sets of indicators and indices that give both a fuller picture of societies, and the tools to enable societies to function more equitably and sustainably.

As we suggested in Chapter 1, poverty is a widely used and understood concept but people often argue about how to define it. The term 'poverty' has several different meanings, depending on the subject under discussion. Poverty, like evolution or health, has both a scientific and a moral dimension. Many of the problems of measuring poverty arise because these concepts are often confused.

In scientific terms, a person or household in the UK is considered 'poor' when they have both a low standard of living and a low income. (Standard of living includes the material and social conditions in which people live and their participation in the economic, social, cultural and political life of the country.) They are not thought of as poor if they have a low income and a reasonable standard of living or if they have a low standard of living but a high income. Both income and standard of living can only be measured accurately in relation to the norms of UK society.

A low standard of living is often measured by using a deprivation index (high deprivation equals a low standard of living) or by consump-

tion expenditure (low expenditure equals a low standard of living). Of these two methods, deprivation indices are more accurate since expenditure is often only measured over a brief period and is not independent of available income. Deprivation indices are broader measures because they reflect different aspects of living standards, including personal, physical and mental conditions, local and environmental facilities, social activities and customs. Figure 3.1 illustrates these concepts. It shows an 'objective' poverty threshold, which can be defined as the point where the differences between people living in poverty and those who are not are at their greatest, and minimises the differences within the respective groups. For scientific purposes, broad measures of both income and standard of living are desirable (see Box 3.1).

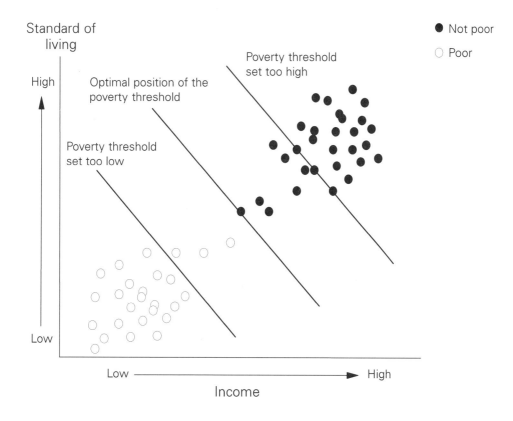

Figure 3.1 *The definition of poverty*

Box 3.1 *Absolute and overall poverty in Britain*

The recent Poverty and Social Exclusion survey of Britain (PSE) attempted to measure the amount of absolute and overall poverty in Britain using both subjective and objective methods (Gordon, 2000). Most 'experts' on poverty thought that overall poverty occurred in industrialised countries, but that absolute poverty was mainly confined to developing countries. One of the key purposes of the PSE survey was to get the views of the British population about these issues and not to rely just on the views of 'experts'.

The PSE survey respondents were shown the UN definitions of poverty and asked if their household income was greater or less than the income needed to avoid poverty and, subsequently, greater or less than the income needed to avoid absolute and overall poverty. In the tables below, those who said their household income was less than that needed to avoid poverty are defined as being in general poverty.

The first table shows that 14 per cent of the sample said they had less income than the level they identified as being enough to keep a household like theirs out of absolute poverty. The income, after tax, they said they needed each week to escape absolute poverty averaged £167 for all households.

Perceptions of the poverty line varied by type of household, as would be expected. More lone parents than any other type of household (40 per cent) said they had an income less than that needed to keep out of absolute poverty. Next were single pensioners (19 per cent) and couples with one child (18 per cent).

A larger proportion (22 per cent) considered themselves to be living in overall poverty. Again, single parents were most likely to claim that they had incomes which fell below this level. It is interesting that the assessment of the mean income needed to keep a household out of general poverty fell somewhere between the absolute and overall standards, which indicates that respondents made distinctions between these subjective thresholds of poverty.

Income needed each week to keep a household like yours out of absolute and overall poverty in Britain in 1999

	Absolute poverty	Overall poverty	General poverty
Mean income needed	£167	£237	£219
Actual income a lot above	46%	34%	31%
A little above	20%	22%	27%
About the same	7%	7%	12%
A little below	7%	9%	8%
A lot below	7%	13%	9%
Don't know	13%	14%	13%
Total	100%	100%	100%

Percentage of each type of household saying their actual income was 'a lot' or 'a little' below that needed to keep out of absolute and overall poverty in Britain in 1999

	Absolute poverty	Overall poverty	General poverty
Single pensioner	19%	26%	21%
Pensioner with partners	12%	18%	15%
Single adult	12%	25%	21%
Couple	13%	15%	16%
Couple, 1 child	18%	27%	14%
Couple, 2 children	8%	15%	14%
Couple, 3 or more children	7%	27%	13%
Lone parent, 1 child	40%	44%	46%
Lone parent, 2 or more children	42%	57%	49%
Other	9%	19%	11%

The PSE survey of the UK shows that the scale of needs in at least one rich industrial society is perceived by its population to be much higher than is generally allowed in national and international debates. This is evidence that these subjective measures of absolute and overall poverty are worth employing in research in other countries. It is important to get the public's views about poverty and not to rely just on the opinions of 'experts'.

Source: Gordon et al, in press

The right tools for the job

From the methods described above and the definitions we referred to in Chapter 1, we can see that the measurement of poverty has developed to include many measurements of social exclusion, rather than just income. It is not just poverty that has demanded more creative thinking. The need to measure newer concepts, such as sustainable development, has prompted several organisations and the government itself to start producing new sets of indicators and indices.

Sets of indicators do not seek to aggregate information into one numerical value. For this reason, some official statisticians prefer them to indices as a transparent way of reflecting progress. The indicators allow statisticians to separate out different aspects of social, economic and environmental wellbeing and measure them in their original unit. Table 3.1 shows examples from the set launched by the Department of the Environment, Transport and the Regions (DETR) at the end of 1999.

Table 3.1 *Examples of DETR indicators*

Issue	Indicator
Environmental	Days when air pollution is moderate or higher
Social	Percentage of elderly in fuel poverty, working-age people without qualifications and in workless households, and children living in families with persistently low incomes
Economic	GDP and GDP per head

Source: DETR, 1999

The government's sustainability indicators cover many aspects of poverty and social exclusion. There are 15 headline indicators that are intended to give a general picture of quality of life by representing key areas; the social indicator in Table 3.1 represents poverty, for example. Elsewhere in the other 150 or so indicators in the set are some on sustainable communities. These include access to various services as well as measures of community spirit – and, in turn, are linked to social inclusion. This set of indicators is generally to be welcomed. What is less clear, however, is whether there is the political will to act on some of the information that the indicators provide. This is crucial in determining their importance, as, ultimately, indicators are only of value if they are acted on.

The new sets of indicators are helpful new tools. But the next stage must be to cull the indicators that do not increase our understanding of poverty or help the fight against it. This process must have at its centre those experiencing poverty itself. It is then for politicians to back these indicators and act upon them in the same way as they have always responded to GDP. It has often been highlighted that many of these new indicators emphasise certain values, the suggestion being that this invalidates them. In reality, no statistics are value-free. As we stressed at the start of this chapter, GDP makes the significant value judgement of assigning a value of zero to everything that does not have a market value.

There may never be straightforward ways to assign values to critical aspects of human wellbeing, whether they be social inclusion or material wealth. But to tackle poverty effectively, we need indicators that show that it is a complex phenomenon, rather than just a product of low incomes.

Human poverty and human development

Besides the move towards broadening measures of poverty, the UNDP had another reason to develop a further index when it created its Human Development Index (HDI) and two human poverty indices. Although social scientific methods and definitions of poverty are useful for making policy within countries, it is often useful to use alternative measures when comparing poverty rates between countries or regions within countries, particularly since detailed statistical data on social conditions are not available in many developing countries. UNDP needs to measure the level of development and the extent of poverty in all countries, so it combines widely measured indicators which highlight the key elements of development and poverty.

The key index produced by the human development report team is the HDI, which was constructed to reflect the most important dimensions of human development. The HDI is a composite index based on three indicators: life expectancy at birth; educational attainment; and standard of living as measured by real GDP per capita. The 1997 *Human Development Report* defined poverty within the human development perspective and introduced the term 'human poverty', defining poverty as 'the denial of choices and opportunities for a tolerable life' (UNDP, 1997). The Human Poverty Index for Developing Countries (HPI-1) attempted to represent this concept by focusing on those groups whose choices are heavily constrained in each of the three areas outlined in the HDI. While the HDI focuses on the average achievements of a country, the HPI-1 focuses on the most deprived. The HPI-1 is made up of five weighted components (UNDP, 1997):

1 The percentage of people expected to die before the age of 40.
2 The percentage of adults who are illiterate.
3 The percentage of people with access to health services.
4 The percentage of people with access to safe water.
5 The percentage of children under five who are malnourished.

There are several aspects of human poverty that are excluded from the HPI-1 due to lack of data or difficulties in measuring them. These include lack of political freedom, inability to participate in decision making, lack of personal security, inability to participate in the life of the community and threats to sustainability and equity between generations.

In the 1998 *Human Development Report* the UNDP produced a Human Poverty Index for Industrial Countries (HPI-2) for use in developed (or industrialised) countries such as the UK. It is made up of four weighted components:

1   The percentage of people not expected to survive to the age of 60.
2   The functional illiteracy rate.
3   The percentage of people living below the income poverty line (50 per cent of the median disposable income).
4   The long-term unemployment rate (12 months or more).

The first three components of this index, which focus on the right to a long life, knowledge and a decent standard of living, are also measured in the HDI and the HPI-1. However, long-term unemployment is included as an indicator of social exclusion (or lack of participation). These are components which are widely measured and aggregated to local level, and so we have chosen HPI-2 to compare British constituencies in this report. Using the HPI-2 and HDI as our main references also allows us to compare the UK's performance with its counterparts in the industrialised world.

Making Comparisons

As a rich country, it is not particularly surprising that the UK is a good overall performer in terms of advancing human development. In UNDP's *Human Development Report* for 2000 we rank tenth in the HDI, close to many other industrialised nations. More importantly, the UK ranks 13 places higher in human development than in income, showing that the UK has done well to achieve a high average national level of human development with the economic resources available. The countries that rank higher than the UK, such as Canada, Sweden and Japan, do better in that their populations as a whole live longer, although the UK has one of the highest primary school enrolment rates. Nevertheless, overall the UK has achieved a very high level of human development, close to the level to which countries should aspire.

However, this does not mean that there are no shortfalls. As highlighted in the previous section, the HDI measures only average achievement. It says little about the disparity and the deprivation that still exist. In fact, for the most developed countries, the HDI is a less meaningful measure of human development than those measures that focus on gender and poverty such as the Gender Development Index (GDI), which adjusts HDI by gender inequality, and the Gender Empowerment Measure (GEM), which measures women's empowerment, or the HPI-2.

Gender equality and empowerment in the UK is less well-advanced than in countries with similar levels of income and human development. Although the UK ranks tenth in the GDI, showing that there is relatively little disparity between men and women in education and health terms, its GEM ranking is as low as 15, which shows that gender empowerment in the UK lags behind countries with similar levels of income or overall human development (see Box 3.2). For example, Finland, Germany and Denmark rank below the UK in the HDI but are at numbers 5, 6 and 4 respectively in the GEM ranking. An

Box 3.2 *Gender inequalities in the UK*

Despite the creation of the Women's Unit in the Cabinet Office, the heart of government, gender inequalities still exist in Britain and have a negative effect on overall human development. Overall, women remain one of the largest groups experiencing poverty in the UK. Women constitute 70 per cent of the lowest earners and 56 per cent of the adults living in poverty in the UK. The groups especially at risk from poverty are lone parents and single pensioners; women form the majority in both groups. Current forecasts predict that there will be two million lone parents in ten years' time.

There is particular concern in the UK about the lack of recognition given to the feminisation of poverty. Poverty in the UK affects far more women than men, but this is not always obvious. Government statistics are not routinely disaggregated by gender. Information on the distribution of income within the household is needed to build up a full picture of the gendered effects of poverty. Despite the absence of data in many areas, a range of quantitative and qualitative research supports the following:

- More women than men are poor.
- Women take most of the responsibility for managing money in the home.
- Many women don't earn enough for a pension, leaving them poor in old age.
- Women can face different and additional barriers to men in their choices around education, health, careers and families which can prevent them from making the contribution to the economy and overall human development that they want to make.
- Girls are still being given educational careers advice which perpetuates stereotyping in the job market.
- Women in paid work still do three times as much housework as men.
- Women are more likely than men to work part-time and below their skill level, especially after having a career break.
- Twice as many women as men care for an elderly parent.

As a result of this, women are facing a deficit, both financially and in terms of the opportunities available to them. They are half as likely as men to obtain a higher educational qualification in science or engineering and are still concentrated in a fairly narrow range of low-income occupations. They are forgoing substantial earnings and incomes due to:

- the 'female forfeit' (the difference between the earnings of childless women and men); and
- the 'mother gap' (the difference between the earnings of childless women and women with children).

Women constantly identify the NHS as the most important issue facing the country and are by far the greater users of NHS services: stress, overwork and domestic violence all cause special health problems for women. The trend toward early sexual experience combined with a lack of information and services increases the risk of unwanted early pregnancy. Taking developed countries as a whole, adolescents have a moderate pregnancy rate in England, Wales and Scotland (46.9 pregnancies per 1000 women aged 15–19 for England and Wales, and 41.6 in Scotland) but it is high when the whole range is considered, and when these rates are compared with those of neighbours such as France (20.2), Belgium (14.1) and the Netherlands (12.2) (Singh and Darroch, 2000).

Recent reforms have had a considerable impact on closing the gap between the educational achievements of girls and boys. Disparities remain in access, achievements and outcomes. In terms of access, teenage mothers in particular are at risk of dropping out of education early. In terms of achievement, girls do well, and better than boys in terms of qualifications, but the subjects they study are still 'gendered'. In terms of outcomes, and despite the success of young women in academic terms and in accessing professional careers in recent years, young women often do not live up to their academic promise and their earnings are not comparable with their equivalently-qualified male peers. The impact of parenthood and the resulting time out of the labour market continues to have a detrimental effect on women's economic independence.

Women must take an equal part in political power and in the important decisions, in order for simple justice to be done but also to ensure that women's views are represented. Without that, women at the grassroots will not be heard. If the differing achievements of women and men are not addressed, progress in human development in the UK will only reflect the needs of half of the population. Human development must incorporate women's distinct experiences and perspectives. Achieving equality needs commitment at the highest level of government and all parts of government must include women's views in the work they do.

Source: Amy Cruse, UNED-UK

important difference in those countries is the higher level of political participation by women; about a third of parliamentary seats are held by women, in contrast to the 17 per cent held by women in the British parliament. Poverty remains a serious problem in the UK, in both income and human dimensions. The UK ranks 16th out of 18 Organisation for Economic Co-operation and Development (OECD) countries for which the HPI was estimated – third from the worst, with only the US and Ireland scoring lower. Income poverty and inequalities are also high. Income poverty is relatively high in the UK, with 10.6 per cent of the population below the poverty line (defined as 50 per cent of median income). This places the UK 5th out of 18 OECD countries in the Luxembourg study of income distribution (2000). The highest rates of income poverty are in the US, Australia, Italy and Canada. Nordic countries tend to have low rates of poverty: in Norway 5.8 per cent of the population is below the poverty line, in Sweden the figure is 5.5 per cent, and in Denmark it is 6.9 per cent. Poverty rates among children are particularly high in the UK. Some 21 per cent of children fell below the poverty line in 1995, the 3rd highest rate after Russia and the US among 25 countries in the Luxembourg study.

As was stressed in Chapter 2, income inequality is also relatively high in the UK, with the ratio of the income of the richest 20 per cent to the poorest 20 per cent being 6.5. This is the fourth highest rate among the OECD countries, behind New Zealand (17.4), the US (9) and Australia (7).

What accounts for this poor ranking? An important factor seems to be high rates of functional illiteracy, with more than a fifth of the population being unable to read instructions on a medicine bottle, fill out a form or read a bedtime story to a child. This is higher than any other of the 18 countries except for Ireland. Recent surveys sponsored by the OECD have assessed how well people can read and comprehend information. In all OECD countries, the inability of people to read effectively is much more widespread than has been commonly perceived, the average proportion being 15.4 per cent.

These figures point to issues of quality and inequality in education, even though the average achievement in education may be high. The UK lags behind other industrialised countries in secondary school enrolment. Net enrolment is 91.8 per cent of the relevant age group while it is more than 95 per cent in almost all OECD countries, except Iceland, Switzerland, Greece and Poland.

It is also interesting to note that many countries spend greater amounts on education per child than the UK. The UK's public expenditure on education amounts to 11.6 per cent of government expenditure and 5.3 per cent of GNP. This is much less than in Canada, Norway and the US, which rank in the top three of the HDI. The corresponding figures were 12.9 per cent and 6.9 per cent in Canada, 15.8 per cent and 7.4 per cent in Norway, and 14.4 per cent and 5.4 per cent in the US.

These indicators show that the UK has achieved one of the highest levels of human development in the world, but that serious issues of poverty and inequality remain, not only in income but in basic human develop-

ment. In comparison to countries with similar levels of income and average human development, the UK has more serious problems of gender disparities in empowerment, human poverty, income poverty and income inequalities. In the next sections the four components of the HPI-2 index will be discussed in turn for Britain, and Northern Ireland where appropriate information is available. We then use the HPI-2 to look at how each parliamentary constituency is performing.

Table 3.2 *How the UK is doing*

	UK rank	UK value	OECD top 3	OECD bottom 3	OECD average
Human Development Index	10	0.918	1 Canada 0.935 2 Norway 0.934 3 US 0.929	44 Poland 0.817 34 Czech Republic 0.843 31 Republic of Korea 0.854	0.893
Gender Development Index	10	0.914	1 Canada 0.932 2 Norway 0.932 3 US 0.937	40 Poland 0.811 33 Czech Republic 0.841 31 Republic of Korea 0.8847	0.889
Gender Empowerment Measure	15	0.656	1 Norway 0.825 2 Iceland 0.802 3 Sweden 0.794	63 Republic of Korea 0.323 46 Greece 0.456 41 Japan 0.490	N/A
HPI-2	16	14.6	1 Norway 7.3 2 Sweden 7.6 3 Netherlands 8.2	18 US 15.8 17 Ireland 15 16 UK 14.6	12.3
Inequality (ratio richest 20% to poorest 20% in income)	4 (where 1 = worst)	6.5	1 Austria 3.2 2 Japan 3.4 3 Sweden, Finland, Iceland 3.6	1 New Zealand 17.4 2 US 9.0 3 Australia 7.0	N/A
Population below income poverty line of 50% of median income	4 (where 1=worst)	10.6	1 Finland 3.9 2 Luxembourg 4.1 3 Norway 5.8	1 US 17.3 2 Italy 12.8 3 Australia 11.9	N/A

Source: UNDP, 2000

Who dies young in Britain?

Details on the circumstances of and age at death have been collected in Britain since the 16th century. In London in the 1530s the parish clerks were required to submit weekly reports on the number of plague deaths. These

'Bills of Mortality' were meant to tell the authorities when public health measures should be taken against epidemics. The first summary of these reports was published as the *London Bills of Mortality* by the Company of Parish Clerks in 1604.

Detailed statistics are available in Britain on who dies young and where they die. The evidence that poverty and inequality in material wellbeing underlie inequalities in health and early death is now overwhelming. In 1980 the Black Committee on Inequalities in Health (DHSS, 1980) concluded that:

'While the health care service can play a significant part in reducing inequalities in health, measures to reduce differences in material standards of living at work, in the home and in everyday social and community life are of even greater importance.' (ibid)

Sir Donald Acheson, in his final report as Britain's Chief Medical Officer, said:

'the issue is quite clear in health terms: that there is a link, has been a link and, I suspect, will continue to be a link between deprivation and ill health . . . analysis has shown that the clearest links with the excess burden of ill health are:

– *low income;*
– *unhealthy behaviour: and*
– *poor housing and environmental amenities.'* (Department of Health, 1990)

More generally, one commentator (Jacobson, 1993) commented in relation to women's health that:

'Two out of three women around the world presently suffer from the most debilitating disease known to humanity. Common symptoms of this fast-spreading ailment include chronic anaemia, mal-nutrition and severe fatigue. Sufferers exhibit an increased susceptibility to infections of the respiratory tract. And premature death is a frequent outcome. In the absence of direct intervention, the disease is often communicated from mother to child with markedly higher transmission rates among females than males. Yet, while studies confirm the efficacy of numerous prevention and treatment strategies, to date few have been vigorously pursued.'

The disease she is referring to is poverty.

It is now widely accepted that poor people die younger as a result of their poverty. Indeed, Frank Dobson, who was Secretary of State for Health between 1997 and 1999, acknowledged this when he said: 'Inequality in health is the worst inequality of all. There is no more serious inequality than knowing that you'll die sooner because you're badly off' (Dobson/DoH, 1997).

There are also detailed statistics in Britain on where people die young and who dies young. We have considerable amounts of data on inequalities in health between socio-economic classes, ethnic groups, unemployed people and those in employment, men and women, and young and old. The 1998 Acheson Report on inequalities in health cites more than 600 studies showing the extent of health inequality in the UK (Acheson, 1998).

In terms of where people experience health inequality, Table 3.3 lists the 15 parliamentary constituencies that contain the million people aged under 65 with the highest age–sex-standardised mortality ratios in Britain between 1991 and 1995 (Shaw et al, 1999). The highest ratio was in Glasgow Shettleston where the chances of dying under age 65 at any time are 2.3 times the national average. Had the mortality ratios of this constituency been the same as for those in the 'best health', the deaths of one million people – including 71 per cent of the deaths of constituents under 65 – would not have occurred in the period under study. Overall, in the areas containing the million people with the 'worst health', 10,921 people would still be alive if they had enjoyed the mortality rates of the million people with the 'best health' over just five years – nearly two-thirds of all deaths under 65 in these constituencies. The second half of Table 3.3 shows the very low mortality rates that are enjoyed by people living in the 'best health' areas, which together contain one million people. It is the conditions in which people can afford to live, given current market and political arrangements, which determine who lives to old age and who dies before their time.

Figure 3.2 presents data on the extent of the geographical gap in map form. The clustering of the 'worst health' areas of Britain in Glasgow, the northern conurbations and in the centre of London is made starkly clear. Even amongst these one million people with 'worst health', however, a north to south gradient in mortality ratios is apparent. In all these areas mortality ratios are very high, but they range from 2.3 times the average at their worst in Glasgow, to 1.6 times the average in Southwark and Bermondsey in London. Conversely, there is much less variation between the million people with the 'best health' in Britain. The position of constituencies across the south of England shows remarkable uniformity of rates, suggesting that there are no particular factors causing mortality rates to be so low in these areas other than general affluence. The pattern is broken by Sheffield Hallam constituency, which illustrates how low mortality ratios in the north could be.

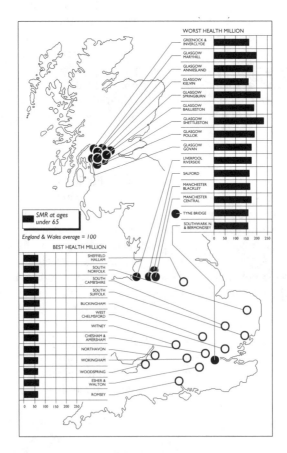

Note: SMR = standardised mortality ratio.
Source: Shaw et al, 1999

Figure 3.2 *Premature deaths in the extreme areas of Britain (1991–95)*

Table 3.3 Constituencies where people are most at risk of premature death (mortality rates under 65) in Britain, 1991–95

Rank	Name	Deaths under 65 years of age	Population under 65 years of age	SMR<65	Avoidable
	Ratio of 'worst health' to 'best health'	**2.3**	**1.0**	**2.6**	
1	Glasgow Shettleston	1405	50,740	234	71%
2	Glasgow Springburn	1438	57,007	217	69%
3	Glasgow Maryhill	1432	67,246	196	65%
4	Glasgow Pollock	1313	62,257	187	64%
5	Glasgow Anniesland	1176	56,757	181	63%
6	Glasgow Baillieston	1267	66,076	180	62%
7	Manchester Central	1597	94,191	173	61%
8	Glasgow Govan	1028	57,286	172	61%
9	Liverpool Riverside	1458	83,267	172	61%
10	Manchester Blackley	1421	78,573	169	60%
11	Greenock and Inverclyde	1051	54,050	164	59%
12	Salford	1285	72,681	163	59%
13	Tyne Bridge	1297	76,678	158	57%
14	Glasgow Kelvin	828	50,304	158	57%
15	Southwark North and Bermondsey	1214	76,811	156	56%
	'Worst health' million	19,210	1,003,923	178	62%
1	Wokingham	588	80,936	65	
2	Woodspring	620	74,251	65	
3	Romsey	593	73,300	65	
4	Sheffield Hallam	481	61,865	66	
5	South Cambridgeshire	636	79,401	66	
6	Chesham and Amersham	673	76,914	67	
7	South Norfolk	710	79,820	69	
8	West Chelmsford	674	83,988	69	
9	South Suffolk	601	68,686	69	
10	Witney	675	82,975	69	
11	Esher and Walton	705	83,333	69	
12	Northavon	742	88,333	70	
13	Buckingham	593	70,344	71	
	'Best health' million	8,291	1,004,147	68	
	Britain	556,957	47,587,310	100	

Key

SMR<65 Standardised mortality ratio for deaths under 65 years of age

Avoidable Percentage of deaths which would not have occurred if the 'worst health' areas had the death rate of the 'best health' areas.

Notes: The population of each constituency is estimated for 1993 from 1991 mid-year ward statistics updated by the 1996 Office of National Statistics age/sex mid-year estimates of population for local authority districts. The mortality figures are assigned to constituencies through the postcodes of the deceased.

Source: Shaw et al, 1999

The geography of the areas with the highest and lowest mortality ratios under 65 requires more comment. Just over half of these 'worst health' constituencies are in Glasgow (and one more is also on the Clyde). Scottish and urban constituencies tend to be smaller than average but even if we were to take this into account it would have little impact on the distribution. This is because many of the constituencies neighbouring these areas also have very poor health and 52 per cent of the million people with the 'worst health' in Scotland. Of the remainder of the constituencies containing the 'worst health' million, three are contiguous areas in central Manchester, containing 24 per cent of the 'worst health' million people in Britain. The other three areas – in the centres of Liverpool, Newcastle and London – contain an equal proportion of the 'worst health' million (a total of 24 per cent). These are the inner areas of some of Britain's largest cities. Expanding the list to over one million would bring in the poorest parts of other cities. By contrast, the 13 constituencies with the lowest mortality ratios are all, save Sheffield Hallam, in the south of England and mainly in suburban and rural areas.

There are, of course, other ways of looking at inequality than the geographic approach we have chosen as our main focus in this chapter. In terms of human development in the UK, perhaps one of the most important pieces of work on health inequality has come from Richard Wilkinson's analysis of the gradient in health inequalities (Wilkinson, 1996). This gradient shows that it is not simply a question of where you live or whether you are exposed to a poor environment that is important. Work on health inequalities in the UK shows that at every point of income below the most wealthy, there is a health disadvantage. In almost all health outcomes the people with the best conditions and/or wealth have better health than anyone with less. This affects child health, adult health and overall health. These inequalities appear in heart diseases, infectious diseases and accidents. As the Acheson Report argues:

'The penalties of inequalities in health affect the whole society and usually increase from the top to the bottom. Thus, although the least well-off may properly be given priority, if policies only address those at the bottom of the social hierarchy, inequalities will still exist' (Acheson, 1998).

The Acheson Report also notes an important aspect of the health inequality data:

'Over the last twenty years, death rates have fallen among both men and women and across all social groups. However, the difference in rates between those at the top and bottom of the social scale has widened. For example, in the early 1970s, the mortality rate among men of working age was almost twice as high for those in class V (unskilled) as for those in class I (professional). By the early 1990s it was almost three times higher . . . In the late 1970s, death rates were 53 per cent higher among men in classes IV and V compared with those in classes I and II. In the late 1980s they were 68 per cent higher. Among women, the differential increased from 50 per cent to 55 per cent' (ibid).

In terms of our future human development it is important to realise that children do not escape the impacts of health inequality. For example, pedestrian injury death rates for children in social class V are five times higher than those for children in social class I, and are higher for boys than for girls.

We also need to note that health inequalities don't just show themselves in deaths, but are also evident in illness. This is important because it shows the trap that poorer people are in. Where there are higher rates of illness, opportunities are affected, and with them chances of human development. For example, for men, major accident rates are substantially higher for manual workers than for non-maual workers. Children in lower income households are more likely to experience accidents in the home. Among women, 25 per cent of professional women report a longstanding limiting illness, while 45 per cent of unskilled women report such an illness.

One of the components of human development most stressed by UNDP has been health security. The UK now has a more extensive database on health inequality than almost every other industrialised country. It was developed by public health epidemiologists, sociologists and practitioners to guide government policy towards more equity, and to evaluate the policy of equitable access to health services set up after the Second World War. The database has become over time, with grim accuracy, the watchdog of UK society. It tracks stories of deaths and illnesses, and the failures of successive policy approaches to deliver equity or health security in a rich country with adequate resources to deliver health for all.

Richard Wilkinson cites Julian Rathbone's summary of the structural situation underpinning the human development dilemma in the UK:

'We live in a criminal society. I mean a society that is structurally criminal. If we removed from our economy every trace of exploitation of the third world and actively worked in the opposite direction . . . if we wiped out all unnecessary pollution . . . if we removed all traces of sexism and racism . . . if there was one single political party interested in structural justice rather than getting their bums onto government seats . . . if, if, if, then we might say our society is not structurally criminal' (Rathbone in Wilkinson, 1996).

Functional illiteracy in Britain

Information on the rates of literacy in Britain does not have as long a history as information about premature deaths. One of the first detailed descriptions were the maps of 'Ignorance in England and Wales as indicated by men's signatures by marks in the marriage registers of 1844', published in 1849 (Fletcher, 1849). This indicated high levels of illiteracy in Wales, East Anglia, Cornwall, Somerset and Liverpool.

Universal free education has resulted in virtually all adults in Britain being able to read and write to a certain extent. However, the International Adult Literacy Survey (IALS) has shown that there are some adults in all developed countries who have great difficulty understanding fairly simple prose and in extracting information from documents or numerical tables. The Adult Literacy Survey of 1996 was the first to be carried out using advanced statistical methods and agreed international standards (Carey et al, 1997). Table 3.4 shows the percentage of people who only attained level 1 (the lowest level) in the survey in England, Scotland and Wales; it shows that between one fifth and a quarter of the adults aged 16 to 65 in Britain would have great difficulty in understanding complex documents or tables. There is little difference in the rates between the three countries in Britain although there appears to be a slightly greater proportion of people in Wales with literacy difficulties than in England or Scotland.

Detailed analysis of the Adult Literacy Survey of Britain revealed that literacy problems were greatest among older people with low levels of education, unemployed people, those in a manual social class and people on the lowest levels of income. For example, 63 per cent of those at level 1 on the document scale had a personal income of less than £5,929 per year and more than a third (37 per cent) of those at level 1 on the prose scale were receiving social security benefits. Unemployed people were twice as likely to have low literacy skills compared with people in paid employment.

Table 3.4 *Percentage obtaining only literacy level 1 in England, Scotland and Wales in 1996*

	Prose literacy	*Document literacy*	*Quantitative literacy*
England	21	23	23
Scotland	23	22	24
Wales	24	26	25
Britain	**22**	**23**	**23**

Source: Carey et al, 1997

Low income in the UK

There is reliable information on income in the UK from the end of the 17th century and it has been shown that since then income has become progressively more equally distributed in Britain (Rubinstein, 1986). Furthermore, the rather sparse evidence available from earlier periods indicates that there has been a trend of a slow but progressive increase in income equality since the 15th century (Wedgwood, 1929; Saltow, 1968). However, during the 1980s and 1990s income inequality increased rapidly in the UK as a direct result of the policies of successive Conservative governments. From this historical perspective, what the Thatcher governments of 1979–90 attempted to do was reverse a trend of increasing income equality which had lasted for half a millennium.

During the past 20 years, there has been no official national survey of poverty in the UK. Those concerned with poverty and inequality at a national level have had to rely almost exclusively on the *Low Income Families* series and its successor the *Households Below Average Income* (HBAI) series, produced by the Department of Social Security (DSS) and the Social Services Select Committee (DSS, 1998). These have generated data on the size and characteristics of the population living on a low income over time and have proved useful in revealing the extent of and growth in financial inequality (Gordon, 2000).

The HBAI statistics have been published by the DSS for 1979 to 1996–97 and are based on an analysis of the annual Family Expenditure Survey (FES) data. The DSS estimates are based on amalgamating two years of FES data to increase the available sample size and this procedure results in their being of limited use for studying the rapid effects of policy changes. However, individual year HBAI estimates from the FES back to 1961 have been produced by the Institute of Fiscal Studies (Goodman and Webb, 1994). Recently, the DSS have also produced single year HBAI estimates for 1994, 1995 and 1996 based on the larger Family Resources Survey (DSS, 1998). The percentage of the population living in households with less than half the UK's average income between 1961 and 1996 is shown in Figure 3.3.

Figure 3.3 shows that during the 1960s the amount of income inequality in the UK remained fairly constant, with around 11 per cent of the population living on an income less than half the average. The recession and 'stagflation' of the early 1970s, triggered by the OPEC oil price increases, caused the numbers living on less than half the average income to rise to a peak of just over 13 per cent. However, the relatively progressive social and economic policies of the mid-1970s contributed to poverty and inequality falling rapidly to a low of under 8 per cent of the population in 1977–78. The 1979 election victory of the Conservative party under Margaret Thatcher

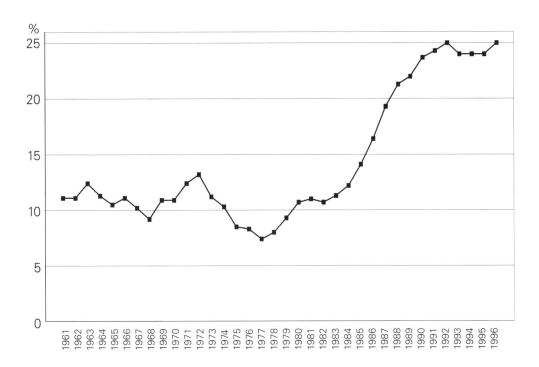

Source: Goodman and Webb, 1994; DSS, 1998

Figure 3.3 *Percentage of the population with less than half the average income after housing costs (1991–96)*

brought a reverse to social and economic policies designed to promote equity and caused a rapid growth in poverty and inequality which increased throughout the 1980s and early 1990s. The marginally more progressive social policies of the 1992 Conservative government resulted in a less rapid increase in inequality during the mid-1990s. However, by 1996, the latest year for which figures are available, a quarter of the British population was living on an income that was less than half the average.

In effect, 18 years of Conservative rule coincided with a trebling in the rate of the British population living on low incomes from 8 per cent to 25 per cent. By 1996, 14,100,000 people in the UK were living in households with incomes below half the average (after the deduction of housing costs). Although, as acknowledged in Chapter 2, this reflected the

driving forces at international level, the more pronounced impact of these forces in the UK compared with other industrialised countries must be due to a certain extent to the government policies of the time.

Table 3.5 shows the change in the share of total income (after deducting housing costs) between 1979 and 1996 that was received by individuals, divided up into deciles of the income distribution.

The results shown in Table 3.5 are unambiguous. Between 1979 and 1996, the share of the total income of those in the top 10 per cent increased from 20 per cent to 28 per cent. The richest 10 per cent of the population received a fifth of the total income in 1979 and more than a quarter of the total income in 1996. The rich are now much richer than they were in 1979. The share of total income

Table 3.5 *Share of the total income received by income decile (after housing costs)*

Income decile	1979 %	1996 %	Change %
Bottom 10%	4.1	2	−2.1
10–20%	5.7	4	−1.7
20–30%	6.2	5	−1.2
30–40%	8	6	−2.0
40–50%	9	8	−1.0
50–60%	9	9	0
60–70%	11	10	−1.0
70–80%	12	13	+1.0
80–90%	15	15	0
Top 10%	20	28	+8.0
Total	100	100	0

Source: Calculated from DSS, 1998

received by all those in the bottom half of society decreased, with the greatest losses occurring in the bottom 10 per cent. Those in the bottom 10 per cent saw their share of the total income fall by more than half, from 4.1 per cent in 1979 to 2 per cent in 1996.

Analysis of the latest HBAI data shows that the poorest 10 per cent were not only 'relatively' poorer in 1996 than in 1979 but also 'absolutely' poorer. Table 3.6 shows the change in real median incomes (that is, after allowing for inflation using the retail price index) by decile group between 1979 and 1996 (at April 1998 prices). DSS data published in 2000 confirm this trend. The number of people living in HBAI rose from 16.9 per cent to 17.7 per cent in Labour's first two years in office.

Table 3.6 *Change in real median weekly incomes 1979–96 by decile group at April 1998 prices (after housing costs)*

Income decile	1979 £	1996 £	Change %
Bottom 10%	81	71	−12
10–20%	104	106	+2
20–30%	121	132	+9
30–40%	139	164	+18
40–50%	157	200	+27
50–60%	177	236	+33
60–70%	199	277	+39
70–80%	227	327	+44
80–90%	263	402	+53
Top 10%	347	582	+68
Total population (mean)	185	264	+43

Source: Calculated from DSS, 1998

Between 1979 and 1996, the income of the British population rose on average by 43 per cent, from £9,620 per year (£185 per week) to £13,728 per year (£264 per week), at April 1998 prices. However, this increase in incomes was not shared equally. The median incomes of those in the bottom 10 per cent of the income distribution scale fell from £4,212 per year (£81 per week) to £3,692 per year (£71 per week) whereas the median incomes of those in the richest 10 per cent increased from £18,044 per year (£347 per week) to £30,264 per year (£582 per week). During these 18 years, the poorest became £520 per year poorer, whereas the richest saw their median incomes more than double, a gain of £12,220 per year.

Table 3.7 shows the distribution of households by region living on very low incomes (under £100 per week) in the late 1990s. The lowest proportion of low-income households are in the prosperous South East and South West of England, and the highest rates of low-income households are in the north of England and in Northern Ireland. The lowest average gross weekly income per person is in Northern Ireland (£126); on average people in South East England have two thirds more income (£207) per week.

Table 3.7 *Distribution of low weekly household incomes, 1995–98*

	% households with income under £100	*Average gross weekly income £ per person*
Northern Ireland	**16**	**126**
Scotland	**15**	**158**
Wales	**15**	**151**
England	**13**	**176**
North East	18	145
North West	15	158
Yorkshire and the Humber	15	152
West Midlands	15	155
London	15	204
East Midlands	12	166
East	12	177
South West	12	173
South East	10	207
United Kingdom	**14**	**171**

Source: ONS, 1999

Long-term unemployment in the UK

Long-term unemployment often results in poverty. It is also used as an indicator of social exclusion as it may cut people off from one possible source of entry to social networks. However, it can be an imperfect indicator of social exclusion as at any given time, 60 per cent of the population is not in paid work because, for example, they are retired, or are young children, or have more important things to do (childcare and so on).

The distribution of employment in the UK underwent a number of significant changes over the second half of the 20th century. During the Industrial Revolution there had been rapid growth in the employment opportunities in major cities and towns and a rapid depopulation of and decrease in jobs in rural areas. Since the Second World War this pattern has reversed and all the major conurbations in the UK have suffered from loss of population and a decline in the number of jobs. Major cities particularly have lost full-time manual jobs in traditional manufacturing sectors which often employed men. Where there has been growth of jobs in cities it has generally been in the service sector in part-time employment for women (Turok, 2000). Much of the long-term unemployment in the UK is a result of the current lack of suitable employment opportunities for unskilled and semi-skilled men in inner city areas.

Table 3.8 shows the distribution of people who were long-term unemployed and receiving benefits in April 1999. In the UK as a whole there were 1,320,100 people unemployed, of whom just under a quarter (24.9 per cent) had been unemployed for more than a year. However, the rates of long-term unemployment varied greatly between region and gender. For example, Northern Ireland had twice the rate of long-term unemployment (42 per cent) as South West England (21.4 per cent). Men in the UK were also more likely to be long-term unemployed (27.1 per cent) than women (18.2 per cent). These differences between regions and between men and women in the distribution of long-term unemployment are a result of the decline in blue-collar manufacturing jobs in the major UK cities and the growth of jobs in the service sector in semi-rural and rural areas.

Human poverty in Britain

In the previous four sections we have highlighted the regional impacts of the four elements of HPI-2: mortality rates, functional literacy, income and employment. In Part IV of this book we present the sets of the UK statistics on which this report is based,

including the calculations of the HPI-2 for all the UK's parliamentary constituencies. Unfortunately, it is not possible to give reliable estimates for human poverty at constituency level in Northern Ireland due to the lack of available data at local area level.

Tables 3.9 and 3.10 highlight the range of human poverty values that exist in Britain. At the top end of the scale is Wokingham with an index of 7.5, whereas Glasgow Shettleston has the worst poverty with a rating of 27.1. As well as illustrating this wide range, the tables show that historic divisions in human wealth and poverty are still very much in evidence. The worse-off constituencies are mainly in the urban conurbations of Glasgow, London, Liverpool, Tyneside, Manchester and Birmingham, while those with least poverty are in the affluent suburbs and comfortable semi-rural areas.

Despite all the talk of a classless society and the growing middle classes, the historic centres of disadvantage are still very much worse off than their wealthy counterparts. Given their traditional support, it is not surprising that the HPI-2 is reflected in the political profile of the constituencies: of the 125 constituencies with the highest rates of human poverty all but two are Labour, while of the 50 constituencies with the lowest levels of human poverty all but five are Conservative.

Given the past year's furore over the lack of investment that Labour had put into the health service and education in its first three years in office, it seems that not only had the party been disregarding the issues that are important to its voters, but also constituents' interests. The HPI-2 suggests that the government has significant potential to improve the lot of its constituents in all the index's elements. Interestingly, it has also been pointed out that the poorest constituencies in terms of the health element in this index were responsible for the least swing to Labour in the 1997 general election (Dorling, 2000).

During the past 20 years the UK has become one of the most socially polarised

Table 3.8 *Percentage of people who were long-term unemployed in April 1999 (claimant count)*

		% unemployed for more one year	Total number unemployed (in thousands)
Males	United Kingdom	27	1010
	England	27	807
	Northern Ireland	47	43
	Scotland	24	107
	Wales	24	53
	North East	27	68
	North West	24	127
	Yorkshire and the Humber	25	102
	East Midlands	24	62
	West Midlands	28	96
	East	24	61
	London	34	155
	South East	24	77
	South West	23	60
Females	United Kingdom	18	310
	England	18	251
	Northern Ireland	26	12
	Scotland	15	32
	Wales	15	16
	North East	17	18
	North West	15	36
	Yorkshire and the Humber	16	30
	East Midlands	15	19
	West Midlands	19	30
	East	18	21
	London	24	54
	South East	18	24
	South West	16	20
All persons	United Kingdom	25	1320
	England	25	1058
	Northern Ireland	42	54
	Scotland	22	139
	Wales	22	69
	North East	25	86
	North West	22	163
	Yorkshire and the Humber	23	131
	East Midlands	22	81
	West Midlands	26	126
	East	23	82
	London	31	209
	South East	23	101
	South West	21	80

Source: ONS, 1999

Table 3.9 *The 20 constituencies which suffer the worst human poverty*

Constituency name	Party	HPI-2
Glasgow Shettleston	Labour	27.1
Glasgow Springburn	Labour	26.0
Glasgow Maryhill	Labour	25.8
Birmingham Ladywood	Labour	25.7
Manchester Central	Labour	24.7
Camberwell and Peckham	Labour	24.6
Glasgow Baillieston	Labour	24.5
Liverpool Riverside	Labour	24.5
Hackney South and Shoreditch	Labour	24.0
Bethnal Green and Bow	Labour	23.6
Poplar and Canning Town	Labour	23.5
Vauxhall	Labour	23.2
Birmingham Sparkbrook and Small Heath	Labour	23.0
Tyne Bridge	Labour	22.9
Southwark North and Bermondsey	Liberal Democrat	22.9
Glasgow Pollock	Labour	22.9
Hackney North and Stoke Newington	Labour	22.3
Holborn and St Pancras	Labour	22.1
Liverpool Walton	Labour	21.6
Bootle	Labour	21.6

Table 3.10 *The 20 constituencies with the least human poverty*

Constituency name	Party	HPI-2
Blaby	Conservative	9.0
Charnwood	Conservative	9.0
Esher and Walton	Conservative	9.0
Solihull	Conservative	8.9
Croydon South	Conservative	8.9
Saffron Walden	Conservative	8.9
Surrey Heath	Conservative	8.8
Mid Dorset and North Poole	Conservative	8.8
Sutton Coldfield	Conservative	8.7
South Cambridgeshire	Conservative	8.6
Beaconsfield	Conservative	8.6
Rayleigh	Conservative	8.5
North East Hampshire	Conservative	8.4
Romsey	Liberal Democrat	8.3
Chesham and Amersham	Conservative	8.3
Buckingham	Conservative	8.2
Woodspring	Conservative	8.1
Cheadle	Conservative	7.9
Northavon	Liberal Democrat	7.9
Wokingham	Conservative	7.5

countries in the industrialised world. As we enter the 21st century, the UK is a society with greater disparities in absolute wealth than at any time in history. During the 1980s and early 1990s, successive Conservative governments actively pursued a range of policies which effectively took money from the poor and gave it to the rich. The long-term trend towards greater equality in income and wealth, which had been evident in the UK since the 15th century, has been reversed during the past 20 years, at least temporarily (Gordon, 2000). The human costs of this increase in inequality have been immense and millions have had to lead lives unnecessarily blighted by the spectre of poverty and want. The UK is becoming a more divided society – a trend that affects all our lives.

The Labour government has committed itself to reducing the amount of inequality, although to date, its policies have had little impact given the scale of the problem. The UK is richer than at any time in its history yet there are still too many families whose lives are blighted by insufficient incomes, long-term unemployment, functional illiteracy and early deaths. As Table 3.9 shows, the problem of human poverty is particularly severe in the

inner city areas of the major conurbations, but no region or area has escaped the blight of human poverty. Even in the most prosperous regions of the country, such as the wealthy South East of England, there remain people who suffer from unemployment, low income, ill health and difficulties in reading and writing. Although there are great differences in the geographical distribution of human poverty in the UK, it is ultimately a national problem which will require national solutions.

As we have also explained throughout this report, human development is about more than these four elements. In Part IV we present some of the indicators that highlight other elements of human development. As many of these have only started being collected recently, there are few for which we can present trends. However, they do highlight the variation that occurs in elements of human development throughout the UK and between European countries, and they show there is room for improvement. In the next section we look at how the government is trying to tackle some of these issues by reviewing the work of the Social Exclusion Unit (SEU) and of the Regional Development Agencies.

The Social Exclusion Unit

The SEU was set up by Tony Blair seven months after the election of a Labour government in May 1997, initially as a two-year experiment with a remit to improve government action to reduce social exclusion. It covered only England, with the intention that the devolved administrations in Scotland, Wales and Northern Ireland would draw up their own strategies for tackling social exclusion. The SEU was not intended to cover issues that fall within the remit of any government department or duplicate work being done by other organisations. In effect, it acts as an

internal government think tank and has no executive powers or budget, although it works with departments to implement its ideas and monitor progress. A more comprehensive strategy for tackling poverty and social exclusion is outlined by the government in *Opportunity for All* (DSS, 1999), the government's annual report on how it is tackling poverty and exclusion. A UK-wide focus on poverty is taken by the Joint Ministerial Committee on Poverty.

The SEU defined social exclusion as 'a shorthand term for what can happen when people or areas suffer from a combination of linked problems such as unemployment, poor skills, low incomes, poor housing, high crime environments, bad health and family break-down' (SEU, 1998), an explicitly common-sense definition that sidesteps some of the academic debates over defining, identifying and measuring exclusion. Significantly, it emphasises areas as subjects of exclusion, rather than individuals. The government has professed a general enthusiasm for the potential benefits of 'joined-up' government, and the SEU embodies its belief that social exclusion, being a complex of related problems, may be particularly appropriate to be tackled in this way.

The SEU's analysis of the causes of social exclusion has been somewhat limited. The SEU has argued that mainstream government programmes have in some cases contributed to social exclusion (SEU, 1998), and that the public sector has been uncoordinated and inflexible, and has not consulted the public sufficiently. It also argued that the private sector has played a role in exclusion through discrimination by area and income or expenditure (SEU, 1998; Kelly and McCormick, 1998). However, it has not referred to market failure, and the role of public funding as potential pump-priming, which was much discussed in the 1980s, and has made only limited reference to the socially and spatially uneven effects of de-industrialisation, in relation to local housing markets (PAT 7, 1999).

Given our emphasis on environmental justice in the previous chapter, it should also be noted that the SEU has not looked at either the distributional impacts of environmental problems and links to social exclusion, sustainable development, or distributional access to environmental resources.

The SEU should not be seen in isolation. It is intended to complement prudent macro-economic management, albeit with acceptance of a reduced government role in the economy, and mainstream initiatives by individual departments. Other government policies in areas such as health and education, and wider social and economic developments, also have an impact on social exclusion.

What the SEU has done so far

The detailed remit of the SEU has been based on specific projects chosen by the Prime Minister, and its agenda has evolved over time. In its first year the SEU focused on rough sleeping, exclusion and truancy from school, and deprived housing estates, probably the most visible and least contentious examples of exclusion or the excluded. In its second year the SEU also looked at teenage pregnancy, provoked by figures showing that the UK had the highest teenage fertility rate in Europe, and the number of 16–18 year olds not in education, employment or training, after informal evidence that large numbers of young people were 'lost' in the system. The review of the SEU in 1999 supported its retention for three years. The unit is currently consulting on the National Strategy for Neighbourhood Renewal and plans for implementation, and has also played a growing role in monitoring the implementation of past SEU reports. There will be a second review in 2002.

The general pattern of work is that the SEU has produced reports on specific issues, on very short timescales and, increasingly, with the help of experts outside government. These have included summaries of existing knowledge but tend to avoid opening up major controversies. They include proposals for action by government and other agencies, and studies of examples of good practice. All of the SEU reports have been published in hard copy and on the SEU's website (www.cabinet-office.gov.uk/seu).

The report on deprived neighbourhoods was particularly significant. It built on the SEU's definition of social exclusion to describe the concentration in poor neighbourhoods of a range of interlocking problems, how the gap with the rest of the country had widened, and analysed why previous initiatives to deal with this had failed (SEU, 1998). This report led

---

Table 3.11 *The 18 policy action teams (PATs)*

Jobs
Skills
Business
Neighbourhood management
Housing management
Neighbourhood wardens
Unpopular housing
Antisocial behaviour
Community self-help
Arts and sport
Schools plus
Young people
Shops
Financial services
Information technology
Learning lessons
Joining it up locally
Better information

Note: Each of these PATs then produced its own report in 1999 and 2000.

on to a further investigation of policy through the establishment of eighteen policy action teams (PATs), which drew in large numbers of academics and practitioners (see Table 3.11).

The first major outcome of the SEU's work was a new urban regeneration programme, the New Deal for Communities (NDC), which drew on the report on deprived neighbourhoods and is led by the DETR. The NDC aimed to reduce unemployment and crime and to improve health and educational achievement in selected areas of 1000–4000 households.

The NDC tries to build on recognised good practice in urban regeneration. It encourages community involvement including, at early stages, the use of some competition to encourage strong proposals; planning and delivery through partnerships of local people, community and voluntary organisations, public agencies, local authorities and business; and modification of mainstream services in the areas over timescales of up to 10 years. It is intended to be experimental and it is hoped that, for example, some community-led partnerships might emerge. Local authorities

high on the index of deprivation (DETR, 1998a) were invited to make bids for neighbourhoods in their areas. The government released £800m for 1999–2002. Seventeen 'pathfinder areas' started work in 1999, and 22 more started in 2000.

Following reports from the PATs in 1999 and 2000 and early experience with NDC, the SEU developed the National Strategy for Neighbourhood Renewal (NSNR) for consultation. This incorporates 'maximum community, voluntary and private sector involvement and leadership', clearer and, possibly, some shared responsibilities for services, and better quality public services, seen as the government's 'best weapons against deprivation'. It aims to reach more areas than the NDC and the Single Regeneration Budget, and fits alongside a general 'Best Value' regime for local authority services (DETR, 1998b).

Is the SEU having an impact?

The SEU has popularised the concept of social exclusion and raised its profile inside and outside government. However, although the NSNR aims to 'revive local economies', the SEU has not yet contributed to the government's thinking on the economy which takes an unequivocal approach to the role of the private sector and to globalisation. The SEU argued that the private sector has played a role in exclusion through discrimination by area and income or expenditure, and PATs examined unequal access to retail and financial services (PAT3, 1999; PAT 13, 1999; PAT 14, 1999). However, in practice these PATs avoided considering the significance of the private sector or making demanding recommendations. The Labour government inherited an improving economy and public finances and relatively low unemployment. The employment-based approach to tackling social exclusion, the supply-side approach to the labour market and the significance and effects of the SEU would be tested much more severely if the economic climate changed for the worse.

To date, the SEU has not had a significant impact on wider initiatives to improve public sector performance so that they are 'exclusion proof'. Largely based on changes introduced in the late 1980s and early 1990s, many of these have used indicators and sanctions that may exacerbate processes of exclusion for a minority of service users (Le Grand and Bartlett, 1993). For example, there are incentives to service providers to exclude or attempt to transfer responsibility for difficult schoolchildren, costly patients, disruptive tenants, asylum seekers, and homeless people – incentives which are inherent in some quasi-market mechanisms in social policy. There is also the use of unweighted league tables to judge performance, and funding restrictions and pressure for 'continuous improvement' and cost reduction through the Best Value regime for local authorities (DETR, 1998b). During the time that the term 'social exclusion' has been common currency, these exclusionary pressures have increased (eg Power and Mumford, 1999). However, while the SEU was not involved in the 1997–98 comprehensive spending review

which set government spending plans for three years, it will be involved in the second review from 2000.

The SEU has had some impact on the activity and infrastructure of the public sector. New units have been established within central government: for example, the Rough Sleepers' Unit in the DETR is overseen by a ministerial committee incorporating all the affected departments and the SEU, and is chaired by the minister for local government and housing. The unit is headed by a high profile 'Tsar' appointed from outside government. In addition to the NDC, individual departments also established some partly crosscutting area-based schemes including education action zones, employment action zones, health action zones, and Sure Start for pre-school children. Overall, about a third of English local authorities have some area-based programmes that are related to the work of the SEU. However, this is largely a continuation of the pattern of urban regeneration funding in the 1980s (Robson et al, 1994).

The NDC and all the PATs were concerned with people in 'poor neighbourhoods' rather than 'poor people', with, initially at least, an implicit emphasis on social housing areas and issues. This area focus (rather than people focus or nationwide approach, as in other government initiatives) has come in for criticism (eg Turok and Edge, 1999; Murie, 2000; Gordon, 2000), reflecting long-running critiques of the dominance of area-based approaches in urban policy and urban regeneration since the 1960s. It has long been argued that much deprivation will remain outside any designated areas (Townsend, 1979), while Robson and his colleagues argued that area programmes may benefit adjacent areas more than the intended areas themselves (1994). It has been argued that the causes of local problems may be at national or even global level, as has been considered in the previous chapter. There has also been criticism of the scale of areas used in urban regeneration policy as addressing only fractions of city and regional labour markets (Turok and

Edge, 1999). Small programmes may also have fewer knock-on impacts than larger ones, lower leverage of private funding and lower sustainability than broader ones. Robson and his colleagues argued that regeneration funding was 'minuscule' compared to the problems (1994). If all the NDC projects lasted ten years, each would received an average of only £2million a year direct funding, although many have supplemented NDC funding with Single Regeneration Budget funding and have attempted to lever in private finance. There is also the suggestion that area regeneration programmes have been used to compensate for or distract from cuts in other public expenditure programmes (Healey, 1992).

The SEU initially focused its concern for poor neighbourhoods on what it thought to be the 'the worst (council housing) estates', but was criticised for overlooking the less visible and politically salient social exclusion outside social rented housing tenure (eg Lee et al, 1995; Murie, 2000), and for potentially contributing to the stigma and exclusion of these estates and their residents. The SEU has considered only to a limited extent exclusion through gender, age, disability, or being a carer, mentally ill or an ex-offender – some of the less visible and

more politically contentious elements. There were also some early concerns about the degree of focus on ethnicity. This and the focus on areas and communities may mean that some of the most excluded individuals and groups are not affected by the SEU's recommendations. The NSNR has not yet been implemented.

It is difficult to assess the impact of the SEU on the level of social exclusion overall and difficult to measure the independent effect of the SEU's work given that there are many other influences on social exclusion. There are also inherent difficulties in defining and measuring the level of social exclusion and there has been little time for initiatives to take effect.

However, the SEU has set the government some targets (see Table 3.12) and these will be watched carefully to see if the SEU is having at least some measurable impact. It is likely that some progress will be made in these areas, particularly on rough sleeping where overall numbers are small. However, there is scepticism about whether the targets can be met and whether they might skew the efforts of agencies working in these areas in an unhelpful way – by changing definitions or means of measurement rather than addressing the problem.

Table 3.12 Targets for SEU outcomes

Date	Outcome
2002	Rough sleeping to be reduced by two thirds from 1998–99 figures
	Truancy and exclusion to be reduced by one third from 1998 figures
2010	Pregnancies under 18 to be reduced to half 1999 figures

Although the SEU was supposed to be based on joined-up government, it suffers from the tensions between government departments, such as the DTI and DETR, which reflect

the tensions at global level. Indeed, this is repeated at regional level in the shape of the recently established regional development agencies.

In the regions

In 1999 the UK took a step closer to devolution with elections for the Scottish Parliament

and Welsh Assembly. In England non-elected bodies were established in the form of regional development agencies (RDAs), whose primary remit is to encourage economic development and regeneration through increasing business efficiency, competitiveness and investment. The boards of the RDAs are dominated by private sector interests and, as a result, economic strategies have tended to emphasise wealth creation, skills and training, employability and enterprise. However, under the terms of the RDA Act (1998), the RDAs have an over-arching responsibility to promote sustainable development and to tackle underlying problems of social exclusion and inequalities.

Each of the RDAs has produced its own vision and strategic priorities, but there are some common themes around equality of opportunity and social cohesion. All acknowledge the importance of addressing the causes of poverty and deprivation, and recognise that it is not sufficient to simply increase GDP. They also appear to understand the need to overcome social and economic barriers which prevent people from sharing in economic prosperity, through positive action measures and targeted support relating primarily to gender and racial discrimination.

Measures which support enterprise and innovation in the social economy should be welcomed, though targets are often couched in business language. The rhetoric of community involvement reverberates throughout the strategies and there are encouraging signs of the RDAs' willingness to work in partnership with voluntary and community sector organisations, especially in addressing social exclusion issues.

The RDAs face considerable challenges, not least in achieving the catalytic and strategic role to which most aspire. Their budgets are modest in comparison with government and European funding reaching the regions, and they have only limited political power. Nevertheless, a crucial feature of the RDAs is a strong commitment to their own regions, alongside an understanding of local strengths, dynamics and issues. This gives them an advantage in tackling complex problems such as poverty, in that they are able to take a holistic approach, drawing in potential partners with different experiences and areas of expertise. Therefore, a more integrated strategy can be developed than would have been possible through the government offices or each of the sectors acting alone.

Although the RDAs lack democratic accountability and have relatively few resources at their disposal, they have the potential to make important links between sustainable development and the alleviation of poverty. The regional economic strategies were written after substantial consultation and incorporate the opinions, priorities and specialist knowledge of wide sections of the population. They represent a valiant, and sometimes ingenious, attempt to devise a coherent, realistic and principled approach to economic, social and environmental problems. In their first year of existence this is no mean feat, and it will be interesting to see whether the early promise can be translated into practical actions which seriously address the causes, rather than just the symptoms, of poverty.

Main Messages of this Chapter

- Overall, the UK has achieved a very high level of human development, close to that to which the countries of the world should aspire; we rank tenth in the HDI.

- However, serious issues of poverty and inequality remain, not only in income but in basic human development. In comparison to countries with similar levels of income and average human development, the UK has more serious problems of disparities in gender empowerment, human poverty, income poverty, and income inequalities.

- A focus on mainly economic measures means that problems such as environmental degradation and social exclusion are under-valued.
- During the past 20 years there has been a move towards developing indicators to measure poverty that do not focus solely on economic criteria.
- Indicators that give a true reflection of what it means to be poor will not be developed successfully without the involvement of those in poverty.
- Poverty damages health: in the constituencies containing the million people with the 'worst health', 10,921 people would still be alive if they enjoyed the mortality rates of the million people with the 'best health' over a period of just five years.
- In a 1996 survey between one fifth and a quarter of the adults aged 16 to 65 in the UK would have great difficulty in understanding complex documents or tables; literacy problems were greatest among older people with low levels of education, the unemployed, those in a manual social class and people on the lowest levels of income.
- Between 1979 and 1996, the share of the total income in the UK of those in the top

10 per cent increased from 20 per cent to 28 per cent. The richest 10 per cent of the population received a fifth of the total income in 1979 and more than a quarter of the total income in 1996. The rich are now much richer than they were in 1979.

- The lowest proportion of low-income households is in the prosperous South East and South West of England, and the highest rates of low income households are in the North of England, in Northern Ireland and Strathclyde.
- Northern Ireland has twice the rate of long-term unemployment as the South West of England. Men in the UK are also more likely to be long-term unemployed than women.
- The SEU's analysis of the causes of social exclusion has been limited.
- The SEU has not contributed significantly to government thinking on the economy.
- The SEU has not had a significant impact on wider initiatives to improve public sector performance to make them 'exclusion proof'.
- The SEU has considered only to a limited extent exclusion through gender, age, disability, or through being a carer, mentally ill or an ex-offender. This and the focus on areas and communities may mean that some of the most excluded individuals and groups are not affected by the SEU's recommendations.

Part II

Key Elements and the UK Policy Agenda

Chapter 4

Food Security: A Challenge for Human Development

The Food We Eat

The remote Hebridean island of Taransay, now famous as the site of the BBC's *Castaway 2000* project, was not always a barren, deserted lump of rock inhabited only by a few sheep and deer. Two hundred years ago Taransay supported a thriving population of more than 100 families, who raised a variety of livestock, grain and vegetables, fished from the sea and collected seaweeds, lichens and shellfish from the foreshore. As recently as the early 1900s, a dozen households remained, mainly producing Harris tweed. By the middle of the century the community had gone, their viability finally undermined by the long-term processes of de-industrialisation, a retreat from living off the land and the globalisation of economies, including the food economy. In 2000 a mixed sample of 30 millennial Britons are facing the self-imposed challenge of repeating their predecessors' achievement of maintaining life from the resources of the land, sea and air around Taransay. On the Hebridean mainland, descendants of Taransay's last weavers look on, bemused.

Across the UK, armchair voyeurs measured the extent of their own alienation from their food supply as they reacted to the TV demonstrations of chicken slaughter or the use of human waste to fertilise the land. They contrasted these challenges with the security of their own food supply, stored away in the kitchen fridge or waiting to be collected from the supermarket down the road. With food-stuffs from all around the world now available for most people no more than a short car ride away, the most challenging aspects of food for many in the UK relate to eating the 'right' foods in the 'right' amounts. There is a major diet and exercise industry which seeks to capitalise on anxieties provoked amongst the affluent about their food consumption.

Malnutrition, in the form of overeating or an unbalanced diet, is at the root of many of the heart and bowel disorders which currently consume a significant proportion of the NHS budget. There is an increasing problem of obesity in children – the WHO estimates that 10 per cent of schoolchildren in industrialised countries are obese. Compared with the past, dietary excess and the costs of treating its consequences, rather than dietary deficiency, are two of the major health problems we now face as a society. Alongside the problems of excess, however, there remain significant numbers of people who experience food poverty and who do not have access to an adequate supply of affordable, quality food.

There is no shortage of food on a global scale and such a great choice has never before been available to so many consumers, especially in the West, but this choice is not evenly distributed. Even though there is more food available to eat, fewer of us are involved in producing it. Many people have never come face to face with the living versions of the animals or fish they like to eat, or have experienced their dinner sprouting from the ground or dropping from a tree. Many are not confident that they can turn a selection of common fresh ingredients into an attractive and tasty meal.

At the same time that we have lost confidence in our individual or communal ability to produce food, we have also lost confidence in those who have the task of providing us with a safe and reliable food supply. Agribusiness and food technology no longer rely on the traditional relationship between the farmer and the land to provide the raw ingredients for the highly processed products which the marketing people will convince us that we want. Anxieties over the consequences of intensive rearing, such as BSE and salmonella, and over genetic modification have revived interest in food production among people who fear for their health if these technologies continue unchecked.

Even though current production methods can provide food to feed the whole world, there is increasing concern that this situation is not sustainable. One aspect of the globalisation of food production is that staples are produced wherever it is cheapest and most economic to do so. The result is that there is the additional impact on energy costs of transporting the food, while any pollution caused by pesticide use is exported from the region buying the food to the area producing it – another example of environmental injustice. Local economies in some of the poorest areas of the world may also be undermined as money flows out of the area into the transnational companies that control big farms. At the same time, the best-quality food is exported while locals are forced to eat what's left.

Developing countries are increasingly challenging the export of the damaging environmental impacts of Western consumption patterns. There is an increasing reaction against the international political structures that reinforce these patterns and subsequent legal developments, especially in patent law, that give multinationals an increasingly free hand in determining our eating choices and in protecting the financial interests of the few over and above the needs of the many.

Food and Human Development

Human development is inextricably bound up with food, how it is produced and accessed and how food choice is determined. One of the oldest forms of human aggression is to starve an enemy into submission; one of the warmest ways of welcoming another individual is to share food with them. The 1970s slogan 'we are what we eat' does not tell us everything about the nature of our humanity but it points up some important relationships which we would be careless to ignore. As this book has already highlighted, during the past 20 years the UK has become an increasingly divided society. Inequalities of income and the access which income provides to the necessities and luxuries of life are major features of that division. Indeed, some observers speak of a 'nutritional underclass' (Leather, 1996).

Food poverty

Food poverty is primarily a problem that is experienced by those who have little money. Some argue, understandably, that food poverty could be eliminated by the single mechanism of increasing welfare payments to ensure that everyone has equality of access to the dominant food market. However, this solution is simply not on offer. Government policy on the reform of welfare contains no reference to the issue of income adequacy in general. Furthermore, an exclusive focus on income diverts attention away from other dimensions of the causes of food poverty and from other possibilities for tackling it across sectors. A concentration on food poverty could, and in some cases does, lead to an exclusive concentration on 'the poor', their habits, their attitudes and the ways in which the costs of these to the wider community can be reduced. This misses out the wider role that food plays in the community and the way in which our treatment of the food supply expresses the kind of society we would like to become.

Since 1992 the Poverty Alliance, an NGO, has been responding to community concerns in Scotland about the problems experienced by low-income households in accessing an affordable supply of quality food. Similar work has been undertaken elsewhere in the UK by Sustain (previously the National Food Alliance). The Poverty Alliance has shown that food poverty is a reality in Scotland, and, indeed, can be found elsewhere in the UK. Evidence is found in Scotland's health record and in the priority which is given to food access issues by community groups and voluntary organisations. At its heart is a national failure to ensure that every person in Scotland has access to an affordable, quality diet.

Whilst this failure could be obscured in the past by the divisions of political responsibility between Scotland and the remainder of the UK, it is likely to become more prominent in the context of a Scottish parliament. We are often willing to judge the values and the efficiency of the governments of developing countries by their ability to feed their populations. Ironically, we have yet to apply this criterion to ourselves and no political party is currently basing its electoral appeal on a programme for securing the basic necessities of life, including food.

Food policy in Scotland today is primarily an export-driven enterprise policy. Second, it is a health policy aimed at reducing the demand for malnutrition services and, third, and particularly prominently at the moment in light of the public concern about BSE and

genetically modified foods, a food safety policy. These are all important issues, but they fall short of securing an accessible, affordable, quality diet for all – a state of food security – which should be a central objective of the Scottish Parliament.

The divided UK is reflected in the very different responses of social groups to the universal need for food. Whilst those who are comfortably-off concern themselves with issues of food safety, the ethics of food production and their personal health, disadvantaged communities are engaged in a wide variety of self-help initiatives such as food cooperatives, community cafés and 'local growing' schemes to compensate for the failures of the food market (see boxes throughout chapter). The irony behind this division is that, despite their differences, both those with money and those without now share a basic concern about the security of their food supply. Development towards a more healthy, sustainable and inclusive UK cannot ignore the issue of food security.

Food security

Food security is a term used most commonly in relation to developing countries. In 1983 the UN defined the goal of food security as being 'to give populations both economic and physical access to a supply of food, sufficient in both quality and quantity, at all times, regardless of climate or harvests, social level or income' (quoted in Oxfam, 1995). We are not suggesting that food poverty in the UK is comparable to the famine or endemic under-nourishment experienced in many parts of Africa or Asia, but the concept of food security is increasingly being applied to the understanding of the problems faced by disadvantaged communities in the West.

Where basic subsistence is not the main issue, definitions of food security have taken on a more empowering character. The Ontario Public Health Association, for example, argues that food security is a state in which people 'can get enough food to eat that is safe, that

---

Box 4.1 *Bath Place Community Venture, Leamington Spa*

Bath Place Community Venture (BPCV) aims to promote healthy eating and encourage volunteering in low-income communities. It offers the local community access to:

- a community café, serving cheap nutritional vegetarian food every day during the week;
- a pre-school nursery each weekday, morning and afternoon;
- a parent/carer toddler group, three sessions weekly;
- a welfare rights adviser, three times weekly;
- a women's art group, weekly;
- youth work;
- summer activities for about 50 local children of all ages; and
- training for women and other disadvantaged groups.

The community café is a much needed and valued resource in the area. For example, in the first quarter of 1999, 1832 adults' and 477 children's lunches were served. Around 9236 lunches will be served throughout the year, nearly 2000 of which will be children's meals. A survey conducted in the café in February this year found that 77 per cent of the users were unemployed and 77 per cent said that the community lunch was their main meal of the day.

The healthy-eating workshops have proved to be very successful. Educating sections of the local community in areas such as healthy eating on a low budget, what ingredients to use and where to buy the food, has proved to be empowering for those attending.

There are plans to open a night café for young people. At least 40 young people said that they would use such a facility. The need for a breakfast club for younger children has also been identified. This will improve not only the physical health of the children, but their ability to learn and their social interaction with the staff and other children. There are also plans for a food cooperative over the next few years.

Bath Place Community Venture receives its core funding from Warwickshire social services and has close links with the health authority. This has enabled access to training opportunities for volunteers and users of the venture. It has also become part of the Open College Network, providing access to a range of accredited courses.

Source: Studies of community projects from the Sustain food and low income database

---

they like to eat and that helps them to be healthy. They must be able to get this food in ways which make them feel good about themselves and their families' (Oxfam, 1995). In 1995 the World Food Day Association of Canada produced the following working definition of food security which identifies the main parameters of the issue and which could provide a useful starting point for the development of food security policy in the UK (Oxfam, 1995).

'By food security we mean that all people at all times have both physical and economic access to enough food for an active, healthy life. This concept encompasses the following principles:

- *that the ways and means in which food is produced and distributed are respectful of the natural processes of the earth and are thus sustainable;*
- *that both the production and consumption of food are grounded in and governed by social values that are just and equitable as well as moral and ethical;*
- *that the ability to acquire food is assured;*

- *that the food itself is nutritionally adequate and personally and culturally acceptable;*
- *that the food is obtained in a manner that upholds human dignity.'*

When these definitions are translated into possible policy dimensions, it quickly becomes apparent that food security relies on more than welfare transfers or health services. Food security moves beyond these considerations to engage with questions of basic human rights, sustainable development, health inequalities, social inclusion, agricultural reform, land use planning, community development, economic development and the capacity of national and local governments to deliver local control of the food supply. A review of food-related systems in the UK would demonstrate that we currently fall well short of food security standards.

Developing food security

In its work on food policy, the Poverty Alliance has organised a wide range of discussions for local community activists, environmentalists, health and community workers and others to explore the nature of these problems and to identify ways in which they might be addressed. As a result its work has included providing support to community-based initiatives to combat food poverty and carrying out an enquiry into the potential for tackling food poverty for a local regeneration partnership.

During the eight years it has focused on food availability in Scotland, the organisation's perception of the dietary problems of those on low incomes has moved from a simple focus on income adequacy and household management skills to a realisation that the problems experienced by people living in poverty are only the most extreme demonstration of a substantive problem which affects Scotland as a nation. Essentially, the problem is that Scotland has minimal control of its food supply and that its food choices, national and individual, are principally determined by interest groups for whom the health and prosperity of Scotland's people are not the main concerns. We have concluded that, whilst community action is essential in defining local food needs, in controlling the excesses of food market operations at the local level and in demonstrating the benefits of alternative approaches to improving the Scottish diet, only government action can provide the framework within which substantive improvements to the Scottish diet and to the ability of people living on low incomes to exercise healthy food choices can be developed.

It is obvious from definitions of food security that the issue goes far beyond the day to day problems of feeding the hungry and making a healthy choice of food available to everyone. Such food poverty programmes are important in tackling current need and in correcting some of the distortions of the market. However, we need to recognise their limitations and also to be aware of the dangers which are inherent in the possible institutionalisation of food poverty (Riches, 1997).

For example, the manager of a major industry-led programme for distributing surplus produce to schemes for homeless people and others once said that she could access produce for distribution to the poor by arguing to food industry research and development people that they could save millions of pounds in consumer testing new products by trying them out on the homeless. 'If they don't like it,' she said, 'who else is going to?' Food banks which, similarly, collect surplus foodstuffs and distribute them to welfare claimants have often meant the difference between hunger and health for families on the brink, but in some countries they have also become institutionalised into the welfare system so that people receive food stamps rather than cash payments and have to accept the choice of foods which is decided for them by the waste policies of the food industry (Webster and Hawkes, 2000). This is not the way for anyone to achieve food security.

Box 4.2 *Cable Street Community Garden, London*

The Cable Street community garden started when a local Friends of the Earth group took over the site in the mid-1970s. Although it is up to individuals to decide what to grow, most grow some food and a few plots are entirely devoted to fruit and vegetables. Some people use the garden to socialise, bringing along their families and a picnic. For others, the garden is an escape from domestic pressures. There is an annual open day during which visitors can come and look around the garden and the half-hectare, 41-plot site is home to people from all over the world – including Japan, Poland and the Outer Hebrides. Around a quarter are of Bangladeshi or Afro Caribbean origin, and around a quarter are Irish, particularly older men. Around half of the gardeners are women.

The gardens are run by volunteers, with funds for maintaining general areas and buying equipment coming from the £12 (£5 for retired and unemployed people) annual rent which plot-holders pay. Individual plot-holders attend regular monthly meetings to discuss issues of concern to do with the garden. While the lack of paid staff can spell disaster for some projects, in this case it may well be the source of its strength. People are involved, and stay involved, because they are passionate about it.

Source: Garnett, 1999

Commodity or Necessity?

Before going on to consider how it might be possible to move forward on this broad-based agenda for food security, it is important to consider the extent to which we think of food as either a commodity or as a basic necessity or social good. This distinction determines the extent to which we regard food issues as primarily a concern for the individual, the market or the political realm.

In its most basic forms, food emerges from the earth, sea and sky around us without any agency on our part. Without access to non-toxic food, water and air, we die. We are not the only species to seek to manage this food supply to ensure our survival through times of scarcity but we are, arguably, the most successful. Even when we are faced with the worst conditions the planet can throw at us, we have the global capacity to sustain all human life through times of drought and famine. The reasons why we do not do this have less to do with our technical capacities than with our unwillingness to share the planet's resources in an equitable way. In achieving our technical

control over the food supply we have developed our agency in the form of agriculture, animal husbandry and fishing to the extent that there is little now available to us, as food, which has not been affected by human intervention.

Human intervention in the food supply is one of the basic sources of wealth. Having moved on from a subsistence economy, this wealth is largely based on the added value that can be attached to basic foodstuffs in the form of convenience, variety or cultural relevance. At the same time that food producers have exploited the potential of adding this sort of value to turn food into a commodity, its role as a basic necessity has kept a downward pressure on prices, except in the specialised niche markets. As we know in the case of BSE, this pressure for cheap food has resulted in cutting corners which has threatened to undermine our confidence in the food supply. In the case of the genetic modification of food, the pressure for cheap foods and high profits also threatens to intervene in the building blocks of nature which will undoubtedly have consequences of which we are not yet fully aware. For example, the idea of using a term- inator gene to prevent plants producing seeds – thus ensuring that farmers will have to purchase a new supply every year rather than collecting their own – brings the concept of built-in obsolescence into the natural world in a way that troubles many people.

The need to reverse some of the common trends in food production was highlighted by participants in a series of seminars on food security held by the Poverty Alliance. They called for a more sustainable approach, describ- ing a state of food security as a highly localised food economy in which:

- Real neighbourhoods (not planners' invent- ions) would have access to affordable food, produced locally.
- People would be able to purchase all the food they needed on a daily basis from a range of shops within walking or easy transport distance of where they lived.
- The emphasis would be on freshly prod- uced food which people could buy when they wanted in order to prepare it, without the necessity for bulk-buying or domestic refrigeration, which are difficult for people on marginal incomes.
- People would appreciate the seasonal nature of the food supply, and that variations in the size and shape of fruits and vegetables do not, necessarily, imply poor quality.
- Priority would be given to locally-produced food including fresh fish and dairy prod- ucts.
- Priority would be given to conserving local food sources, such as fish, and using them

for direct food consumption, rather than indirect consumption such as animal feeds.
- Where food could not be produced locally, priority would be given to supporting developing world economies according to fair trade principles.
- Food services would be provided by a mixture of commercial and community- based agencies, including food cooperatives and community cafés.

Food is both a necessity and a commodity, but it is a commodity unlike almost any other in that it is ingested into our system in a way which does not apply to commodities like cars and fridges. Food security is concerned not only with supply but also with people's nutrit- ional welfare and with the psychosocial security that is essential for social cohesion. Because of this, food is a commodity whose supply cannot be left entirely to the market because market failure would, ultimately, mean starvation and social collapse; it is also a necessity whose production places specific requirements on the market in relation to safety and supply that go further than normal market conditions would require. Because individuals are unlikely to have the range of influence to ensure food security, and because the range of decisions we can make about food in our own lives are determined largely by the parameters estab- lished by the food industry, it is essential that government plays a central role in ensuring food security. For governments, food security and the health and welfare of individuals and society should take precedence over the prior- ities of the food industry.

Lessons from the Past

This is not the first time these issues have been raised. Writing in 1937, Sir John Orr, director of the Rowett Institute in Aberdeen, who was familiar with the poor nutrition and general

living standards of many people in the years following the First World War, argued the need for a revolution without bloodshed to 'raise the standards of living of the poorest without depriving the more fortunate of any of their material possessions' (Orr, 1937). He saw this revolution as fundamental to improvements in the health and welfare of the nation. Orr, as an ardent nationalist, addressed himself particularly to the concerns of Scotland, but his views were relevant to the social disparities which affected the UK as a whole. He wrote:

> *'If we are going to have a revolution . . . we must have a definite objective. Let us have a modest, simple objective that all classes will understand, and let us set down in our plans only what we know we can accomplish. Let us limit it to food and housing. For food we will set out to get nothing extravagant, no luxuries, merely a diet on the standard which the Government Advisory Committee on Nutrition has said is necessary for health.'*

Essential to Orr's vision was a return of people to the land to produce the healthy foodstuffs which would support dietary objectives, but these people would not be required to experience the rural poverty of the past. 'As good a living must be made on the land,' wrote Orr, 'as in the towns.'

Orr was not dewy-eyed about the possibility of achieving these goals. 'An attempt to carry through a national scheme of reorganisation would be resisted by powerful vested interests,' he wrote.

> *'In this country the people who have the power and influence think mainly in terms of money making and profit, and the Government must do the same. Apart from war, the balancing of the budget, imports and exports and other trade considerations must be the primary interests of the Government of a country of traders. The third of the population consisting of unemployed and poorly paid workmen, whose standard of living is far below what the present material*

> *wealth of the country warrants, cause a certain amount of uneasiness. The well to do don't like to think of them, for we are a kindly people. We soothe our consciences by charitable organisations and the poor are kept from rising and asserting themselves by periodically giving them a little more. A little extra on the "dole", a few more houses, a third of a pint of milk at half-price to prevent gross malnutrition amongst children and other such social measures take the edge off the bitterness of poverty and help to keep the masses quiet. Our labour [that is, union] leaders think they have achieved something worthwhile when they have got these crumbs, when the people they represent might secure their full share of the loaf, which is big enough to supply sufficient for everybody.'*

John Orr envisaged a Scotland which was largely self-sufficient in food. Written before the days of the globalisation of food production, and food culture through advertising, his remedies would be even harder to achieve today. Yet we find that many people still search for similar solutions: food which contributes to the health of individuals as part of a fulfilling lifestyle; to the health of the nation by supporting people's ability to benefit from education and their capacity to contribute to economic development through work; and a food economy which is localised, which is environmentally friendly and which meets basic needs without causing psychosocial stress.

These ambitions are in line with the broad objectives of the organic food movement in the UK and with the objectives of those promoting land reform and rural development in Scotland. There are examples from our Nordic neighbours of significant improvements in health outcomes as a consequence of government schemes that support the production of local fruits and berries combined with health education and community development programmes (Ross et al, 1999). What measures are in place in Scotland or the UK as a whole that contribute to making this vision of food security a reality?

Despite the comprehensive rethinking which has gone on in the UK from 1997–2000 about almost every area of government policy, little has emerged which could be said to address the issue of food security. The Prime Minister's advice to farmers to diversify seems to signal an acceptance that UK agriculture, as well as fishery and livestock production, no longer has a privileged position in the nation's food supply. The government's quality of life indicators contain no reference to the accessibility of an affordable supply of quality food. Government policies to promote biodiversity fail to highlight the effects on wildlife of production methods that depend on high levels of pesticide use, and the potential benefits of alternative methods of food production.

Although the reports of the low income team of the Department of Health's Health of the Nation committee and the Acheson Report (Department of Health, 1996; Acheson, 1998) recognised the problems faced by disadvantaged groups in maintaining a healthy diet, the anti-poverty strategy document *Opportunity for All* includes no specific food policy (SEU, 1999). However, the government has now agreed to place responsibility for the availability and affordability of food on the agenda of the Food Standards Agency. The SEU has addressed the issue of food and low-income communities but only at the level of promoting retail activity and self-help food cooperatives in disadvantaged areas. Overall, there is nothing that could be described as a comprehensive, integrated food policy in the UK.

Before the 1997 general election, the burden on the NHS created by the high incidence of health problems related to diet in Scotland led to a programme of work on the Scottish diet. It was based on a committee chaired by Professor Phillip James, Sir John Orr's successor at the Rowett Institute. The James Report and the subsequent work of the Scottish Diet Action Group provided a comprehensive review of the ways in which dietary habits impact on the health of Scottish people, especially in the areas of coronary, digestive and dental health (Scottish Home and Health Department, 1993).

The work of the Scottish Diet Action Group also focused on some of the barriers which prevent Scottish people from making their health a priority. In particular, the Scottish Diet Strategy focuses on the role of dietary education for all ages, the role of institutions in influencing diet, the role of the food retail sector in providing a more healthy choice of foodstuffs and the role of communities in addressing aspects of food choice and supply from the bottom up. One of the most obvious outcomes of this work has been the setting up of the Scottish Community Diet Project which provides support and networking opportunities for developing community-based dietary initiatives. The next stage in the government's programme in Scotland is the appointment of a Scottish Diet Coordinator to promote coordinated action and to promote and disseminate good practice.

However, set against the criteria for food security policy, there are some serious deficiencies in this strategy. They reflect the general lack of joined-up thinking in the UK about policies related to food. The principal weakness of the recommendations for action is that, beyond inviting producers, retailers, caterers, local authorities, health boards and others to use their capacities to promote healthy eating, there is a failure to address the structural factors which have contributed to the problems which we face. The role of government in improving the Scottish diet is reduced to a reliance on voluntary and free market principles to generate change, and the allocation of a modest amount of funding to support community self-help initiatives. What is missing from the strategy is a recognition of the role played by government, through its planning and economic development powers, to create the framework within which the possibility of healthy eating can become a reality for everyone.

There is also no recognition of the role which could be played by the government through its tax and benefits policies and other policies to ensure equity of access to the basic necessities of a healthy life. Finally, the strategy ignores the question of whether the structures and arrangements which currently constitute the food economy of Scotland contribute positively to the government's agenda for sustainable development, social inclusion and health for all or are appropriate to delivering the dietary targets that the government has determined.

A fundamental problem with the government's approach to the nation's diet is the apparent assumption that, because poor diet results in disease, methods which are appropriate to tackling disease, especially preventative measures, will be sufficient to address the problem. This may be the case for the minority of the population who are not barred from accessing the components of a healthy diet but who persist in eating badly, but it is not necessarily true for those for whom this access is restricted by income, locality and ability and so on, or who are excluded from access by the operations of the free market (McGlone et al, 1999).

The government's current approach to food poverty compares with the treatment in the past of the health problems associated with living in damp, cold housing. Whilst efforts to address these health problems focused initially on teaching people to avoid causing condensation by opening windows and to wrap up warmly in winter, it is now appreciated that the fundamental problems are related to the construction of the houses. It is also recognised that this poor construction came about largely because of the relaxation of the postwar Parker Morris building standards in response to industry pressure, together with the imposition of severe spending restraints on public sector housing authorities. Now it is starting to be recognised that eradicating fuel poverty needs investment in housing stock, as we discuss

in the next chapter. When we have finally exhausted the capacities of individuals and communities to radically alter their own diet we might then address the structural factors which have such an influence in determining the food choices we can make.

Food security should be recognised as an essential feature of sustainable development. Indeed, the subject of food arguably provides a more accessible way into understanding the environmental dimension of sustainable development for most people than issues such as climate change. Control of the food supply and an ability to exercise free, responsible food choices are basic underpinnings of personal and community empowerment. Food plays a significant part in both national and international economic life. Despite the centrality of food to people's lives, however, it is – with the exception of various scandals – relatively ignored as a focus of public policy and action.

An accessible supply of affordable, quality food can be environmentally sound. Growing the right kinds of food for health can help to reduce fuel consumption, pollution, transport and packaging costs and promote biodiversity, especially if food is grown as near as possible to where it is consumed. This can help create local jobs, especially in rural areas. These links are likely to be highlighted towards the end of 2000 when the WHO will consider the adoption of a food and nutrition action plan for Europe which integrates food and nutrition concerns with the objectives of the Health 21 programme and of Local Agenda 21.

Food security, local, national and global, should be at the centre of policy development from the UN CSD down to the activities of local communities everywhere. Individually, through our institutions and political structures we are all able to influence choices which make the difference between food inequalities and malnutrition caused by economic greed, and equitable and sustainable development for all; choices which recognise food security as a fundamental human right.

Main Messages of this Chapter

- Both those with money and those without now share a basic concern about the security of their food supply.
- Development towards a more healthy, sustainable and inclusive UK cannot ignore the issue of food security.
- Only government action can provide the framework within which substantive improvements to diet and to the ability of people living on low incomes to exercise healthy food choices can be made.
- The government's quality of life indicators need to refer to the accessibility of an affordable supply of quality food.
- Government policies to promote bio-diversity should highlight the effects of production methods dependent on high levels of pesticide use on British wildlife and the potential benefits of alternative methods of food production; an accessible supply of affordable, quality food can be environmentally sound.
- Growing the right kinds of food for health can help reduce fuel consumption, pollution, transport and packaging costs and promote biodiversity, especially if food is grown as near as possible to where it is consumed. This can help create local jobs, especially in rural areas.
- The UK needs a comprehensive food policy that encompasses all the above issues, especially a programme to eradicate food poverty.

Chapter 5

Housing

A Key to Human Development

Safe shelter is fundamental to the idea of human development, allowing people to live dignified healthy lives and giving them a secure base from which they can make a contribution to society. This view has held true for international and domestic policy: the last major UN conference of the 20th century, Habitat II, adopted as part of its global plan of action the goal of achieving adequate shelter for all, while in the UK the benefit of secure housing has been long been recognised in traditions and slogans: 'An Englishman's home is his castle', or Lloyd George's promise of 'homes fit for heroes' after the First World War. Historically, housing projects have been seen as a means of social engineering and a promise of a better life. Indeed, the current government has declared that housing is at the heart of its social policy.

In housing terms, sustainability has several aspects. The DETR uses the definition from *Our Common Future* (WCED, 1987): 'development which meets the needs of the present without compromising the ability of future generations to meet their own needs', as does this book. This translates in practical terms to providing warm, safe and affordable quality housing that meets people's needs, the building and use of which has minimal impact on the environment. A sustainable city has been defined as

'one in which its people and businesses continuously endeavour to improve their natural, built and cultural environ-ments at neighbourhood and regional levels, whilst working in ways which always support the goal of global sustainable development' (Haungton and Hunter, 1994).

This notion also takes in that of sustainable communities, in terms of transport, work and general infrastructure. There is insufficient space to discuss all these issues here but they should be taken as implicit when we are describing sustainable housing.

Homeward bound

Postwar governments have built on the historic association of home and security with a continual drive towards home ownership and, until the 1980 Housing Act, a role for the state as a major provider of housing in the rented sector. Although support for home ownership has continued, the idea that social housing should be provided by local authorities was challenged in the 1980s when the Conservative government granted council tenants the right to buy their homes, without putting the money raised towards new council housing.

With the 1988 Housing Act, local authorities were encouraged to hand over their housing stock to registered social landlords, such as housing associations, while private renting restrictions were also relaxed. By 1998–99, 14 million households (69 per cent) in England owned their own home, compared with less than 10 million (57 per cent) at the start of the 1980s. Around a fifth (21 per cent) rented from the council or registered social landlords, compared with 32 per cent in 1981. However, within this rental sector decline, which was mainly due to the right-to-buy policy, the relatively small percentage of people renting from registered social landlords more than doubled. Renting in the private sector has changed relatively little with 11 per cent renting privately in 1981, following a long-term decline, a low of 8.6 per cent in 1991, and now a level of 10 per cent (Green et al, 1997; DETR, 2000). This probably reflects the lifting of renting restrictions in the 1988 Housing Act and the number of people who rented out property at the start of the 1990s to increase their income when the recession kept their properties in negative equity. However, although the number of private tenancies has remained fairly stable over the past five years, the types of lettings have become less secure. At the same time homelessness has risen.

For many people, the emphasis on home ownership has created a constant financial pressure that has reduced rather than increased their feelings of security and, indeed, has reduced the sustainability of housing in a financial sense. The finance of housing has shifted from investing directly in building to funding housing through individual payments such as housing benefit and giving tax relief on mortgages. The effect of this has been to create an open-ended funding commitment for the government in many instances. As a result, the elements of this individualistic approach are in turn now under review or in the process of being abandoned.

In planning terms, the needs of the 21st century are different from those of the mid-20th, and those changing needs are reflected in the current changes in housing policy. From 1945 until the end of the 1960s dense terraced housing was replaced by high rises, estates on the edges of towns and cities, and new towns. Industrial and residential districts were separated. Suburbs, though not a new phenomenon, continued to grow in their various guises: for example, the public transport suburb tied into the main conurbation's infrastructure, the car suburb, the lower-density detached housing on the edge of town that relies on inhabitants owning a car to get between home, work and leisure opportunities, or the social housing suburb, the large estates on the outskirts of many of our towns and cities (Gwilliam et al, 1998).

At present there are two forces driving housing in planning and building terms. First are the social and demographic patterns that have given us a rising demand for housing, yet with different household structures. This reflects two main changes: people are living longer (in 1998–99 there were 2.5 million households headed by someone over 75, compared with 1.6 million in 1977–78); and more people are living alone, from less than a million in 1971 to 1.7 million 20 years later. These changes are creating a demand for more units but not necessarily for the same models that dominated the 20th century. Second, since the Earth Summit in Rio in 1992, we have seen an increasing pressure to promote sustainability in housing, as in other areas. Indeed, one of the other commitments of Habitat II was 'improving living and working conditions on a sustainable basis'.

Sustainable Building

The latest DETR-backed research suggests that up to 26,500 extra homes could be provided annually by converting and redeveloping older houses (Llewelyn-Davies and University of Westminster, 2000). It is crucial to understand that the first step in a sustainable approach to building should be to consider how best to improve and recycle the buildings and materials we already have (see Box 5.1). Although this chapter concentrates on sustainable construction, this emphasis on new buildings is not to negate the major role to be played by renovating and recycling. Instead, it is used to illustrate the types of techniques involved.

All stages of construction have an effect on the environment and each stage of a building's life pollutes the environment to some extent. To minimise these effects and reduce the impact, the whole lifecycle of a building needs to be considered: the choice of materials, the building process, its use, and ultimately its demolition. The aim of sustainable housing should be to lessen the impact on the environment during the whole of the building's life cycle.

Box 5.1 *The National Sustainable Tower Blocks Initiative*

Many people believe that high-rise housing is unsafe and unattractive, and that it is mostly inhabited by marginalised and excluded people. The National Sustainable Tower Blocks Initiative is a grouping of four NGOs seeking to discover and implement ways to make tower blocks better and more sustainable places to live.

There are still more than 4000 tower blocks in this country, providing homes for around 800,000 people. They tend to suffer from a wide range of problems relating to the physical conditions of the blocks, to management and allocations policy, and to service provision issues. The majority of blocks are owned by local authorities, which have often seen demolition as a favoured option, this being cheaper than refurbishment. Refurbishing a tower block can cost £5 million or more, whereas demolition may cost less than a tenth of that. This is compounded by funding regimes where finance is easier to come by for housing association new-build than for the refurbishment of local authority stock. Demolition simply means that more new houses will have to be built, usually requiring more land for development. Some blocks are now owned or managed by housing associations; this will increase markedly in the next few years, although many associations have no experience of the specific problems related to high-rise.

If conditions in tower blocks are to improve, the state of the physical environment and the social qualities of the community must inch forward together. While negative perceptions are commonplace, they are by no means universal, and many residents are proud of where they live.

Tower block accommodation is not suitable for one large section of the population – families with children. Broadly speaking, this leaves two other main types of household: young people without children, and middle-aged to elderly people. It is generally possible to make tower blocks cater successfully for these groups. Tower blocks can be particularly popular with elderly people, provided that a high standard of security is maintained.

Demolition may be necessary or the best option if the block is structurally unsound, or mired in such deep social problems that the best hope lies in giving the residents a new start in new (though not necessarily new-build) homes.

The first report of the NSTBI concludes that to improve tower blocks an integrated approach is necessary, through:

- long-term community development;
- the provision of good quality services; and
- physical improvements to the stock.

Tower blocks have some distinctive features that can be advantageous for developing sustainability.

- As a high density form of housing they allow housing need to be met while minimising land use.
- Tower blocks can provide security from crime.
- Tower blocks have the potential to leave a smaller 'ecological footprint'.
- The defining feature of a multi-storey block – many homes within a common building – gives it special qualities, forming a self-defined unit.
- The possibilities for operating common systems within one unit can have benefits in anti-poverty terms, including one-stop housing and advice shops.

Support for change is needed at many points. This could come from the landlord, be it a local authority or housing association; from regeneration partnerships; or from NGOs. Agencies themselves may need to go through a process of education and capacity-building in order to develop a culture and approach that supports community democracy.

The report recommends that:

- The government, local authorities and regeneration agencies should recognise the potential value of these blocks, review current financing mechanisms, and establish more sustainable management practices.
- Effective security systems are an essential starting point for sustainability.
- No tower block of satisfactory construction should be demolished without the carrying out of a rigorous option study and joined-up cost analysis.
- Good practice is emerging as increasing numbers of tenants' groups take on management roles. The development of a national network of tower block residents groups should be encouraged and supported.

High-density inner city housing is likely to become a priority for the UK over the next ten years, both for young professionals and for older people. Use of the best available refurbishment techniques alongside community development would show that there is a lot more that can be done with the UK's high-rise housing stock.

Source: National Sustainable Tower Blocks Initiative, 2000

Buildings use around half of the UK's energy output (the remainder being equally split between transport and industry). About 30 per cent of the UK's energy is used in homes and 20 per cent in offices. There is undoubtedly considerable potential for reducing the level used in their production and during their habitation. The principles that need to be borne in mind when designing a building start with the choice of site and run through to the appliances used in it. For example, when designing a new building or extending an old one, site orientation and south-facing glazing can take advantage of the sun's 'free' energy. The design needs to be for life; the structure needs to be easily adaptable so that the internal layout can be changed easily, for instance. The design also needs to take account of the health and comfort of the people who live in the building in terms of daylight, temperature and ventilation.

The actual building materials used need to be selected to minimise the energy used in their production and transport, as well as improve the building's energy efficiency. Recycling or reclaiming materials also reduces the need for energy, resources and use of landfill space.

Making buildings energy efficient is crucial if housing is to be regarded as sustainable. They need to be insulated well and the products used in them chosen for energy efficiency (see the DETR's Energy Sense Information Pack

(1999), for example). The initial costs of added insulation and low energy products may be higher than their conventional equivalents but any additional cost will be paid back within a few years because of the saving on running costs, important for preventing fuel poverty in future generations. Ideally, such products should be subsidised and VAT removed from them in order to encourage people to buy them. Indeed, the government took a first step towards this when it reduced VAT for the installation of energy-saving materials to all homes in the March 2000 budget. Electricity should be from renewable sources, such as solar, wind, hydro- or geothermal power, while building materials should be naturally durable, thereby helping to avoid the use of hazardous chemicals. Careful design will reduce the need for preservatives.

The aim of a sustainable building or development is to achieve a closed-loop system where waste is recycled and water use minimised. Harvesting rainwater and recycling 'grey' water (the output from baths and washing machines), for example, is possible even in an urban site.

Costs for sustainable housing can be comparable to those of conventional building and should fall for many materials and products as the market for ecoproducts develops and economies of scale come into play. This does not mean that all systems will be appropriate on all sites. The variation within the site itself and its geography have to be considered when designing systems to service a project. But if the true costs were taken into account – in terms of the health service for treating asthma and chemical sensitivity, for example, or cleaning up after polluting technologies – then a very different economic picture would emerge.

Although the government is, in theory, supportive of sustainable building development, there remains a long way to go before the sort of techniques we have described here all become the norm. The construction industry, with an annual output of £58 billion (1997) and employing 1.4 million people, has a great deal invested in current systems of building, in its workforce training, and in the vast volume of the businesses that support it, from quarrying raw materials through to manufacturing and production. The DETR's consultation paper on sustainable construction found a very mixed level of awareness of the issues in the industry, with small- and medium-sized companies particularly lagging behind in their understanding and practice (1998). On its website, the DETR says it is paying more attention to housing standards in the context of sustainable communities and sustainable environments, but set against its commitment to 'balance between quality and quantity' it's unclear that political will is strong enough to withstand the conventional volume builders' and manufacturers' lobby groups. In the March 2000 budget the Chancellor did, however, send a signal to the industry of the government's interest in encouraging recycling and sustainability by introducing a levy on aggregates.

There are several steps that can be taken to encourage the UK building industry to take a sustainable direction. For example, the building regulations could be revised to ensure that the minimum standards for such areas as insulation are raised; at present we fall well behind our European counterparts in this respect. The next generation of builders and craftspeople also need training that ensures they are familiar with the techniques for creating sustainable housing. Many of these are traditional skills, which are in danger of being lost. One useful step forward would be to develop a standard design for sustainable building to encourage the major building companies to embrace environmentally sound practices. This would also make it easier to create appropriate training programmes.

Non-renewable fuels are becoming cheaper, especially as no account is taken of environmental costs, so much more support needs to be given to the renewable energy sector, both in research and development terms and in reducing or removing VAT from this sector.

Encouragingly, the climate change levy will not apply to electricity generated from renewable sources.

The limits of the environment itself are likely to continue to be driving forces behind technological developments. One of the predicted results of climate change in the next 20–30 years is a shortage of water in the South East of England, so water availability will limit the number of households that the region can support. Therefore there will be a pressure on the big volume builders to demand efficient water recycling technology in order to be able to continue to work in the area.

One way the government could make a significant move in the direction of sustainable housing is in its criteria for the new building work that is planned for the next couple of decades. The long-term economics of setting new standards that support sustainable development should not be cost prohibitive in the current market, let alone when economies of scale come into play. Several projects are already under way to create sustainable developments that encompass many if not most of the sort of requirements set out above, and show ways forward (see Box 5.2). These include the DETR's Construction Research and Innovation Programmes, one element of which is identifying and promoting best practice in sustainable construction. Housing Quality Indicators being developed to assess social housing, whether new-build or refurbished properties, and eventually private housing, also encompass an element assessing energy, green and sustainability issues. The DETR is also supporting the Sustainable Homes project to coordinate and raise environmental standards.

Box 5.2 *BedZED*

The BedZED (Beddington Zero Energy Development) project in Sutton, Surrey, is the result of a joint effort between environmental specialists BioRegional, the Peabody Housing Trust, architect Bill Dunster and the local authority, to both meet Local Agenda 21 criteria in their area and produce a design for a mixed development urban village that would be easily reproducible elsewhere. The key elements include use of mostly brownfield land, south-facing buildings and the use of natural materials and products with low embodied energy. These materials are sourced where possible within a 35-mile radius of the site while the buildings will be powered by a combined heat- and powerplant running on tree surgery waste to achieve an overall zero CO_2 emissions. A car pool will be incorporated in the development, and cycling and walking will be encouraged by the layout of the site, with secure cycle stores in homes and workplaces.

Water consumption will be reduced by the products installed in the buildings and rainwater will be collected from roofs and stored in tanks below the buildings. Wastewater is being treated in rooftop reedbeds housed in a glasshouse. The housing itself is a mix of tenures and its energy efficiency should be reflected in a unit's running cost. For example, a three-bedroomed house's annual bill for heating and electricity should be around £250 rather than £750 for a conventional design. The Sutton development will have a residential population of 148 per hectare but the architects say the main elements of the design minus the car-parking provision could be transplanted to an inner city site to give a density of 309 per hectare. Though a suburban area, these densities are comparable with parts of central London. The intention behind intensifying suburban housing density and adding new workplaces is that it encourages commuting out from the city on what are currently nearly empty trains, thus doubling the carrying capacity of the existing transport system without further investment, while minimising the pressure to build new dormitory suburbs in the green belt. Work started in April 2000 and the first phases of the project are due for completion in spring 2001.

Sustainable Living

Most importantly, especially in the context of this book, a sustainable building programme should provide homes that people can afford to live in. This is illustrated clearly by considering the issue of energy efficient homes. Warm housing is also a particularly important topic for the UK, as cold weather is an important public health issue in this country. The UK sees a significant number of extra deaths each year during the winter months – around 40,000 extra people die between December and March. This seasonal swing is much more pronounced than in most other countries in Europe, despite the fact that our winters are generally less severe. Various reasons have been suggested for this but it seems likely that the quality of housing plays a part. This theory is reinforced by recent research which shows that the poorer quality housing, in terms of thermal efficiency and heating systems, is 'associated with increased vulnerability to winter death from cardiovascular disease' (Wilkinson et al, in press). Older properties are particularly vulnerable. The researchers conclude that 'substantial public health benefits can be expected from measures which improve the thermal efficiency of homes and the afford-ability of heating them'.

While 21°C is a comfortable indoor temp-erature, it only needs to fall below 18°C for it to be uncomfortable and for there to be a risk of an impact on people's health in terms of bronchitis, heart attacks and stroke. Yet the energy report of the English House Condition Survey in 1991–92 found that even in a mild winter only a quarter of the homes they had measured had indoor temperatures which met the standard temperatures recommended by the DETR, meaning that cold homes repre-sented the primary health risk associated directly with the condition of the housing stock (Department of the Environment, 1996). Yet since 1980 there have been no minimum

heating standard for homes in building regul-ations or environmental health standards. Of the 3 million least efficient buildings, nearly one in ten have high loss of heat and a similar number have inefficient heating systems. The least energy efficient homes are older prop-erties, generally in the private rented and owner-occupied sectors.

Not being able to afford to heat your own home is known as 'fuel poverty', the result of a combination of low income and the lack of an energy efficient home. More than 4 million households have a degree of fuel poverty (DETR, 1999). It has been acknowledged as a national scandal by the UK Environmental Audit Committee (1999), which commented: 'It should be addressed with the sort of urgency and determination usually reserved for more sudden crises here and abroad.'

At the same time, however, the UK is also pledged to reduce its CO_2 emissions as part of efforts to combat climate change, CO_2 being one of the gases that contribute to global warming. The 1997 Kyoto Protocol to the UN Framework Convention on Climate Change commits it to reducing its 1990 levels of CO_2 emissions by 12.5 per cent by 2008–12, although the government now says it will have cut emissions by 21.5 per cent by then. There-fore, simply reducing the cost of fuel, as the government did by reducing VAT on domestic fuel in 1997, although easing the burden on those in fuel poverty in the short term, will actually encourage fuel use and discourage people implementing fuel saving measures. This will also add to CO_2 emissions, a major blow to sustainability. Ultimately, decreasing fuel costs encourages greater use of fuel, especially in homes that aren't heating-efficient.

Yet, as has been pointed out, the aims of reducing fuel poverty and limiting CO_2 emissions are not necessarily in opposition, provided there is a long-term strategy rather than a short-term focus (Boardman et al, 1999). Although domestic energy prices will have to rise in the long term to meet environmental considerations, the priority in the short and medium terms must be improving housing stock to increase its energy efficiency. The combination of these measures should both lift people out of fuel poverty and go some way to meeting environmental concerns – and therefore be sustainable in the long term.

The government has committed itself to producing a coherent strategy to end fuel poverty. Such a strategy would require efforts across a number of areas but should pay for itself in environmental and purely financial terms. The benefits of investment in producing energy efficient homes are, for example, the savings to the health service in cold-related illness, the benefits of job creation in the building trade, and the reduction in CO_2 emissions. The Campaign to End Fuel Poverty has calculated that a 15-year rolling programme of energy efficiency works would cost £18.75 billion but save £19.6 billion in terms of health, housing and unemployment costs.

The government's main focus for improving domestic energy efficiency has been the Home Energy Efficiency Scheme (HEES), a revised version of which, the New HEES, has now been developed. Although the New HEES is for England, similar programmes are being developed in Scotland, Wales and Northern Ireland. It provides packages of insulation and/or heating improvement measures for households on income or disability-based benefits that are adapted to different types of properties. The New HEES aims to produce a more targeted approach than its predecessor by helping the most at-risk groups in private rented accommodation and young owner occupiers; 85 per cent is intended for the private sector.

The strength of this approach is that those most at risk should benefit first, but it is likely that the sums involved will prove insufficient for older properties in poor repair. There also remains the difficulty of actually reaching those who are entitled to benefit. However, it provides a basis on which to build further policies to improve current stock.

Making homes energy efficient is obviously in the interests of people in low-income households. But reducing the amount of fuel used is not in the interest of those selling fuel, so government action is needed to require the regulators to ensure that the pricing framework supports the interests of the government and householders. The Green Paper on Utility Regulation in March 1998 suggested that regulators of the gas and electricity industries should have a duty to consider the interests of low-income consumers when focusing on consumer interest. For example, at present, reductions in the cost of fuel when customers agree to pay by direct debit are unlikely to benefit those on low incomes, who cannot often commit to that payment method. Standing charges are also disproportionately expensive for those with low bills. Instead, making cheaper payment methods available to those on low incomes and increasing the cost of fuel in line with the amount that is used, for example, would help tackle fuel poverty while, in the latter case, discouraging waste (Boardman et al, 1999).

There is evidence to suggest that the government is moving towards a coherent strategy for tackling fuel poverty while improving energy efficiency. The Energy Efficiency Best Practice Programme monitors, evaluates and encourages new technologies, as well as promoting design options that make full use of traditional measures such as good insulation, efficient heating systems and good controls. However, there remains much scope for more methodical structures to be set up to ensure that the funds set aside for this work are both targeted and made use of, and to ensure that the different statutory bodies all play their part. For example, although environmental indicators are being developed for housing developments, both built and proposed, there remain relatively few elements of either regulatory or pricing policy that encourage a more sustainable approach to building. Yet using the driving force of sustainability can be a positive pressure for promoting affordable housing. Providing people with a home that they can afford to live in while minimising impact on the environment is the key to sustainable housing policy.

Meeting Demand

Urgent attention should be paid to such measures if the demand for housing is to be met during the next couple of decades in any sustainable way. Current housing predictions are that an extra 4.4 million new homes will be wanted in the UK by 2016, compared with the 1991 housing stock. The demand is highest in the South East of England where the Regional Planning Conference (SERPLAN) concluded there was a likely demand for about 900,000 extra homes and the government's inspection panel, headed by Professor Stephen Crow, subsequently suggested the requirement is for more than a million. The reason for this focus on London and South East England is that between 1994 and 1997, 70,000 people moved to the South East and, without major intervention to reverse the process, this population movement is expected to continue.

However, the SERPLAN and Crow recommendations were rejected by the government in March this year, when the DETR announced that 860,000 new homes will be built over a 20-year period, with housebuilding in the South East increasing by 10 per cent, and by 22 per cent in London. There has, however, been recognition by the government that the old model of simply predicting housing need and encouraging development is no longer sufficient, and the plans for the region will be reviewed at least every five years.

Both the way we use land for building and the infrastructure that supports communities have come under closer scrutiny in the past decade, as well as the material from which the houses are built. Much of the debate has centred on the sort of land that any new properties should be built on, specifically either greenfield (that is, previously undeveloped land, usually outside urban areas) or brownfield sites (land that has been used previously, whether for domestic or commercial purposes). The debate has been characterised as a split between those wanting to use brownfield sites to minimise damage to the countryside, and those who say there is a need to build on new land as brownfield development won't meet the demand for housing. In fact, these sides are not really in opposition, although they emphasise their different interests. As has been highlighted elsewhere (Bate, 1999), there is more agreement than difference between them.

To sum up the main points of the debate: developing brownfield sites is more desirable from an environmental point of view as it reduces the impact on the countryside, is more likely to be able to make use of the infrastructure already in place, and can help regenerate urban areas. Its downside is that the previous use of a site may have left it in a polluted state which is expensive to clean up, that it risks overloading the current infrastructure if further investment does not take place in sewerage, transport and so on, and, consequently, that the cost of developing a brownfield site will mean that affordable housing may be squeezed out.

The current government target is for 60 per cent of new housing to be built on brownfield sites – an apparently achievable target given that the actual proportion rose from 38 per cent in 1985 to 50 per cent in 1995. The UK Round Table on Sustainable Development proposed 75 per cent. Nevertheless, there is widespread acknowledgement that brownfield sites, including the space over shops and so on, will not be sufficient to meet all projected housing needs although they should remain the preferred option.

The government is currently promoting the extension of urban conurbations from present sites, especially along the corridors provided by public transport networks. Some regional plans have already adopted these principles. The advantage is that use can be made of existing infrastructure, including transport, and so the development is less likely to encourage extra car use. However, as has been pointed out, this will not necessarily persuade people to abandon their cars if there is no incentive to use the public transport provided (Bate, 1999). There is a general feeling that adding to urban sites is preferable to creating new settlements.

However, despite the government's willingness to move planning policy in favour of brownfield development, planning agreements will have to enforce a percentage of social and affordable housing in a higher proportion of urban developments if there is not to be a mismatch between the housing provided and those who can afford to live in it. Although one of the grounds given for the rejection of SERPLAN's proposals was their failure to take account of the need for affordable housing, there are no targets in the new plans. The recent Green Paper on housing highlights the risk of losing key workers from an area and recommends that local planning authorities ensure there is an element of affordable housing in new developments (DETR and DSS, 2000). New money needs to be found, however, if affordable housing providers such as housing associations are to be able to buy into these developments. The government's rejection of the DETR's Urban Task Force recommendation to provide low-tax incentives for local authorities and developers to encourage urban regeneration is a further cause for concern.

Conclusion

Although government housing policy refers repeatedly to the desirability of sustainable development, there are several barriers that are preventing faster progress. First, there remains a lack of financial commitment, in the form of, for example, tax incentives, and in investing money to ensure that sufficient affordable housing will be built or retained. The volume-builders also lack the experience and skills to produce the conversions and new builds that we have described here. The lower costs associated with building on greenfield land mean there is a constant pressure to release new land for development while we struggle with the problems associated with half a century of car-orientated planning. Indeed, this latter issue is representative of the way in which the huge pressures of economic growth and consumer societies are antithetical to sustainable practice, illustrated for example in the conflict between the DETR wanting to discourage out-of-town shopping centres while the DTI sees them as encouraging economic growth and competitiveness. Nowhere is this conflict illustrated more clearly than in the fact that in conventional economic terms, fast rising housing prices are held to represent a buoyant market, and are therefore a 'good thing', when in fact they represent a rapid increase in the gap between the haves and have-nots in housing terms. One way in which inequalities in the UK are made visible is in people's housing options.

However, the new building programme provides an opportunity to redirect this country's building practice. At the same time, environmental pressures are set to drive the technology forward by creating a demand from builders for solutions to, say, water shortages. There need, therefore, to be two components to the policies to meet these challenges: first, to ensure new-build is based on the best sustainable practice, while preventing further deterioration in the stock; and second, to ensure people have access to quality affordable homes. This takes us closer to ensuring that future housing demand is met, and that people can afford to live in their homes – that their housing is sustainable for them financially. It is an investment for both people and their environment.

Main Messages of this Chapter

- Changing demographics and sustainable development are driving forces in planning and building homes.
- The first principles in sustainable construction should be recycling, renovating and reclamation.
- A new building should be designed for its entire lifecycle.
- Building standards should include sustainability criteria.
- Construction training programmes need to include sustainable building techniques.
- The government must put a high priority on improving the energy efficiency of the housing stock.
- Providing people with a home that they can afford to live in while minimising the impact on the environment is key to sustainable housing policy.

Chapter 6

Employment Integration for the Least Advantaged People in the UK: Opportunities and Risks

Into Work

'Financially, the reason I'd gone back into work was that after having been ill I felt I needed it for my confidence and to socialise in company, and a lot of it was for me, but in practical terms, by the time I had to pay a percentage of the rent – and it is a lot of rent . . . so much towards the council tax, petrol and my new clothes for an office job – you've got to look respectable – I was worse off.'

Teresa's story is the reality for many people trying to get back into employment at the lower paid end of the marketplace; a difficult balancing act between taking the first step back into paid work while ensuring they will still be able to afford the basics, as well as the extra expenses of work clothes, travel and so on that are part and parcel of working outside the home (see Box 6.1).

Ensuring that people have the material means to lead dignified lives is a key issue for human development, just as having access to secure paid work is a crucial element in people's lives. Lifting people out of poverty by getting them back into work is an important plank in the government's policy of tackling social exclusion. To do this the government has instituted three main policy changes: the Welfare to Work incentives, the national minimum wage and the New Deal training programmes. They are aimed at 'making work pay', making it seem to be a better option than a life on benefits.

The central policy themes are opportunities and responsibilities. In practice this means:

- An emphasis on free markets and the flexibility of labour, although the government acknowledges that relying solely on the market results in social exclusion.
- A shift from passive welfare to active citizenship and a focus on responsibilities.
- An aspiration to be 'one nation'; to combat the causes of social exclusion, and give opportunities to all. The twin themes of education and work are emphasised through flexible labour markets and education and training opportunities.

To fully assess the UK government's employment programmes, it is important to understand what kind of factors are driving the labour market. Just 60 per cent of the workforce are employed in full-time permanent jobs, while part-time employment rose from 3.3 million in 1971 to 5 million in 1995. Between 1984 and 1994 the proportion in temporary employment rose from 4 per cent to 6 per cent of the workforce. A quarter of men and half of women are in non-standard employment (a rise from 30 per cent to 38 per

Box 6.1 *Teresa's story – one lone parent's experience of getting back to work*

The last job

'It was 25 hours per week . . . it was ideal, because it was on the doorstep, a two-minute ride . . . my son was in school and you've got adult company and something to get up and dressed for in the morning and something to occupy your mind.'

The problem: flexible hours and long hours

'We were expected to cover when the other person was off (and frequently to work over the stated hours) . . . Husbands and that can bath the kids or do something with the homework while [wives are] doing the tea, whereas I've got it all to do . . . SATS . . . They are giving more responsibility to the parents. I've told the school I feel that I'm back at school again, I'm an unpaid teacher as well as everything else.'

Costs and benefits of working and budgeting

'I was about £30 a week better off when I was in work, income-wise, but I was paying £35 a week towards the rent, about £12 a week for the council tax and then the childcare was only about £7 a week during term time, but holiday time. . .it was £50-odd a week and the Family Credit work it out as an average. That's great on the weeks when you're paying £7 a week . . . but on the weeks when you've paid £50, when you've not allowed for that, you've got to take it out . . . You've got about £7 for school dinners as well and that's without outside activities that they want to do . . . I felt like I was working for nothing and everybody you ask who goes for work goes to work for the money, and not just for the enjoyment.'

Living on benefits

'I've still got debts from club books and being a woman on my own I wanted a decent car as I didn't want to break down, and as my son can't walk with his disability. So that's on a loan, so that takes a chunk of the money but luckily his disability benefit covers that, but we've got to reapply for that . . . If we don't get that [disability benefit] we'll be even more financially stuck which you can't understand as . . . he'll have his disability all his life.'

The impact of means-testing

'At the moment I'm on income support and I'm still receiving Family Credit . . . Because I'm not working the DSS take the Family Credit off my income support; your child allowance is also classed as an income. It really annoys me . . . why should it be that everyone with children under 16 gets that whether they're on £5000 or £50,000 a year?

I got my childcare book back this week . . . she'd taken nearly £3 off me because that's the lone parent rate. I don't know the regulations about it, I've only got their word for it but as far as I'm concerned I'm still a lone parent.

I've got the DSS coming round in a couple of months . . . they say it's got to be done, but why? I don't understand their laws, why? Why do I have to let them in, what's happened to being a king of your own castle and having privacy? I've got nothing to hide but at the same time I think I should have a say in who crosses the doorstep. They just assume they own you and your house and everything in it because they're paying you a miserly sum each week.

There's a lot of stigma attached to being a lone parent, especially one on benefits. I've never felt so degraded because they all talk down to you at that department.'

The impact of payment systems complexity

'It's always a book you've got to fill in; it's pages and pages and it's so intimate . . . and so personal; they shouldn't be allowed to ask [such things].

One week they'd say I'd get so much benefit, another week so much, then they'd write to you in the next month saying they've backdated it and it should have been such and such . . . The housing [department] wrote to me seeking repossession because it hadn't been paid . . . I was upset and angry and I don't need this stress in my life . . . One department pays you in arrears, the council pay the housing two weeks in arrears, then two weeks upfront, so I couldn't get it to balance with what they said was outstanding . . . If they did it weekly and worked it out that'd be great . . . even though I've got qualifications I can't work it out.

I had a handwritten letter [from the DSS] the other week saying I would get a computer-written letter saying I was not eligible for income support anymore, and this first letter said to ignore it because they'd made an error, so on one hand they are saying I can't have it any more and on the other I can.

The Child Support Agency (CSA) are a rule unto themselves . . . [maintenance] is so irregular you can't rely on it as an income, but yet the DSS . . . they take that into account. If one month I don't get any CSA [payments], well then I've hardly got anything coming in. They had to send me three months [of payment] together because they hadn't paid it.

It's stressful. I'm always on the phone or writing letters . . . In a lot of these systems you're in a queue but the different departments, the CSA, the invalid care, the child benefit, none of them work together.'

Training for the future

'I wouldn't know where to start. I need extra training to do what I want and also the extra confidence. It's a barrier that I have to sort out all my benefits.'

Full-time or part-time work and the benefits trap

'I'm looking again at the moment but for part-time work. But the dilemma is that the vacancy I've applied for is . . . 15 hours a week and I'm only allowed to earn £15 per week unless I do over 16 hours. In the case of working 15, which is £1 an hour, (it) doesn't cover the childcare which is below the minimum wage . . . and then . . . it's got to be over 16 to stay on the new Working Families Tax Credit . . . I wouldn't work for £3.60, my childcare is nearly £2 . . . I don't want to go for less than £4.

I don't go out much, I don't drink and I don't smoke. They just pay you for an existence . . . [but] I can't afford to work full time as I would lose all my benefits, and then it would be more childcare costs . . . and I haven't got good enough health . . . I don't know the kind of job a woman would earn a lot [in] . . . I don't want to live to work, I do want to have a life.'

Source: interview with a single mother on benefits

cent of the labour force 1981–1993; Rix at al, 1999; see also Table 2.6 in Appendix 1).

Despite this drive towards giving employers flexibility, the UK is not the most flexible in all respects. The Netherlands has more people in part-time employment, and in 1993 12 out of the 15 EU member states had more temporary employment than the UK. The US has relatively low atypical employment (part-time and temporary work) but the greatest wage flexibility. However, the UK leads the EU in ease of hiring and firing, and long working hours. Current developments at company level are a consequence of the deregulation by governments in the 1980s and 1990s that were trying to create the low-cost enterprise centre of Europe. As a result, the UK labour market is now one of the least regulated among OECD countries with regard to restrictions on terms and conditions of employment, working time, and hiring and firing rules (Vickery and Wurtzberg, 1996).

Sustainable livelihoods

What does sustainability mean in employment terms? There are two key aspects: the results of the actual job – that is, whether the work supports or contradicts sustainable development; and the ability of a person to sustain him- or herself in work. There is insufficient space here to explore both of these aspects so we are concentrating on examining whether the government's employment policies help people to achieve a sustainable livelihood; whether they enable them to both move into, and stay in, secure employment. Secure employment allows people to build up their assets, which is important in providing a cushion against life's shocks and enables people to influence policies and institutions; assets empower people. The concept of a sustainable livelihood is also a dynamic one which is orientated towards people, encouraging them to participate at many levels of society and to work in partnership with individuals and organisations.

Incentives to Take Up Employment

At the end of the 1990s there were 1.3 million recipients of Jobseeker's Allowance (JSA), one million lone parents on income support, and 2.8 million people of working age receiving disability or incapacity benefits (DSS, 1998). The government accepts its own evidence that the majority of benefit recipients want to work but don't, firstly because of the poor delivery of the benefit system (see Box 6.1), and, secondly, because of the gap that can open up between the levels of financial support they receive on benefit and the wages that are necessary to provide them with at least the same level of support. To combat the former, the government is trying to streamline the system by providing a 'single gateway' to benefits and finding a job.

To try to get people back in to paid work, the government is using a carrot-and-stick approach. Extra support includes the working families tax credit (WFTC), more assistance towards childcare costs and the national minimum wage (see next section). The 'stick' is an increasing emphasis on means-testing and the compulsion to accept any job on offer. Thus the government's priority is to forge an entirely new culture that focuses on work and transforms the way people think about the welfare system.

One key way of increasing the incentive to work is the JSA. This is a regime with two routes into a single benefit: one based on insurance, the other on means-testing. Unemployment benefit was an insurance-based right, paid to those who became unemployed; but now, after six months, the two routes into the JSA converge on the means-tested income-based allowance. Despite the fact that there is little evidence to suggest that unemployment insurance benefits have an impact on labour market entry and exit, the JSA introduced more rigorous policing of entitlement conditions and means-testing of the allowance.

Because the JSA is conditional, those in receipt of it are required to follow a particular course of action, such as training or looking for work. From April 2000 anyone receiving the JSA will be interviewed about their prospects of finding work and be faced with stiffer penalties for refusing work. This merging of the right to an income and the obligation to work is a significant change to the UK's benefit system. For those who face difficulties in accessing and retaining paid employment, compulsion threatens their human dignity and means-testing invades their privacy.

The risk of stigmatising and alienating people may reduce real opportunities for social inclusion through helping the least advantaged back into paid work, especially since people are already unhappy with the current degree of compulsion and penalty. Research on people whose claim had been disallowed or benefit temporarily withdrawn found that nearly all felt the penalty was unfair. Those who responded to the survey sometimes believed job centre staff had acted with malice, and they feared

hardship and debt; those who had paid regular national insurance contributions felt cheated (Vincent, 1998). When MORI interviewed 127 16 and 17 year olds to investigate the effects of the JSA, they concluded that the JSA process works well for those in transition between school and work or between jobs, but not for a minority of young people with deep-rooted problems and temporary addresses or no fixed address (MORI, 1998).

It is difficult to build human and social capital where the conditions that allow people to have self-respect, dignity, security and privacy are absent, and while compulsion measures erode the individual rights of the least advantaged. Further marginalisation occurs in the stigmatisation of unemployed people by repeated reference to fraud and 'dole cheats'; the government's fear of the moral hazard of unemployment seems greater than their concern with the risks to human dignity. For example, the government sees neither irony nor insult in its statement that 'we have no intention of referring people who are awaiting major operations for a discussion of work prospects' (DSS, 1998), when reforms to the all-work test for incapacity benefit have instilled the fear of being forced to work in people with a disability.

Low Pay and the Minimum Wage

Benefit reform is one part of the government's strategy to make work pay; the national minimum wage is a more positive incentive.

In the UK, low pay is more common for the unskilled, less educated, for women and part-time workers. The North East has the largest concentration of those affected (11.6 per cent) and London has the least (4.3 per cent). Low pay is more common among people working in wholesale, retail and catering sectors; the main occupations affected are hotel and catering (29 per cent), and cleaners and security guards (24 per cent) (*The Economist*,

1999). Industries that were paying below the minimum in 1997 were hospitality (40 per cent of employees), private social care (36 per cent), and retailing (19 per cent) (Kitching, 1999). Japan and the UK are the only two countries in the OECD in which older workers are significantly more likely to be low-paid than workers in their prime (OECD, 1997).

If low pay is defined as those earning below two thirds of median earnings, then 39 per cent of full-time workers were low-paid in 1986 and 1991 (compared with 8 per cent in Denmark and 58 per cent in the US). Between 1975 and

1995, the incidence of low pay increased only in the UK, the US and Australia. And the more difficult it is to move up the job ladder, the more unequal the earnings distribution. Mobility out of low pay is greatest for young people, while low-paid women, and older and less educated workers, are more likely to get stuck in poorly-paid jobs, or the cycle between low-paid jobs and not working. The longer a person has been low-paid, the more likely they are to stay that way, and many of those who escape low pay find that it is a short-lived change. So, for these workers, the pressure to enter paid employment is less likely to be rewarded by sustainable protection from poverty. This may explain why more low-paid workers leave the labour market altogether than other groups (OECD, 1997).

Without a minimum wage, downward pressure on wages can undermine income supporting measures of tax and benefit reforms. A minimum wage prevents a race to the bottom in a vicious cycle of wage and benefit cuts that is likely not only to destroy financial assets and plunge people into debt, but also to put pressure on their ability to deploy human and social capital assets. Furthermore, in poor communities, there are likely to be knock-on effects on the life quality in the area, as private capital in the form of shops and banks withdraws in the face of a reduction in the amount of money in circulation and an increasingly downgraded environment.

Despite its benefits for individuals and communities, a minimum wage may not target the most needy households very well. For young people, low-paid jobs may be a stepping stone to better jobs, while women may be members of households with high household income. So, while equity may require individual rights to a decent income, the minimum wage has little effect on low-income families headed by a low-wage male worker earning just above the minimum wage, and does nothing for no-wage households (40 per cent of low-income individuals in OECD countries live in no-job households). Nevertheless, low-paid employment is strongly related to low family income and, within countries, low pay correlates with poverty. This connection may come about because of social choices, rather than for economic reasons. For example, countries may have relatively generous welfare benefits, compressed earnings structures and few low-paid jobs, as some Scandinavian countries still do. Ireland and the US are the two OECD countries that have a higher incidence of poverty and low pay than the UK, and whereas the working poor are around 10 per cent of the full-time workforce in most EU countries, they are a quarter of the workforce in the US (OECD, 1997). The latter model seems to be the one preferred by the present UK government.

However, the government feels that a minimum wage that is set too high might cost jobs, so it originally set it at £3.60 for those aged 22 and over, £3.20 for those on training programmes, and £3.00 for those aged 18–21. The subsequent increase of 10p per hour on the basic rate has been criticised by anti-poverty groups for being too small, and for the failure to commit to raising the rate each year to protect even this small sum against inflation. Indeed, the minimum wage was set at a low level, at 46 per cent of median earnings, below that of continental Europe but above the federal rate in the US. Yet there is evidence that some employers in parts of the UK are evading minimum wage rates by changing employees' hours of work and other aspects of their contract (Edwards and Gilman, 1999).

Nevertheless, despite government fears, there is little evidence that the minimum wage will cost jobs. A survey of UK firms found employers intended to make efficiency savings if a national minimum wage was introduced (Edwards and Gilman, 1999). Most mentioned tighter labour controls and changes in production organisation, or investment in more training. A comparison between the experiences of France, the Netherlands, Spain and the UK with a minimum wage found some evidence that it reduced income inequality between those in work, but little evidence of job losses (Machin and Manning, 1997).

The incidence of low pay does seem to be connected to a country's labour market institutions; it is less likely in highly unionised countries with relatively generous unemployment benefits. Higher minimum wages are associated with a lower proportion of low-paid jobs, and lower earnings inequality between men and women, and between younger workers and adults. While there appears to be some tendency for unemployment to be higher in countries with a lower incidence of low pay, there is not much evidence of a causal relation, though labour market regulation undoubtedly plays some part. And there is evidence that employment trends for low-skilled workers are the same whatever the wage trends (OECD, 1997). There does seem to be scope for a higher minimum wage to cut inequality and increase the opportunities for poorer people to build up their assets. Taking home a decent wage increases human dignity.

In-Work Benefits

Rather than increase the minimum wage, the government has chosen to top-up low wages with means-tested benefits. However, the current Family Credit benefit has not been as successful as the government hoped in encouraging people into employment. Any form of means-testing introduces poverty traps due to the combination of the loss of benefits and an eligibility for tax. Those most at risk are lone parents. For them and some other disadvantaged groups, there are a number of risks associated with the decision to enter the labour market. They also have least to gain, being very unlikely to earn enough to get out of the poverty trap and begin to accumulate financial assets (see Box 6.1).

The UK has reduced the steepness of the benefits 'taper' – that is, the rate at which benefit is withdrawn as income from other sources increases – in order to reduce the impact of the poverty trap. Thus the government has recently replaced Family Credit with the more generous working families tax credit (WFTC), targeted at the low-paid employed. Where there is at least one wage earner, it offers a top-up in order to guarantee £200 per week for a household with children. However, it has numerous drawbacks as an equitable and efficient means of assisting poor families. It is not very useful to part-time workers who cannot work the minimum number of hours required to become eligible for the benefit. Therefore it may not reach the least advantaged people. Unlike the Family Credit which it replaced, WFTC is usually paid through the wage packet, so it is now more likely to be received by fathers and less likely to be received by mothers – and so reach children. Added to that, given the different regional possibilities of gaining work, WFTC could be discriminatory, in that it will be more accessible to low-income families in regions where there is plenty of work. Given the tight private housing market and the very restricted access to attractive social housing and schools, the mobility of poor families out of asset-poor regions into asset-rich regions is very constrained.

The WFTC does not eliminate the perverse effects attached to means-tested benefits and is not very useful to those who cannot get clear of the poverty trap. WFTC also has the unwanted side-effect of shifting the high marginal effective tax rates further up the income distribution, making the leap to better-paid work more difficult. Further, in countries such as the UK and the US with high earnings inequality, these schemes are expensive as there is a large pool of potential beneficiaries. Moreover, wage top-up schemes such as WFTC may put downward pressure on low pay, subsidising the worst-paying employers the most. The OECD has stated that overall, low income will not be reduced to the extent suggested by the initial effects (OECD, 1997).

To these disadvantages must be added the denial of the right to privacy as applying for a means-tested benefit involves giving access to financial records. Consequently, WFTC is a threat to human dignity. Belgium, France and the Netherlands have chosen instead to put more emphasis on increasing minimum wages and cutting income tax (which is higher than in the UK) for the low-paid.

Unemployment and High Risk Groups for Unemployment

The UK's seasonally adjusted International Labour Organization (ILO) unemployment rate was 5.9 per cent for July–August 1999 and 4.2 per cent by September. Claimant-count unemployment rates only count those who are entitled to unemployment benefits and are registered as seeking work; the ILO rate counts all those seeking work through several defined routes (see also Tables A2.5–A2.8 in Appendix 2). In recent years, unemployment rates in the UK have compared well with other EU countries. In May 1999 the average ILO rate in the EU was 9.3 per cent when on the same measure UK unemployment was 5.3 per cent (Skills and Enterprise Network, 1999). The impact of global trends on the structure of industry, preparations for European monetary union, and labour market regulations including social protection measures, may all contribute to unemployment differentials in the EU. Although unemployment is now falling almost everywhere in the EU, there are labour market groups who face additional disadvantages in accessing employment. In the UK these include lone parents, black and minority ethnic groups, disabled people, young people (under 25 years of age) and older workers (Deve et al, 1998; Shropshire et al, 1999; Watson et al, 1998; Arthur et al, 1999; Stone et al, 2000; McKay and Middleton, 1998; Kozak, 1998). What is clear is that the possession of human capital is not enough. Those with greater vulnerability and weaker social capital networks, whether because of personal characteristics, isolation or prejudice, confront additional disadvantages in accessing employment.

Active Labour Market Policies

Globalisation and technical change have increased the rate at which UK industry and its workforce will have to adapt to compete in world markets. The government's response has been twofold: an employment-friendly social protection policy as described above, and increasing the skills of the labour force. Part of the process of achieving the latter is overhauling the education system to promote numeracy and literacy, work-readiness, higher targets for every level of qualification and better retention and achievement rates. The priorities include improving the skills of those at risk of exclusion and those of the labour force generally, and providing information and guidance to potential trainees, employers and trainers. Within the next two years the government intends to double to 500,000 the numbers of those receiving training in basic numeracy and literacy.

Given the unemployment experience of the groups referred to above, active labour market policies for the least advantaged must address quite complex issues. The government's response has been to launch the New Deal for the Unemployed, with the initial aim of getting a quarter of a million young people off benefit and into work. As youth unemployment has fallen, the New Deal has been extended to other groups, such as lone parents, those aged over 25, disabled people and partners of all these groups. Employment programmes are packaged into a plethora of schemes, and they change quite frequently. Consequently, information about training opportunities in itself may be considered an asset. The government has also recognised the need for measures to support people undertaking training, such as the national childcare strategy and childcare tax credits. However, these measures do not meet the full cost of childcare and the latter are irrelevant for those too poor to pay tax. The government also provides some assistance with the costs involved in looking for a job.

Like JSA, the New Deals involve sticks as well as carrots. There are compulsory job skills, availability and advice interviews with benefits agency staff, penalties for refusing job offers, advice on education and training opportunities, and calculations to demonstrate the financial attractiveness of work to most people who are currently unemployed or outside the labour market. There is also a £60 per person per week incentive to private sector employers to take on people under 25 years old who have been unemployed for six months or more.

The New Deal for the Young Unemployed (NDYU) has been in operation longest. It offers three elements: gateway, options and follow-through. The gateway involves advice on job search and careers guidance. In general, participants have been positive about their sessions with personal advisers. Post-gateway options for those who do not get jobs include subsidised employment, full-time education or training, work in the environment task force and work in the voluntary sector.

One survey showed that:

- 25 per cent of participants had taken up a subsidised job. Taking a subsidised or unsubsidised job was most common amongst those with shorter spells of unemployment.
- 50 per cent had taken a course of full-time education or training. Most were aiming for NVQ/SVQ Level 2. The least skilled were well-represented in this option.
- 13 per cent had taken a job in the voluntary sector and 12 per cent a job with the environment task force. Not much is known about what is going on in these options (Atkinson, 1999).

The NDYU client group are less qualified than young people who have been unemployed for less than six months. They are also predominantly male and white, although they include a disproportionately high number of those from Pakistani-British families. There is evidence that the government's job search and guidance initiatives do help people find jobs, but, clearly, the least advantaged young people are most distant from unsubsidised paid jobs. Further, the level of demand in the local labour market is important to opportunities for paid work and this client group disproportionately lives in areas that have experienced large job losses. Therefore there are more long-term unemployed (LTU) young people, and NDYU has a double hurdle: poor work histories plus low labour demand. The task is more difficult because of the UK's troubled history in smoothing the transition from school to work.

It is not surprising, therefore, that a recent report suggested that in its first 18 months there has been a high drop-out rate from the largest New Deal option, education and training courses. Only one in ten participants completed them; drop-outs tend to get recycled through the other non-market job options. The government disputes the report's claim, which arose from parliamentary answers, that in its first year only just over 8 per cent of New Deal leavers from this option got unsubsidised jobs.

Restricting analysis to those who can be traced, the government's figures suggest 46 per cent of leavers got jobs lasting more than 13 weeks (Morgan, 2000).

According to *Social Trends* 29, in 1996–97 42 per cent of lone parent families were in the bottom fifth of the income distribution (TUC, 1998). Yet to make work pay, alongside the support for re-entry to the labour market for lone parents there has been a cut in benefit for new claimants, and a requirement that teenage single mothers go through the 'single gateway' port to training. Despite this pressure, the New Deal for lone parents is having limited success in placing lone parents in employment. Between July 1997 and February 1999, of the 243, 971 invitation letters issued, 21 per cent of those lone parents invited for interview attended. While 83 per cent of those who attended an interview agreed to participate in the New Deal, fewer than 18 per cent of those participating obtained jobs (3 per cent of those originally invited for interview). As Box 6.1 shows, lone parents face particularly difficult decisions concerning taking paid work.

It is too soon to draw conclusions about the New Deal's contribution to new jobs. Evidence from Workstart pilots in the early 1990s suggests that 30 per cent of jobs created were for the LTU. However, most of this gain (24 per cent) was achieved by substitution to the LTU from other workers – the other 70 per cent would have happened anyway (Hasluck, 1999). Further, if the economy is below full employment, then training alone will not reduce unemployment; it will be necessary to expand aggregated demand for goods and services. Opportunities for trainees vary by region and by type of programme. Those with better access to physical capital (work-rich areas) and human capital are more likely to get the best opportunities to take paid work or augment their human capital. Adults leaving work-based training in the South East region during the last months of 1998 were more likely to get jobs (47 per cent of leavers) than leavers in the North East (34 per cent).

During 1998, 70 per cent of young people leaving their work-based training programme went into a job and 11 per cent went into further education. However, the 49 per cent taking the modern apprenticeship route were most likely to get a job, as were leavers in the South East and Eastern region. The 30 per cent of young people on other training (OT) were least likely to get a job. The worst-performing region was Yorkshire and Humber, in which 45 per cent of OT leavers got a job (Skills and Enterprise Network, 1999).

There is further evidence that those with least assets are least likely to get on training programmes. Payne and colleagues (1999) looked at the Training for Work (TfW) programme which was a part of work-based training that was targeted at those claimants unemployed for more than six months; their study excluded people with special needs. They found that although the programme increased participants' chances of getting a job generally, the greatest impact was for people in their first spell of unemployment. Placements were the most effective route to getting a job, yet the least advantaged groups are least likely to access these. Participation in TfW was voluntary and oversubscribed; those who were least likely to make it onto the scheme were from two groups: the least advantaged, and the vocationally better-advantaged and mobile. Therefore, they included: women with pre-school children; people with long-term health problems or disabilities; tenants in social and private housing; people with no higher-grade GCSE or GCE 'O' level passes; people who had never had a job; people of Indian ethnic origin; people with a driving licence and access to a vehicle; and people with NVQ vocational qualifications higher than level 2.

To improve the accessibility of training programmes, the government may have to reconsider their interaction with the benefits system, links to workplaces and the prejudices of employers and trainers. Above all, they may have to look again at the security and attractiveness of paid jobs as this kind of training programme does not appear to improve participants' suite of assets in a way that leads to sustainable employment. Qualifications gained while on TfW, except for the small percentage of people achieving NVQ level 4 or higher, did not improve participants' likelihood of getting a job compared with that of non-participants. TfW also had little effect on pay.

Flexibility

Many UK employers have adopted flexibility to gain short-term cost savings through a closer fit between labour demand and supply at any given moment. Training and development is less often given to atypical workers (the Netherlands has introduced regulations to counter this). For the past 15 years, the National Institute for Economic and Social Research (NIESR) found that production has been of a lower quality in the UK than in Germany across a range of manufactured products; there is also a large domestic market for low-specification goods and services. This is a vicious circle since this market will grow because of the low wages involved. The NIESR argues that this kind of production is unlikely to lead to highly skilled workforces with lifelong learning, trust and soft human resource management – what the OECD has referred to as the 'high performance workplace'. In other words, the UK approach to flexible employment may undermine the national policy objective of improving the skills of the workforce. Moreover, more than half of all workers are not trained to do a job other than their own. Sectors with high proportions of non-traditional or flexible workers include business services, retail, hotel and catering, and oil and gas (Barrell and Genre, 1999; Casey, Keep and Mayhew, 1999).

Furthermore, the National Association of Citizens Advice Bureaux (NACAB) has suggested that employers are using flexibility and deregulation to worsen pay and benefits and employment security, in order to minimise statutory and contractual obligations (1997). The resort to flexibility of this sort may be an admission of the failure to modernise and increase skills. Income insecurity is generally a bigger problem than low pay. For the countries in an OECD study which included the UK, the share of workers paid poorly at any one time during 1986–91 was one and a half to two times as great as the proportion who were continuously badly paid (OECD, 1997). Income insecurity is clearly a threat to individuals' ability to accumulate assets and achieve a sustainable livelihood. Top-up benefits such as WFTC, even for those eligible, are less effective in sustaining people in paid work in an insecure environment where benefit payments lag behind changes in incomes. Combating poverty involves ensuring that livelihoods are secure.

Employability

Despite the importance of security, employability has become the key concept for the government. The idea of employees 'managing [their] personal risk' is now widespread (Skills and Employment Network, 1999); the result is a culture of constant change. The new employment pattern is made up of downsizing, delayering and employability, while periods of unemployment are assumed to be part of people's working lives and a working week has become an elastic concept.

Yet a socially inclusive society would find a place for routine work, recognised and paid with dignity and would also provide dignified security for those who can't take paid work and for those who are legally excluded from paid work, such as asylum seekers. It is important that the government recognises the diversity of individuals and the way they can best make their contribution at any time. For example, individuals with certain kinds of learning disabilities make valued contributions in repetitive jobs, while it has been noted that 'for some individuals variety is not effective and change can appear threatening' (Watson et al, 1998). This has implications for the government's lifelong-learning approach and its expectation that everyone is adaptive, efficient at managing risk, and happy with a portfolio career path that involves periods of training, job change and unemployment.

Rajan and colleagues (1999) defined employability in terms of obtaining and retaining employment, coping with changes in employment and having relevant skills and motivation. They identified four types of employee: franchise builders (job hoppers), career builders (wanting to progress within a given workplace), flexible workers (part-timers and contract workers) and job satisfiers (who seek more fulfilment outside work than in it). According to Rix and colleagues, a number of studies have raised the issue of whether a new deal operates between employer and employees in which employers confer enhanced employability on workers in exchange for enhanced flexibility and the forgoing of employment security (1999). Rajan and colleagues found that while employers believe that the first two of the four kinds of employees identified above require an incentive to be retained and are suitable beneficiaries of training (which enhances their employability), the latter two groups are not considered worthy of training. Rix and colleagues suggest that there may be no new deal but rather a new form of market failure in which employers provide less and less transferable training to employees they do not plan to retain.

Clearly, the risks of exclusion from training and therefore career opportunities are not evenly distributed. Employer attitudes and beliefs may discriminate against women, who are more likely to be perceived to be, or to be included in, Rajan's latter two categories (flexible workers and job satisfiers). They are therefore denied opportunities to progress in the changing labour market. According to Burchell and colleagues, 'people who can cope with stress will be less afraid of redundancy. But even these individuals will be strongly influenced by family and social responsibilities' (1999). Therefore insecure work also impinges negatively on those in poorer health for whom stress may result in a worsening of their condition.

So, flexibility of the sort encouraged in the UK may inhibit the incentives to upskill the labour force. The government will confront a major difficulty in extending to all the means to cope with permanent revolution in the workplace: lifelong learning and career opportunities which have so far been the preserve of a minority (for much of our industrial history this has also been true of job security).

Furthermore, flatter organisation structures reduce promotion opportunities, and the payoff to seniority is reduced. Younger workers will not experience the pay increments that older workers have had, and studies show that upward mobility is falling, especially for lower earnings but generally across all skill groups. Buchele and Christiansen (1998) compared the impact of unregulated/deregulated labour markets on employment and unemployment and earnings inequality in the US and France, Germany, Italy and the UK. They concluded that labour market institutions that increase unemployment in Europe also contribute to more rapid earnings growth and greater earnings equality. The overall impact of different routes on social cohesion will depend on a particular country's culture.

Skills training cannot be regarded as the long-term solution to all labour market problems. The extent and persistence of low pay differs too much between countries to be attributed simply to differences in the supply of skills. Moreover, not everyone will benefit from extra training and in the foreseeable future there will not be a significant decline in the number of low productivity jobs on offer in OECD countries (OECD, 1997). Anyway, where productivity is a function of a job's requirements, then, independent of its occupant's abilities, human dignity and asset accumulation for some people will depend on their access to decent incomes being detached from their productivity status.

Conclusion

This chapter has focused on paid employment, so it has not considered the broader notion of work, paid and unpaid. Unpaid work, in people's own homes and as volunteers, must be central both to sustainable working lives and to sustainable communities. In particular, neglect of this factor may undervalue the contribution of women and unwaged people to sustainability and therefore underestimate threats to this source of sustainability. Nevertheless, considering sustainable livelihoods allows us to consider the impact of the government's active labour market strategy in combating poverty and social exclusion. Within the framework of this approach, this chapter has introduced the idea that there is a suite of assets necessary for social and economic cohesion. We would suggest that this is a coherent and fruitful framework for assessing policy for the least advantaged. However, as this chapter has also indicated, security and dignity are the fundamental foundations on which asset accumulation is predicated. It would be perverse to undermine them in attempting to engineer the accumulation of particular kinds of assets.

Main Messages of this Chapter

- Financial assets are likely to be a prerequisite to certain other kinds of asset.
- Access to training and employment opportunities depends on people's circumstances and where they live.
- The evidence on access to training programmes suggests that if one has access to one type of capital, one usually has access to others.
- Despite its benefits for individuals and communities, a minimum wage may not target the most needy households very well. However, there is little evidence that the minimum wage will cost jobs. There is scope for the minimum wage to be set at a higher rate to cut inequality and increase the opportunities for poorer people to build up their assets.

- To improve the accessibility of training programmes, the government may have to reconsider their interaction with the benefit system, links to workplaces, and the prejudices of employers and trainers. Above all, they may have to look again at the security and attractiveness of paid jobs.
- The UK approach to flexible employment may undermine the national policy objective of improving the skills of the workforce and the quality of the goods it produces.
- Skills training cannot be regarded as the long-term solution to all labour market problems.
- To combat poverty we need to ensure that livelihoods are secure.
- Security and dignity are the fundamental foundations on which asset accumulation is predicated.

Part III

The Way Forward

Chapter 7

From Vision to Reality

Meeting Needs

We introduced this book by restating the two key concepts of sustainable development: meeting the needs of those in poverty and staying within environmental limits. The acceptance that the environment has ecological limits reinforces the moral argument for equitable access to resources for countries, communities and individuals. We also introduced the idea of human develop- ment, a wider concept than simply meeting economic growth targets. These are the central themes of this book and are fundamental to the way those who produced it see our future, in the UK and globally. In this final chapter we want to return to these themes and address some of the ways in which we can make – and, in some cases, are already making – people's vision a reality.

An Equitable Environment

Chapter 2 underlined the importance of integrating anti-poverty measures and protect- ing the environment, highlighting people's right to environmental justice. It stressed the importance of participation and equitable access to resources and benefits to ensure that people's right to environmental justice is achieved.

There is considerable precedent for a rights- based approach to development. Indeed, the US Environmental Protection Agency defin- ition of environmental justice includes both the right to a healthy environment and the right to participate in the decision-making process to uphold that right. Since the Rio Summit in 1992, international human rights law has also started taking account of these principles (see Box 7.1). Principle 10 of the Rio Declaration emphasises the importance of citizens' part- icipation in handling environmental issues.

The newly-signed Aarhus Convention also implies substantive environmental rights, and guarantees procedural environmental rights to European citizens. Its first objective states that:

'In order to contribute to the protection of the right of every person of present and future generations to live in an environ- ment adequate to his or her health and wellbeing, each party shall guarantee the rights of access to information, public participation in decision making, and access to justice in environmental matters in accordance with the provis- ions of this Convention' (UNECE, 1999).

Ratification and implementation of the Aarhus Convention should ensure that people have greater access to the environmental information necessary to make informed decisions and choices. The UK should establish comprehensive

---

Box 7.1 *Draft principles of the UN sub-commission on human rights and the environment*

International Substantive Rights

- Freedom from pollution, environmental degradation and activities that adversely affect the environment or threaten life, health, livelihood, wellbeing or sustainable development.
- Protection and preservation of the air, soil, water, sea-ice, flora and fauna and the essential processes and areas that are necessary to maintain biological diversity and ecosystems.
- The highest attainable standard of health.
- Safe and healthy food, water and working environments.
- Adequate housing, land tenure and living conditions in a secure, healthy and ecologically sound environment.
- Ecologically sound access to nature, and the conservation and sustainable use of nature and natural resources.
- Preservation of unique sites.
- Enjoyment of traditional life and subsistence for indigenous peoples.

International Procedural Rights

- The right to information concerning the environment.
- The right to receive and disseminate ideas and information.
- The right to participation in planning and decision-making processes, including prior environmental impact assessment.
- The right of freedom of association for the purpose of protecting the environment or the rights of persons affected by environmental harm.
- The right to effective remedies and redress for environmental harm in administrative or judicial proceedings.

Source: from Boyle, 1998

and publicly accessible pollution inventories for industrial processes, traffic and other pollution, and for products.

There are also proposals already on the table in the UK about how these rights can be advanced. One of the main recommendations of the Acheson Report is that all policies should be evaluated for impacts on health inequalities and formulated to reduce them (Acheson, 1998). Subsequent policies should then be formulated to favour the disadvantaged in an attempt to reduce inequalities. In addition, Europe has several region-wide treaties that deal with environment and health protection at the level of rights, including the European Convention on Human Rights.

This national focus requires expansion, as one country can impose environmental injustices upon another, and one generation can impose injustices on another. For example, as a response to the difficult problem of how environmental resources should be distributed in a world of ecological limits, member groups of the international environmental network Friends of the Earth in Europe, Southern America and Asia, have advocated the use of 'equal distribution of resource consumption between countries on a per capita basis' (Carley and Spapens, 1997). This would have major implications for the UK. Halving the planet's emissions will require nearly a 90 per cent cut in the UK's carbon dioxide emissions if all people in all countries have equal rights to a share of the global commons, such as the atmosphere. This massive reduction in the use of environmental resources will need to be achieved while meeting all the UK population's needs – which implies a major revolution in the efficiency with which we use environmental resources and is also an argument for equitable distribution of those resources within the UK.

This work on environmental justice highlights the fact that conflicts between and convergence of trade, human development and environmental protection agendas cannot be resolved solely at a national level. The UK has to pursue a more globally responsible path with greater emphasis on fair and ecologically beneficial trading practices with other nations. Many NGOs believe this can be achieved in part through greater consultation between government departments, particularly those of trade and industry, environment, health and education. This can also be achieved through increased participation of the key government departments for health and environment in trade agreement negotiations, and in Europe (see Box 7.2).

Box 7.2 *European influence*

Many people in Britain see European decision-making as separate from or even superseding national policy, but activists are beginning to see the potential for European cooperation to bring a positive influence to global institutions. Europe's Common Foreign and Security Policy (CFSP) sees EU member states working within the UN taking a lead in reconstruction in the Balkans. It was the EU delegation which talked toughest to increase the emissions limit agreed at Kyoto.

The European parliament itself took a positive position on UN reform in 1999, has played a key role in preparation for the major UN conferences, and passed the most influential resolution in opposition to negotiations on the Multilateral Agreement on Investment.

Of course, the EU does not always speak with a single voice. The UK called for the WTO to launch a 'development round' and gave substantial technical assistance to developing countries during the negotiations in Seattle, while the EU delegation defended protectionist interests in agriculture. But a resolution on international regulation for multinational companies passed in January 1999 is an example of European action generating interest in an issue blocked in global institutions.

This is the view of the EU with its commitment to a social model, as a progressive force leading international negotiations. The human rights and democracy clauses the EU builds into trade and cooperation agreements with third parties provide a ready-made mechanism for engaging in real debate on these questions. The EU's agreement with 71 African, Caribbean and Pacific countries is a unique example of North–South partnership in our world. European action can be a stepping stone to a global change.

Source: Richard Howitt MEP, Development Committee, European Parliament

---

Fair Shares

Chapter 3 highlighted how traditional economic indicators emphasise growth. It also underlined the unfair distribution of the UK's wealth throughout this report. In order to address social, economic and environmental dimensions of poverty seriously, one needs to look again at the driving forces. And, just as importantly, one needs to end what has been called our 'patchwork assault on poverty' and look at how we value our society as a whole (Jowell et al, 1999).

A focus on economic growth is not enough to eradicate poverty, as can be seen by looking at both UK and international data over the past 50 years. The focus has to change from the quantity of economic activity to its quality, which consists of prioritising economic development that meets people's needs, particularly those of the poorest people, whilst protecting the environment and taking only a fair share of global resources. Table 7.1 shows some ways of going about this.

Table 7.1 *A fairer share of resources*

Issue	Mainstream approach	Sustainable approach
Overuse of materials	Recycling centres	Community recycling. There are 500 schemes in the UK where members of the community learn about and benefit from recycling
	Increase efficiency in resource use	Promote equality in the use of resources
Low cost finance	Don't lend to poor groups	Credit unions. 200,000 people in England, Scotland and Wales are members of these financial cooperatives. They get access to cheap loans and other financial services
Low cost, nutritious food	Out of town hypermarkets. Bulk buying with cars	The UK has around 20 food cooperatives, where members' collective buying power saves money
Community needs	Targeted by grants and assistance from statutory bodies	Over 1000 local currencies, including LETS and 'time money', operate in industrialised countries allowing needs to be met locally without cash
Individual needs	Assessed through measures of society as a whole	Considered as a proportion of the 'environmental space' available if the world's population is to live sustainably

As we have discussed in the previous chapters, poverty takes different forms, and so does the solution. Poverty is related not only to a lack of income, but also to the lack of a social, economic and natural infrastructure. For example, money put into a community may disappear because there are no local shops, no access to good value food, or poorly insulated homes (see Box 7.3). Initiatives like food cooperatives, self-help DIY schemes and volunteering help to provide the missing infrastructure. A good illustration is the village shop. A recent survey revealed that in rural areas local food producers often start their food production businesses on a small scale and could not do so without the outlets the small shops provide.

Box 7.3 *Plugging the leaks*

Imagine a poor community in the UK – one that would be a candidate for a regeneration programme. It could be a village or a housing estate. In that community, imagine painting a pound coin red and watching where it goes. Every time it changes hands within the community, it means income for a local person. In other words, if something is bought locally then some of that money will be re-spent in the local economy.

Currently regeneration strategies tend to look at how to attract more money into these types of areas, even though this has been difficult to achieve. A major challenge is that money flows much too quickly out of the community, just like water running out of a leaky bucket. In fact, in some of the poorest urban estates money comes in and leaves immediately, since there are no businesses – not even a local shop.

Simply pouring more money into these leaky economic buckets is not in itself going to bring about long-term change. This means that even when local authorities successfully attract external investors – businesses, supermarkets, additional tourists – frequently they only remain for a short period, or they extract more from the community over time than they put in. For example, the National Retail Planning Forum has published a survey of 93 out-of-centre food stores and concluded that in each case within a 10-mile radius there was a net average loss of 270 local retailing jobs (Porter and Raistrick, 1998).

Neighbourhood renewal strategies must therefore also include helping money to circulate more effectively within a community. This is also a much easier economic development strategy for a poor community to control. The strategy of plugging the leaks means mapping how different parts of the local economy link together and how money leaks out of an area, followed by finding ways of keeping the money within the community. This could include: using local building materials, favouring local firms who tender for contracts, or supporting the village shop.

Source: Bernie Ward, New Economics Foundation

At national policy level this phenomenon means that local money flows need to be taken into consideration when the impact of a particular action is being assessed, and those actions need to maximise local money flows. This could lead to a variety of policy changes. For example, we could use social service expenditure to foster the development of services that employ local people, such as creches, services for older people, or the cleaning of estates. We need to examine the potential impact of post office and bank closures, since it is clear that once the last financial institution in a community closes down the remaining outlets in the area will also suffer. We could follow Norway's lead and limit the development of large shopping centres outside city centres. Or ensure that micro-finance and technical advice are available to small enterprises.

The possibilities are vast but the basic principle is simple: if you are trying to regenerate a poorer community, then the money you spend is worth more to that community if it is spent locally.

As Table 7.1 illustrates, there is a growing number of sustainable responses to poverty. They have emerged organically as a result of people's needs and inspiration. Chapters 4–6 looked at different areas of national policy, at how current government policies contributed to sustainable development, and at how policy could be improved to meet sustainability criteria. Later, this chapter will explore further how change can be brought about at national level, but first it will look at what can be done locally and how we can strengthen communities to bring about change.

How can we Empower Communities?

There is no doubt that the major characteristic of poor neighbourhoods is a lack of money but, as this book has emphasised, material improvements alone do not guarantee effective regeneration. Normal practice tends to inhibit the effective integration of community involvement with regeneration plans. There are two main obstacles:

1 The prevailing view of community involvement and its development to date as an add-on to other social issues, not as a field with objectives in its own right.
2 The conventional economic wisdom which believes that only paid employment produces material empowerment and that everything else is a cost or is 'non-economic'.

Regeneration policies, although they have grown dramatically in the past couple of years, still tend to focus on the secondary effects of community involvement, as it assists development planning, the economy and public services, rather than on community activity as a benefit in its own right. Yet it is only by fostering community activity that community life will become vibrant enough to have these secondary effects.

Community development's roots in the small scale and the face-to-face remain a great strength. Society can be seen as comprising three sectors of equal significance: the public, private and community sectors. Each sector has both primary and secondary roles – areas in which it leads and areas in which it helps. The overall value of the third sector can be summarised as follows:

• Mutual aid and micro-social cohesion.
• Representing community interests.
• Social provision complementing public services.
• Assisting economic development.

The first two are intrinsic to community action; they are the sector's main reasons for existing. The second two are primarily the products of the other sectors. But the four aspects tend to depend on and reinforce each other. However, their extent and effectiveness are very patchy and can vary enormously from one locality to another. Policy alone can't make community action happen, but given the tendency of some people, in all neighbourhoods, to get together to do constructive things, as well as the willingness of considerably more people to be 'dragged in' more or less enthusiastically, policy has a critical role in providing the right conditions.

It is now generally recognised that if a local partnership or development scheme wants to foster empowerment, it needs to build up the community sector as a whole throughout the area, by supporting networks, projects and forums which in turn support and help the development of the whole range of small groups. They in turn provide more opportunities for individuals to get involved in constructive activity.

Trying to foster community involvement is not about trying to make local communities homogeneous or completely self-sufficient. It is about the tolerance of differences and enabling everyone to have an equal opportunity to participate in the task of running society and in the benefits of doing so. This demands a wide network of autonomous, varied community activities, providing many alternative access points for local people. As this report has stressed, social inclusion must include the opportunity to be connected to society's decision-making systems, from the locality upwards. Most locally-based citizens' initiatives and community organisations are about directly improving local life, and have real economic and social value.

In an empowered locality most local inhabitants would:

- be involved in their own local networks and organisations;
- care about what happens in their locality;
- know what developments are taking place in their locality;
- know how to monitor the activities of official agencies and private companies;
- have ways of making their influence felt in developments;
- contribute their own initiatives, voluntary effort and cooperation; and
- feel ownership of what is achieved and be prepared to preserve it.

Box 7.4 *Human development: models for change*

People with physical and/or sensory impairments, mental health service users and people with learning difficulties are groups which in the UK and elsewhere experience very high levels of poverty and unemployment. Led by the disabled people's movement, they have developed their own analysis of the exclusion and prejudice which they face.

They frame this in terms of social oppression rather than poverty and seek to challenge the discrimination they face by working for their civil and human rights as full and equal citizens in society. The disabled people's movement has developed the social model of disability, which distinguishes between the impairments which individuals may have and the disability or social oppression which they experience in society as a result, and which is the main reason for the restriction of their opportunities, rights and choices.

The disabled people's movement pioneered the idea of independent living to make it possible for people to have personal support and assistance to live as they wish, including the choice of being in employment, rather than being restricted to a poverty-level income from the welfare and benefit systems.

A wide range of user-led and user-controlled organisations and services have developed in the UK and internationally as a result of this. There are centres for independent living, arts and cultural organisations and activities, and parliamentary and direct action campaigning. These have focused on improving the support people have, particularly through direct payments or personal assistance schemes which disabled people themselves run, and through countering the broader discrimination and social exclusion that they have traditionally faced. In the UK this has resulted in legislation to give people more control over the support they need, as well as laws to increase people's access to the built environment, employment, education, training, public transport and information in appropriate formats. In the US it led to the passing of the Americans with Disabilities Act; in the UK the Disability Discrimination Act and the establishment of a Disability Rights Commission.

This is a large-scale development but one based on creating alternatives which tend to be participatory, democratically structured, bottom-up rather than top-down, locally accountable, small-scale and humanistic, challenging conventional consumerist approaches to meeting needs and prioritising people's human and civil rights. This approach to human development and challenging poverty has been doubly effective. It means that all disabled people, including people with learning difficulties and mental health service users, have developed their own support services and training, which help give them access to general employment opportunities, but which also provide them with new sustainable employment opportunities as support workers, trainers and managers. By gaining evaluation and research skills and experience, these groups are also developing their own alternative social and economic critiques which have a wider relevance for challenging poverty and working towards greater sustainability.

Source: Peter Beresford and Fran Branfield, Centre for Citizen Participation, Brunel University

Once a significant proportion of people are involved at some level, and the forms of involvement are increasingly well-connected, the development becomes a joint effort between people and local or national authorities instead of something done to or for communities by others. But this approach to empowerment requires two things:

1 teams of specialist workers skilled in facilitating people's activities and micro-organisations; and

2 a willingness on the part of those with authority and resources to share power widely among those whom they represent and serve.

Box 7.5 *A local programme*

Central to work on both poverty and sustainability is the need to restore community pride and build social capital and a strong local identity, which can help mobilise local energy and commitment. This can be done anywhere. The London Borough of Hackney's Local Agenda 21 (LA21) plan (one of the first in the UK to tackle poverty seriously) includes a vision of sustainable development built on the strengths identified in the borough:

- A robust and flexible culture, capable of welcoming change.
- Dense and integrated development patterns allowing maximum exchange with the minimum of movement.
- A distinctive sense of place.
- Proximity to the centre of a world city giving easy access to a wide range of resources and markets.

This same plan identified specific areas of concern, including:

- The current gulf between the well paid and the marginalised and unemployed.
- The need to identify and challenge the processes by which individuals are forced into debt and excluded from the legal economy.
- The short-term and insecure nature of much employment.
- The failure of long-term youth unemployment to respond to job market improvements.

It stressed that attempts to improve the environment were likely to be unsuccessful if these issues are not kept in mind by those running such attempts. Among the ideas for action that emerged were:

- Revitalise local centres and street markets.
- Increase local spending and employment.
- Expand the sustainable and green economies in the borough.
- Increase local savings, credit unions and Local Exchange Trading Schemes (LETS).
- Develop local food production.

It also stressed that short-term goals such as maximising benefit take-up, and providing good debt advice and service delivery, were key parts of a sustainability strategy.

Source: Chris Church, Community Development Foundation

Setting Up Systems to Build Sustainability

Making sustainable development happen requires practical schemes to combat poverty that can generate jobs: public transport, waste minimisation and recycling, energy efficiency and cultural and leisure activities all have a role. Reduced pollution, warmer homes and active leisure will improve everyone's health too, while many jobs thus created will be accessible to people with a range of skills, thus helping to tackle growing economic polarisation. All this will happen at a local level, so it is important to have a clear local focus as well as a national one.

Some LA21 projects have tackled these issues, but there is a great deal more to be done. Many LA21s find it difficult to build links between environmental and anti-poverty initiatives within local government. This is an area where leadership is badly needed, and there is also much that LA21 activity can do to enable the involvement of people from disadvantaged communities. As LA21 develops and supports emerging work on community planning, so the need for such cross-sectoral work becomes more important. Some ideas on how a local programme might develop are discussed in Box 7.5.

As stressed in the previous chapter, community involvement is the minimum requirement in planning environmental, health and social welfare programmes. Therefore, any project involving the participation of individuals or community organisations should have a plan to encourage that participation. Any such programme should identify disadvantaged groups among the stakeholders and build in work that will specifically target such groups. We have to dispense with the still-common idea that announcing 'our project is open to all and therefore anyone can participate' is sufficient in dealing with under-involvement (see Box 7.6). All participation work should have adequate money and staff time allocated to it by the lead organisation.

The initiators of any new project seeking involvement from within the community, or as professionals working with it, should agree with local representatives as early as possible what the project may realistically achieve, what resources are allocated to it, and how community involvement may make a difference. Professionals should seek to involve local organisations in the management of the project wherever possible, and local people should have a choice over when and how they get involved (see Box 7.7).

Sustainable regeneration

Some of the best practice at local level is coming from regeneration initiatives which have developed programmes that seek to give people confidence, work experience and self-help appropriate to local conditions so that they can in turn make a valuable contribution to improving local quality of life and sustainability. Rebuilding the local economy, using the innovative ideas that have come from the sustainable development movement, must go alongside community development in building people's confidence and self-respect.

Environmental improvements in deprived areas have in the past been seen as less important or even as marginal aspects of regeneration, but there is now a substantial body of evidence that suggests that improvements to housing, training and the local economy in problem areas may not be enough if they are not linked to environmental work, not least because people who have been empowered by such developments may simply move away from what they see as an unpleasant area to live. Lack of green space, poor transport, high crime and so on are all powerful incentives to move.

In addition, tackling poverty requires measures which are sustainable by being appropriate for both the local environment and

---

Box 7.6 *Barriers to participation*

These are some guidelines designed to help those living in poverty to make life easier for themselves, and to help those who do not understand the barriers faced by those in poverty.

Patience

1   There are a lot of good things that come with patience. For example, when people are speaking they tend to use abbreviations that other people don't understand – and so they lose interest in what is being talked about. Or when they join an organisation or meeting that has been running for a while, it is very hard to get the gist of what is going on. There has got to be time allowed for this and people need to be patient when others ask for the meaning of abbreviations. Sometimes I suspect the people using them don't themselves know what the abbreviations mean. However, grassroots people must also give respect to others at meetings, regardless of whether they are paid or not – we are all learning from each other.

Understanding

2   People must have time to speak and be understood. When they don't understand something they must be able to feel that it is all right to ask. Not everyone will feel happy about speaking in a room full of people, and so it helps if people are available to talk outside the meeting as well.

Confidence building

3   Being part of the process of changing the way people see each other is one of the most exciting ways of building one's confidence. But getting to that point is a long and hard process as people often think they don't have anything to say that is worth listening to, or that they might say or do something silly and be thought stupid. To combat this, people must be given the opportunity to bring someone with them, and be given support by everyone.

Support

4   Financial support, which people need to travel to events, and support when they make a public appearance, are very different but equally important. The type of support needed should be discussed thoroughly beforehand between the volunteer and their support person.

Dignity

5   Grassroots people very often don't like to ask about money – for example how much they need to get to a meeting, or whether they can claim for coffee or bus fares. As there are so many things a volunteer needs to know, it would be better if organisations which worked with volunteers a lot produced booklets that told them what they are entitled to. There should also be a way to pay people expenses in advance as they will not necessarily have the money needed in the first place.

Respect

6   Everyone has to understand that volunteers are the equal of paid people in every way; they have as much right to have their say and be heard and should be valued as much as everyone else in the organisation.

Source: Karen Dugdale, Communities Against Poverty

Box 7.7 *Steps to participation*

Working with volunteers

Community-based activity is built on voluntary activity, but many difficulties exist in this field. Some communities feel demeaned by being invited to volunteer by professionals who are being paid; and the traditional view of the volunteer as unpaid supernumerary assistance still lingers. Yet unpaid work can be an important way to deliver change and build the confidence of excluded people; the challenge is to ensure that the experience of volunteering is a positive and valuable one.

The value of volunteers should be recognised. Any project working with volunteers should budget properly for adequate volunteer expenses and training, plan volunteering opportunities to meet the needs of disadvantaged groups, and ensure that volunteers are aware of and take up opportunities to acquire skills that will be of value to them.

Training

Working on environmental issues in disadvantaged areas often poses new problems. Training programmes can help solve those problems, and basic training in community development, dealing with conflict, and race awareness should be provided for any environmental project worker in these areas. In addition training should be available for community activists, and they should be encouraged to define their own training needs.

Professionals working with community-based projects

Local councils, NGOs, and other professionals working with community-based projects need to be open and realistic. For any project or process they should make clear what they have to offer and avoid raising false expectations. They also need to spend time assessing the priorities of local people before finalising project plans and targets; this may seem obvious but it is by no means common practice where short-term economic targets are prioritised.

Source: Chris Church, Community Development Foundation

resources. The debate about the North–South divide in the UK and differences in the official statistics between regions highlight the need for local initiatives within national policy.

As well as general participation in the community, those in poverty can productively shape the services that are provided to them. Indeed this is an important feature of a sustainable economy. The idea is that more effective action and learning takes place where stakeholders are involved in decisions that affect them (see NEF, 1997). Table 7.2 shows a participation continuum. Participation and possibilities increase from left to right.

Perhaps the single most important conclusion from work on these issues is that there is an urgent need to improve the involvement of disadvantaged communities and to enable people within them to take effective action. However, almost all community-based projects receive some support from professionals, and many of the best environmental projects now running in disadvantaged areas exist because such support workers were prepared to go the extra mile and to work closely with small groups of people to turn ideas into action. The need for increased professional responsibility is central to enabling more community activity.

But however successful local efforts are, to sustain projects at the local level communities need to be working within a wider framework that supports their efforts. This chapter concludes by returning to developments at regional and national levels.

Table 7.2 *Participation continuum*

Passive	Information transfer	Consultation	Involvement	Partnership	Empowerment
People in poverty receive a service and have no say in priorities	People in poverty are told how things are going to be	People in poverty are asked 'How do you think things should be?' Often funding is fixed so not much scope for change	People in poverty are involved in the ongoing work of a project, but direction is still from the outside. Community forums for regeneration projects can fall into this category	People in poverty are asked 'What are your ideas for projects?' Two-way learning and shared control over direction, for example, some NGO-funded community projects	People in poverty shape membership of the group and determine actions. Resident-initiated housing associations are such an example

Source: Adapted from Partnerships in Participation, 1999

Regional Level

As was highlighted in Chapter 3, regeneration and development agencies have substantial financial power in many deprived areas, although it is as yet too early to evaluate their progress. This power needs to be used to promote genuinely sustainable development, although the economic priorities in their remit mean that environmental concerns are marginalised. The RDAs should respect the wishes of affected people and communities on matters relating to the local environment, and accept that their operations may have an impact on a much wider environment. Agencies should also ensure that local organisations working on sustainable development issues have an input to overall policy decisions; such NGOs may have a valuable role to play in ensuring that new developments do not conceal long-term mistakes.

National Level

At government level there is still little, if any, specific linkage between poverty and sustainable development. If environmental policies are to be genuinely sustainable, they must decrease inequity and narrow the gap between rich and poor. This is difficult because single measures tend to have limited benefits; the policies that are needed should be presented as a package, with the impact of each considered in the light of the others.

There is now an agreement from all sides to tackle financial incentives. Energy policies need to focus on tackling fuel poverty as well as carbon taxes and global warming, and getting the balance right may not be easy. Similarly, local and national transport policies need to improve access, and provide socially necessary public transport. Many environmental solutions currently advocated (such as energy efficiency measures) involve capital expenditure, but the poor lack capital; assessment of policy packages must include their distributional effects, both in relation to daily expenditure and to capital investment.

The government still has policies and programmes that are undermining its commitments to sustainable development, both in the UK and worldwide. The tension between access and mobility is one obvious area; despite commitments to improve public transport, and access for those without cars, many excluded communities in both urban and rural areas still have very unsatisfactory public transport, which can increase their exclusion by cutting their residents' access to facilities. Many anti-poverty schemes still see the level of car ownership as an indicator of poverty, rather than considering the ease of access to key services. Loans for public transport season tickets are still taxable, making subsidised company cars a favoured option while it increases pollution and road congestion. Similar perverse subsidies exist in other sectors; these should be a priority for change.

The Welsh National Assembly has conducted a major public consultation in the first half of 2000 to gather views on sustainable development. *A Better Wales*, a draft plan to integrate sustainability into all of the work of the Assembly, was launched in January 2000. This highlights a comprehensive commitment to incorporate sustainable development into all the activities of government in Wales, focusing on the need for all programmes to promote equality and sustainable development and tackle poverty. A central element of this is the production of a detailed set of sustainable development indicators which are intended to help in shaping policy in all areas of government activity.

There has been rather less activity in Scotland. *Down to Earth: A Scottish Perspective on Sustainable Development* was released by the Scottish Office in early 1999. The need to establish the particular priorities for Scotland within the UK's strategy for sustainable development was stressed, but has yet to be acted upon. A Scottish sustainable development commission has not yet been established, and no comprehensive set of indicators to guide policy formulation has been put in place. The emphasis in *Down to Earth* and other Scottish Office documents is on the capacity of economic growth and private sector activity to play a major role in achieving social and environmental improvements.

Participation, volunteering and training may all be important, but for long-term change new policies in a national framework are essential. Some of these have been discussed above, but there is another policy area that is less clear but may offer great potential to support change. Equal opportunities policies have become day-to-day practice for all large organisations. Clear criteria and programmes exist to help implement this work, but this is currently linked primarily to employment and access within the organisations. Any organisation that is serious about tackling the under-involvement of disadvantaged groups may wish to start considering how to apply its equal opportunities policy to project work involving NGOs, community-based organisations, and the wider public.

We also need to recognise that businesses are social institutions as much as they are money making bodies. As a result they have social responsibilities to a range of stakeholders – those that influence them and are influenced by them. These include staff, communities, and the environment, as well as shareholders.

We acknowledge that business has a vital role to play in any anti-poverty strategy. Policy action teams, set up by the SEU, have argued that business can have a positive effect on poverty by adopting a more responsible approach. Some of this responsibility is encouraged by the use of tools like social auditing. This helps to measure, understand and improve an organisation's impact on its stakeholders.

The challenge of enabling people to work across sectors can only be a long-term one. At its core is the same lesson that professionals focused on the developing world have learnt –

that it is the professionals themselves who must change their outlook and their ways of working to establish genuinely honest and effective working relationships with the people they are seeking to help.

Active and high-level commitment to tackling inequalities and injustice will be required if the current trends of globalisation are not to make these injustices worse. It will not be enough to have a level playing field; the equal treatment of unequals will merely exacerbate injustice.

Both the WHO and UNEP now share views on the difficult links of trade, health and environmental protection. As the WHO put it in 1997, 'a trading system that favours the optimal distribution of global production can potentially contribute to sustainable development, provided sound management practices and policies are adopted'. UNEP also noted that many international NGOs now share the concerns of the UN agencies focusing on health, human development and environmental sustainability. For example, the NGOs of the sustainable production and consumption caucus to the Commission on Sustainable Development expressed their concerns about

the trade liberalisation negotiations by the WTO, which were concerns widely voiced last November during the WTO meeting in Seattle.

As well as fears about the conflict between trade liberalisation and the more inclusive vision of human development, there remains the threat posed by environmental degradation to human societies and widespread environmental injustice. The inequality gap continues to widen. This global and national context, does not, however, preclude the UK itself making changes and seeking to influence its neighbours. Indeed, the UK government is starting to make profound commitments. Within the past year it has pledged to eradicate child poverty within 20 years, to cancel a large part of its developing world debt, has acknowledged its overconsumption of fossil fuels and pledged to reduce CO_2 emissions by 20 per cent by 2010. If the UK implements policies to meet these and other similar targets, and sets about a systematic programme to target all types of inequality, national, international and generational, then it will be joining more progressive countries which have a longstanding record of support for the principles of human development.

Main Messages of this Chapter

The main messages of this chapter are those of the whole report. The UK is a rich country with a good overall record on human development. However, it still suffers from dramatic inequalities that undermine that development and prevent sustainability; we still have poverty in plenty. The challenge posed in this report is for joined-up government to recognise the inconsistency in trying to tackle social exclusion while assuming that market forces will provide social stability and economic growth will reduce poverty.

Changing this situation requires us to take on messages about participation and equity from local to global levels. If a new, concrete

view of empowerment can genuinely be brought about, it will make a major contribution both to solving social and economic problems and to bolstering democracy. Indeed, it is likely that the social, economic and democratic needs of the 21st century will not be met without it. Society will either become more inclusive, participative and equitable or increasingly and dangerously polarised.

There is much that local communities can do to empower themselves to take on the rights and responsibilities associated with human development. But this process needs to be set in a national policy framework that acknowledges the urgent need to give people equitable access to the benefits of our country's wealth and uses the concept of human development to provide an ethical and viable way of making decisions about the future of our society. If we can achieve this we can meet the aspirations of the many individuals and organisations who have contributed to this report: a sustainable society in which all citizens can thrive.

Part IV

Reference Section – HDR-UK Report Statistics at Regional Level

Appendix 1

Environment and Health

Table A1.1 *Atmospheric pollution 1977–78, 1987–88 and 1997–98*

City[1]	Pollutant	Micrograms per cubic metre 1977–78[2]	Micrograms per cubic metre 1987–88[2]	Micrograms per cubic metre 1997–98[2]	Percentage change 1977–78 to 1997–98
Newcastle	Black smoke	149	124	41	–72
	Sulphur dioxide	252	163	79	–69
Manchester	Black smoke	188	78	53	–72
	Sulphur dioxide	266	127	38	–86
Barnsley	Black smoke	301	122	58	–81
	Sulphur dioxide	301	170	161	–47
Mansfield Woodhouse	Black smoke	311	154	60	–81
	Sulphur dioxide	257	168	93	–64
Stoke-on-Trent	Black smoke	256	94	56	–78
	Sulphur dioxide	274	121	70	–74
Norwich	Black smoke	93	61	40	–57
	Sulphur dioxide	89	39	20	–78
Stepney	Black smoke	98	40	38	–61
	Sulphur dioxide	311	178	89	–71
Slough	Black smoke	85	72	42	–51
	Sulphur dioxide	175	87	24	–86
Swindon	Black smoke	82	61	39	–52
	Sulphur dioxide	106	59	20	–81
Cardiff	Black smoke	148	52	51	–66
	Sulphur dioxide	175	64	108	–38
Glasgow	Black smoke	146	93	44	–70
	Sulphur dioxide	229	67	49	–79
Belfast	Black smoke	304	133	53	–83
	Sulphur dioxide	142	201	141	–1

Notes:
1 One site chosen for each UK Statistical Region.
2 Measured in OECD units; measurements in British Standard Units are equivalent to 0.85 × OECD units (refers to black smoke only). Figures shown are for the 98th percentile daily mean concentration, ie the level which is exceeded by the highest 2 per cent of daily mean concentrations during the year.

Source: National Environmental Technology Centre, 1999

Table A1.2 *River and canal pollution in 1995 (percentage rated poor or bad)*

	Biological quality (percentages) in 1995; poor/bad[1]	Chemical quality (percentages) in 1994–96; poor/bad[2]
Wales[3]	1	2
Scotland	2	1
Northern Ireland	–[4]	12[5]
England	8	11
North East	14	14
North West	22	16
Midlands	8	11
Anglian	3	13
Thames	5	9
South	2	10
South West	1	4

Notes:
1 Classification based on the River Invertebrate Prediction and Classification System (RIVPACS).
2 Based on the chemical quality grade of the General Quality Assessment (GQA) scheme.
3 In England and Wales the boundaries of the Environment Agency regions are based on river catchment areas and not county borders. In particular, the figures shown for Wales are for the Environment Agency Welsh Region, the boundary of which does not coincide with the boundary of Wales.
4 In Northern Ireland, 1991 survey.
5 In Northern Ireland, 1989–91 survey.

Source: Environment Agency/Department of the Environment, Northern Ireland, 1999

Table A1.3 *Percentage of bathing waters not complying with mandatory EU coliform standards in 1999*

Coastal region	Percentage of bathing waters not complying
Wales	1
Scotland	32
Northern Ireland	0
England	
Northumbria	3
North West	32
Yorkshire	9
Anglian	6
Thames	0
Wessex	5
South	6
South West	11
United Kingdom	9

Note: The EU mandatory coliform standard is 10,000 per 100ml for total coliform and 2,000 per 100ml for faecal coliform.

Source: Environment Agency, 1999

Table A1.4 *Water pollution incidents in 1997 (total number of incidents and prosecutions)*[1]

Region	Nature of pollutant/ number of prosecutions	All	Major[2]
Wales[3]	Industrial	592	5
	Sewage and water related	704	2
	Agricultural	262	2
	Other	689	2
	Total	2247	11
	Number of prosecutions[4]	6	
Scotland	Industrial	857	66
	Sewage and water related	1126	36
	Agricultural	449	48
	Other	1103	29
	Total	3535	179
	Number of prosecutions[4]	21	
Northern Ireland	Industrial	365	21
	Sewage and water related	351	14
	Agricultural	549	34
	Other	558	4
	Total	1823	73
	Number of prosecutions[4]	85	
England	Industrial	3131	48
	Sewage and water related	4661	34
	Agricultural	1622	33
	Other	7910	68
	Total	17324	183
	Number of prosecutions[4]	61	
North East	Industrial	465	9
	Sewage and water related	876	8
	Agricultural	170	4
	Other	893	8
	Total	2404	29
	Number of prosecutions[4]	9	
North West	Industrial	506	24
	Sewage and water related	482	5
	Agricultural	255	12
	Other	917	9
	Total	2160	50
	Number of prosecutions[4]	12	
Midlands	Industrial	814	4
	Sewage and water related	1229	4
	Agricultural	407	6
	Other	1961	11
	Total	4411	25
	Number of prosecutions[4]	3	

A1.4 *Water pollution incidents in 1997 (total number of incidents and prosecutions)[1] (continued)*

Region	Nature of pollutant/ number prosecutions	All	Major[2]
Anglian	Industrial	383	2
	Sewage and water related	555	1
	Agricultural	193	1
	Other	1280	24
	Total	2411	28
	Number of prosecutions[4]	10	
Thames	Industrial	324	4
	Sewage and water related	436	4
	Agricultural	89	1
	Other	1068	4
	Total	1917	13
	Number of prosecutions[4]	13	
Southern	Industrial	138	2
	Sewage and water related	294	8
	Agricultural	101	3
	Other	641	7
	Total	1174	20
	Number of prosecutions[4]	2	
South West	Industrial	501	3
	Sewage and water related	789	4
	Agricultural	407	6
	Other	1150	5
	Total	2847	18
	Number of prosecutions[4]	12	
United Kingdom	Industrial	4945	140
	Sewage and water related	6842	86
	Agricultural	2882	117
	Other	10260	103
	Total	24929	446
	Number of prosecutions[4]	173	

Notes:
1 Data relate to substantiated reports of pollution only. Figures for Scotland relate to the financial year 1996–97.
2 Major incidents are those corresponding to category 1 in the Environment Agency's pollution incidents classification scheme. For Scotland the term 'significant incidents' is used.
3 In England and Wales, the boundaries of the Environment Agency Regions are based on river catchment areas and not county borders. In particular, the figures shown for Wales are for the Environment Agency Welsh Region, the boundary of which does not coincide with the boundary of Wales.
4 For England and Wales, total prosecutions include cases concluded and prosecutions outstanding. Prosecutions concluded relate to cases which had been brought to court by March 31 1998. In Scotland, this figure relates only to legal proceedings which resulted in a conviction during 1997–98.

Source: Environment Agency/Scottish Environment Protection Agency/Department of the Environment, Northern Ireland, 1999

Table A1.5 *Previous use of land changing to urban use in 1993*[1]

	Land changing to urban uses, total hectares	Land changing to urban uses, hectares per 100,000 population[2]	Percentage previously in rural use
North East	775	30	35
North West	1925	28	33
Yorkshire and the Humber	1535	32	43
East Midlands	1200	29	58
West Midlands	1315	25	37
East	1835	35	48
London	635	9	10
South East	2240	29	41
South West	1325	28	57
England	12785	26	41

Notes:

1 The information relates only to map changes recorded by the Ordnance Survey between 1993 and 1997 for which the year of change is judged to be 1993.

2 Based on mid-1993 population estimates.

Source: DETR, 1999

Table A1.6 *Percentage of land covered by trees, 1995*

	%		%
North East		South East (government office region)	
Northumberland	15.6		
Tyne and Wear	3.7	Berkshire	13.8
Cleveland	6.2	Buckinghamshire	8.6
Durham	6	East Sussex	15.9
North West		Hampshire	16.6
Cheshire	3.9	Isle of Wight	9.9
Cumbria	8.3	Kent	11.6
Greater Manchester	2.2	Oxfordshire	6.3
Lancashire	3.9	Surrey	19
Merseyside	2.7	West Sussex	17.7
Yorkshire and the Humber		South West	
North Yorkshire	7	Avon	5.3
Humberside	3	Cornwall	5.5
South Yorkshire	7.2	Devon	8.3
West Yorkshire	4.9	Dorset	9.6
East Midlands		Gloucestershire	10.5
Derbyshire	5.3	Somerset	5.8
Leicestershire	3.3	Wiltshire	7.5
Lincolnshire	3.3	Wales	
Northamptonshire	5.3	Clwyd	9.4
Nottinghamshire	7.3	Dyfed	11.1
West Midlands		Gwent	13.4
Hereford and Worcestershire	7.8	Gwynedd	11.3
Shropshire	7.4	Mid Glamorgan	16
Staffordshire	6.4	South Glamorgan	6.4
Warwickshire	3.6	West Glamorgan	22.2
West Midlands		Powys	13.3
(metropolitan county)	2.2	Scotland	
Eastern		Borders	17
Bedfordshire	5.4	Central	16.4
Cambridgeshire	2.1	Dumfries and Galloway	24.7
Essex	4.3	Fife	12.2
Hertfordshire	7.7	Grampian	18.1
Norfolk	8.2	Highland	12.6
Suffolk	7.7	Lothian	9
London	3.9	Strathclyde	19.6
		Tayside	12.5
		Northern Ireland	7.3

Notes:
Counties (prior to local government reorganisation) for England and Wales. Local authority regions (prior to local government reorganisation) for Scotland, Northern Ireland.
Within Great Britain, figures are estimates projected from the 1980 Census of Woodland. For Northern Ireland, figure relates to 1992.

Source: The Forestry Commission/Department of the Environment, Northern Ireland, 1999

Table A1.7 *Greatest threats to the countryside, 1997*

	Greatest %	Next greatest %
Land and air pollution, or discharges into rivers and lakes	36	21
Building new roads and motorways	15	15
Litter and fly-tipping of rubbish	13	13
New housing and urban sprawl	11	12
Superstores and out-of-town shopping centres	8	9
Industrial development	8	13
Changes to traditional ways of farming and of using farmland	2	7
Changes to the ordinary natural appearance of the countryside	2	5
Number of tourists and visitors	1	1
None of these (includes don't know and not answered)	3	5
All	100	100

Note: Respondents were asked to indicate which of nine possible threats they believed to be the greatest and the second greatest threats.

Source: National Centre for Social Research, 1997; Social and Community Planning Research, 1997

Table A1.8 *Average daily motor vehicle flows by road class, 1998*

	Motorway	Major roads, non built-up	Major roads, built-up	Minor roads, non built-up	Minor roads, built-up	All roads
Wales	50.3	7.8	9.8	0.5	1.7	2.0
Scotland	35.9	4.2	10.8	0.6	2.0	2.1
England	71.9	13.7	16.2	0.9	2.1	3.8
North East	44.9	14.3	13.5	0.6	2.2	3.1
North West	66.4	11.8	15.8	0.9	1.9	4.1
Yorkshire and the Humber	58.9	12.2	15.7	0.9	2.0	3.5
East Midlands	76.6	12.0	13.9	0.8	1.7	3.3
West Midlands	80.1	11.1	16.7	0.8	2.5	3.9
East	80.8	17.2	13.8	1.0	2.2	3.8
London	93.8	53.4	23.4	23.4	2.3	6.0
South East	79.3	17.4	15.5	1.4	2.4	5.0
South West	59.9	10.2	13.5	0.6	1.8	2.5
Britain	67.3	10.7	15.1	0.8	2.1	3.4

Note: Average daily flow is the annual traffic divided by road length multiplied by 365. Traffic estimates are derived from roadside traffic counts which take two forms: occasional 12-hour counts at a large number of sites to estimate the absolute level of traffic (the rotating census) and frequent counts at a small number of sites (the core census) to estimate changes in the amount of traffic.

Source: DETR, 1998

Table A1.9 *Fatal and serious road accidents in 1997[1]*

	Fatal and serious accidents on all roads (numbers) 1997	Fatal and serious accidents on all roads (rates per 100,000 population) 1997	Fatal and serious accidents on major roads (numbers) 1997[2]	Fatal and serious accidents on major roads (rates per 100 million vehicle kms) 1997
Wales	1541	53	847	5.5
Scotland	3648	71	1869	7.6
England	34439	70	17616	7.2
North East	1184	46	503	4.8
North West	4449	65	2232	6.7
Yorkshire and the Humber	3470	69	1642	7.0
East Midlands	3258	78	1680	7.4
West Midlands	3971	75	1860	6.8
East	4129	77	1947	6.1
London	6401	90	3951	20.2
South East	4988	63	2508	4.9
South West	2589	53	1293	4.9
Britain	39628	69	20332	7.1
Northern Ireland	1273	77	542	7.0

Notes:

1 An accident is one involving personal injury occurring on a public highway (including footways) in which a road vehicle is involved and which becomes known to the police within 30 days. The vehicle need not be moving and it need not be in collision with anything. Persons killed are those who sustained injuries which caused death less than 30 days after the incident. A serious incident is one for which a person is detained in hospital as an inpatient, or any of the following injuries whether or not they are detained in hospital: fractures, concussion, internal injuries, crushing, severe cuts and lacerations, severe general shock requiring medical treatment, injuries causing death 30 or more days after the accident.

2 Major roads are motorways, A(M) roads and A roads.

Source: DETR/Royal Ulster Constabulary, 1999

Table A1.10 *Cigarette smoking among people aged 16 and over, 1996–97*

	Proportion who smoke	Proportion of smokers having their first cigarette within less than 5 minutes of waking
Wales	27	12
Scotland	32	22
Northern Ireland	29	16
England	28	14
North East	31	23
North West	30	16
Yorkshire and the Humber	27	19
East Midlands	26	17
West Midlands	28	15
East	26	10
London	29	12
South East	26	10
South West	27	13
United Kingdom	28	15

Source: ONS, 1996; Northern Ireland Statistics and Research Agency, 1996

Table A1.11 *Standardised mortality ratio in 1997*

		Standardised mortality ratio (UK=100)
Males	United Kingdom	100
	Wales	104
	Scotland	117
	Northern Ireland	107
	England	98
	North East	112
	North West	109
	Yorkshire and the Humber	103
	East Midlands	97
	West Midlands	102
	East	90
	London	97
	South East	90
	South West	89
Females	United Kingdom	100
	Wales	102
	Scotland	115
	Northern Ireland	105
	England	98
	North East	109
	North West	107
	Yorkshire and the Humber	100
	East Midlands	98
	West Midlands	99
	East	94
	London	94
	South East	95
	South West	91
All persons	United Kingdom	100
	Wales	103
	Scotland	115
	Northern Ireland	106
	England	98
	North East	110
	North West	107
	Yorkshire and the Humber	101
	East Midlands	98
	West Midlands	101
	East	92
	London	96
	South East	93
	South West	90

Note: Standardised mortality ratio (SMR) is the ratio of observed deaths to those expected by applying a standard death ratio to the regional population. The SMR compares with overall mortality in a region with that for the UK. The ratio expresses the number of deaths in a region as a percentage of the hypothetical number that would have occurred if the region's population had experienced the sex/age specific rates of the UK in that year.

Source: DETR, 1999

Table A1.12 *Percentage of children immunised, 1981, 1991–92 and 1996–97[1]*

	1981[2]	*1991–92[3]*	*1996–97*
Diphtheria	82	94	96
Tetanus	82	94	96
Whooping cough	45	88	96
Poliomyelitis	82	94	94
Measles, mumps, rubella[4]	52	90	92

Notes:

1 Data shown in this table for 1991–92 and 1996–97 for England, Wales and Northern Ireland relate to children reaching their second birthday. Data for 1981 in England, Wales and Northern Ireland relate to children born two years earlier and immunised by the end of the second year. For Scotland, rates prior to 1995–96 have been calculated by dividing the cumulative number of immunisations for children born in year X and vaccinated by year X+2, by the number of live births (less neonatal deaths) during year X; rates for 1995–96 have been calculated by dividing the number of children completing a primary immunisation course before their second birthday by the total number of two-year-old children.

2 Data exclude Scotland.

3 Data for Scotland are for 1992.

4 Includes measles-only vaccine. Combined vaccine was not available prior to 1988.

Source: Department of Health/Welsh Office/National Health Service in Scotland/Department of Health and Social Services, Northern Ireland, 1999

Table A1.13 *Percentage reporting a limiting long-term illness in 1997*

	%
Wales	26
Scotland	21
Northern Ireland	21
England	22
North East	25
North West	22
Yorkshire and the Humber	24
East Midlands	22
West Midlands	21
East	21
London	21
South East	19
South West	23
United Kingdom	22

Note: Longstanding illness is measured by asking respondents if they have a longstanding illness, disability, or infirmity. Longstanding means anything that has troubled the respondent over a period of time that is likely to affect the respondent. A limiting longstanding illness/infirmity is one which limits the respondent's activity in any way.

Source: ONS, 1999; Northern Ireland Statistics and Research Agency, 1997

Appendix 2

Economics and Employment

Table A2.1 *Percentage of households that could not afford certain items in EU countries, 1995*

	Eat meat or vegetarian equivalent every other day, %	New clothes, %	A week's holiday, %
Portugal	6	47	59
Greece	35	32	51
Spain	2	9	49
United Kingdom	10	15	40
Irish Republic	4	7	38
Italy	6	15	38
France	5	10	34
Belgium	4	10	26
Austria	8	10	24
Denmark	2	5	16
Netherlands	2	13	15
Luxembourg	3	5	14
Germany	5	15	12

Source: Eurostat, 1995

Table A2.2 *Percentage of households in receipt of benefit, 1997–98*

	Family Credit or income support	Housing benefit	Council tax benefit	Jobseekers' allowance	Retirement pension	Incapacity or disability benefits	Child benefit	Any benefit
Wales	18	20	27	5	32	23	28	76
Scotland	16	22	27	6	28	18	29	72
England	15	17	23	4	28	14	29	69
North East	21	26	33	7	28	22	29	77
North West	18	21	29	5	30	20	29	74
Yorkshire and the Humber	17	20	27	5	30	16	28	72
East Midlands	15	16	21	4	27	15	28	67
West Midlands	17	17	24	4	29	15	30	70
East	11	13	18	3	28	11	28	66
London	18	22	26	5	24	11	30	68
South East	9	12	15	3	27	10	29	63
South West	11	13	20	3	32	13	26	68
Britain	15	18	23	4	28	15	29	70

Source: DSS, 1998

Table A2.3 Distribution of weekly household income, 1995–98

	Households under £100 %	Households £100 to £150 %	Households £150 to £250 %	Households 250 to £350 %	Households £350 to £450 %	Households £450 to £600 %	Households £600 to £750 %	Households £750 or over %	Average gross weekly income per household (£)	Average gross weekly income per person (£)
Wales	15	12	20	15	10	12	7	9	360	151
Scotland	15	12	19	13	13	12	8	9	371	158
Northern Ireland	16	13	20	13	12	12	7	8	336	126
England	13	11	16	13	12	13	9	13	417	176
North East	18	14	18	14	10	11	7	8	333	145
North West	15	11	17	13	12	13	9	10	384	158
Yorkshire and the Humber	15	13	19	12	12	12	8	9	360	152
East Midlands	12	11	17	14	13	15	7	12	401	166
West Midlands	15	11	17	15	12	14	7	10	381	155
East	12	11	16	14	12	14	9	12	419	177
London	15	11	12	13	10	14	9	17	491	204
South East	10	9	14	13	12	13	11	19	474	207
South West	12	11	15	14	15	14	8	11	405	173
United Kingdom	14	11	16	13	12	13	8	12	408	171

Source: ONS/Northern Ireland Statistics and Research Agency, 1998

Table A2.4 Percentage of households with different types of savings, 1997–98[1]

	Current account[2]	Post office	TESSA	Other bank/building society	Gilts or unit trusts	Stocks and shares	National savings	Save as you earn	Premium bonds	PEPs
Wales	81	11	10	51	4	18	6	1	19	10
Scotland	77	8	9	57	6	24	5	1	15	11
England	85	12	14	65	7	30	9	2	30	13
North East	80	9	11	56	4	24	6	1	23	12
North West	82	10	12	55	5	25	7	2	23	11
Yorkshire and the Humber	81	12	14	62	6	27	8	1	27	11
East Midlands	84	13	14	66	5	29	8	2	28	11
West Midlands	80	11	13	65	6	26	8	2	26	12
East	90	15	18	72	9	36	11	3	37	16
London	84	10	13	62	6	29	8	2	28	13
South East	92	14	16	73	8	37	11	3	38	18
South West	91	17	16	70	9	31	13	2	37	16
Great Britain	84	12	14	64	7	29	9	2	28	13

Notes:

1 Households in which at least one member has an account.

2 A current account may be either a bank or building society account.

Source: DSS, 1998

Table A2.5 *Percentage unemployed (claimant count)[1] in April 1999 at county and unitary authority level[2]*

	%		%
Darlington UA	5.9	Cambridgeshire County	2.3
Hartlepool UA	12	Essex County	3.3
Middlesbrough UA	9.5	Hertfordshire	1.9
Redcar & Cleveland UA	9.7	Norfolk	4.4
Stockton-on-Tees UA	7.8	West Berkshire UA	3.5
Durham County	7.2	Suffolk	4.9
Northumberland	6.2	London	1.4
Tyne and Wear	7.8	Bracknell Forest UA	6.6
Blackburn with Darwen UA	5.5	Brighton and Hove UA	6
Blackpool UA	5.5	Isle of Wight UA	5.3
Halton UA	6.6	Medway Towns UA	2.1
Warrington UA	3	Milton Keynes UA	1.1
Cheshire County	3	Portsmouth UA	3.5
Cumbria	4.7	Reading UA	2.1
Merseyside	4.8	Slough UA	2.8
Greater Manchester	3.9	Southampton UA	4.3
Lancashire County	9.1	Windsor and Maidenhead UA	1.5
East Riding of Yorkshire UA	4.6	Wokingham UA	1
Kingston upon Hull UA	8.7	Buckinghamshire County	1.7
North East Lincolnshire UA	7.8	East Sussex County	4.2
North Lincolnshire UA	4.8	Hampshire County	2
York UA	2.9	Kent County	3.9
North Yorkshire County	2.7	Oxfordshire	1.5
South Yorkshire (Met. County)	7.2	Surrey	1.2
West Yorkshire (Met. County)	5	West Sussex	1.8
Derby UA	5.4	Bath and North East Somerset UA	2.7
Leicester UA	5.2	Bournemouth UA	5.2
Nottingham UA	5.5	Bristol UA	3.8
Rutland UA	1	North Somerset UA	2.8
Derbyshire County	4.7	Plymouth UA	5.1
Herefordshire UA	2.5	Poole UA	2.4
Leicestershire County	3.4	South Gloucestershire UA	1.8
Lincolnshire	2.8	Swindon UA	2.3
Northamptonshire	4.9	Torbay UA	6
Nottinghamshire County	2.8	Cornwall and the Isles of Scilly	5.5
Stoke-on-Trent UA	5	Devon County	3.3
Telford and Wrekin UA	3.5	Dorset County	2.5
Shropshire County	3	Gloucestershire	2.9
Staffordshire County	3.7	Somerset	3
Warwickshire	2.7	Wiltshire County	1.9
West Midlands (Met. County)	6.4	Blaenau Gwent	11.3
Worcestershire County	3.1	Bridgend	5.9
Luton UA	4.8	Caerphilly	7.3
Peterborough UA	2.9	Cardiff	4.4
Southend-on-Sea UA	6.1	Carmarthenshire	6.2
Thurrock UA	5.1	Ceredigion	3.9
Bedfordshire County	2.8	Conwy	5.9

A2.5 *Percentage unemployed (claimant count)[1] in April 1999 at county and unitary authority level[2] (continued)*

	%		%
Denbighshire	4.7	Fife	7.6
Flintshire	4	Glasgow City	6.4
Gwynedd	6.1	Highland	5.3
Isle of Anglesey	8.4	Inverclyde	6.9
Merthyr Tydfil	7.8	Midlothian	4.9
Monmouthshire	3.6	Moray	4.5
Neath Port Talbot	7.2	North Ayrshire	10.2
Newport	5.6	North Lanarkshire	8.7
Pembrokeshire	7.6	Orkney Islands	3.1
Powys	3.4	Perth and Kinross	3.6
Rhondda, Cynon, Taff	7.3	Renfrewshire	5.8
Swansea	5.9	Scottish Borders, The	4.4
The Vale of Glamorgan	4.5	Shetland Islands	2.6
Torfaen	4.6	South Ayrshire	6.2
Wrexham	4.1	South Lanarkshire	6.7
Aberdeen City	2.3	Stirling	4.6
Aberdeenshire	3	West Dunbartonshire	10.9
Angus	6.2	West Lothian	5
Argyll and Bute	5.2	Ballymena	5.5
Clackmannanshire	8.9	Belfast	6.2
Dumfries and Galloway	5.9	Coleraine	8.6
Dundee City	7.7	Craigavon	5.7
East Ayrshire	9.7	Dungannon	7.1
East Dunbartonshire	6.2	Enniskillen	8.2
East Lothian	4.3	Londonderry	10.6
East Renfrewshire	6.7	Mid Ulster	7
Edinburgh, City of	3.3	Newry	9.9
Eilean Siar (Western Isles)	8.7	Omagh	8.4
Falkirk	7.4	Strabane	11.6

Notes:

1 The claimant count rate is the number of people claiming unemployment-related benefit as a proportion of claimant count and workforce jobs in each area.

2 Unitary Authorities and counties for England, Unitary Authorities for Wales, New Councils for Scotland and Travel to Work areas for Northern Ireland.

Source: ONS, 1999

Table A2.6 Percentage unemployed (ILO definition) 1994–98

	Spring quarter of 1994	Spring quarter of 1995	Spring quarter of 1996	Spring quarter of 1997	Spring quarter of 1998
Wales	9.3	8.8	8.3	8.4	6.7
Scotland	10.0	8.3	8.7	8.5	7.4
Northern Ireland	11.7	11.0	9.7	7.5	7.3
England	9.5	8.6	8.1	6.9	6.0
North East	12.5	11.4	10.8	9.8	8.2
North West	10.3	9.0	8.4	6.9	6.6
Yorkshire and the Humber	9.9	8.7	8.1	8.1	7.0
East Midlands	8.3	7.5	7.4	6.3	4.9
West Midlands	10.0	9.0	9.2	6.8	6.3
East	8.2	7.5	6.2	5.9	5.0
London	13.1	11.5	11.3	9.1	8.1
South East	7.1	6.4	6.0	5.2	4.3
South West	7.5	7.8	6.3	5.2	4.5
United Kingdom	9.6	8.6	8.2	7.1	6.1

Note: The International Labour Organisation (ILO) definition of unemployment is measured through the Labour Force Survey and covers those who are looking for work and are available for work. The ILO unemployment rate is the percentage of economically active people who are unemployed.

Source: ONS/Department of Economic Development, Northern Ireland, 1999

Table A2.7 *Percentage of unemployed people who were long-term unemployed in April 1999 (claimant count)*

		Over 26 weeks and up to 1 year	*Over 1 year and up to 2 years*	*Over 2 years and up to 3 years*	*Over 3 years and up to 5 years*	*Over 5 years*	*Total number unemployed (thousands)*
Males	United Kingdom	17.6	13.5	4.1	3.8	5.7	1010.3
	Wales	17.9	12.4	3.8	3.6	4.3	53.3
	Scotland	18	13.1	3.6	2.9	4.2	107.1
	Northern Ireland	16.1	15.2	5.8	7	18.6	42.5
	England	17.6	13.6	4.1	3.8	5.2	807.3
	North East	17.7	12	4	4.1	6.7	68.1
	North West	17.4	12.1	3.6	3.2	5.2	127.2
	Yorkshire and the Humber	18.1	13.1	4.1	3.4	4.6	101.6
	East Midlands	17.3	13.9	3.5	2.7	3.6	61.5
	West Midlands	17.3	14	4.5	3.6	6	95.9
	East	16.7	12.4	3.8	3.7	4.5	61.1
	London	19	16.8	5.3	5.2	6.5	154.6
	South East	16.6	12.6	3.8	3.4	4.1	77.2
	South West	17.1	12	3.4	3.6	4.2	60.1
Females	United Kingdom	17.3	10.2	2.9	2.4	2.7	309.8
	Wales	16.9	8.5	2.3	2	2.3	15.5
	Scotland	16.6	9.3	2.4	1.7	2	31.9
	Northern Ireland	18.3	10.4	3.8	3.9	7.8	11.9
	England	17.3	10.4	2.9	2.4	2.5	250.6
	North East	16.8	8.7	2.5	2.4	3	17.8
	North West	16.6	8.5	2.4	1.9	2.2	35.6
	Yorkshire and the Humber	17.3	9.2	2.5	1.9	2.3	29.6
	East Midlands	16.9	9.5	2.4	1.7	1.8	19.1
	West Midlands	16.8	11	3	2.2	2.9	29.6
	East	15.9	9.9	2.8	2.4	2.4	20.5
	London	20.1	13.8	4.1	3.5	3	54.4
	South East	15.5	10.2	2.9	2.4	2.3	23.6
	South West	16	9	2.5	2.3	2.3	20.3
All persons	United Kingdom	17.5	12.7	3.8	3.5	4.9	1320.1
	Wales	17.6	11.5	3.4	3.2	3.9	68.8
	Scotland	17.7	12.2	3.3	2.6	3.7	139
	Northern Ireland	16.6	14.1	5.4	6.3	16.2	54.4
	England	17.6	12.8	3.9	3.4	4.6	1057.9
	North East	17.5	11.3	3.7	3.7	6	85.8
	North West	17.2	11.3	3.3	2.9	4.5	162.8
	Yorkshire and the Humber	17.9	12.2	3.7	3.1	4.1	131.2
	East Midlands	17.2	12.9	3.2	2.4	3.1	80.7
	West Midlands	17.1	13.3	4.1	3.3	5.2	125.5
	East	16.5	11.8	3.5	3.4	4	81.7
	London	19.3	16	5	4.7	5.6	209
	South East	16.3	12	3.6	3.2	3.7	100.8
	South West	16.9	11.2	3.2	3.3	3.7	80.4

Source: ONS, 1999

Table A2.8 *Percentage of employees with 'flexible' work contracts in spring 1998*

	Males	*Females*
Wales	16.3	26.1
Scotland	17.7	22.1
Northern Ireland	20.5	29.1
England	16.4	25.0
North East	18.4	26.7
North West	17.3	24.8
Yorkshire and the Humber	16.4	27.3
East Midlands	16.5	24.5
West Midlands	17.2	24.1
East	14.2	23.9
London	14.7	22.9
South East	16.6	24.8
South West	17.8	28.1
United Kingdom	16.6	24.9

Note: Includes term-time working, job sharing, nine day fortnight, four and a half day week, flexi-time, annualised hours, and zero hours contract (not contracted to work a set number of hours but paid for actual number of hours worked)

Source: ONS/Department of Economic Development, Northern Ireland, 1999

Table A2.9 Households accepted as homeless: by reason, 1997[1]

	No longer willing or able to remain with parents (%)	No longer willing or able to remain with relatives or friends (%)	Break down of relationship with partner (%)	Mortgage arrears (%)	Rent arrears or other reason for loss of rented accommodation (%)	Other reasons (%)[2]	Total (=100%) (numbers)
Wales	21	9	23	6	26	15	6403
Scotland		33	34	3	14	16	17600
Northern Ireland		26	20	1	12	41	4997
England	15	11	25	6	25	18	102410
North East	20	9	35	5	17	14	4430
North West	13	8	31	5	18	25	12800
Yorkshire and the Humber	14	11	30	6	21	18	8960
East Midlands	13	7	38	7	23	12	7980
West Midlands	14	11	32	5	18	20	14500
East	17	9	22	10	33	9	8020
London	17	17	16	3	23	24	24850
South East	18	10	20	8	33	11	12070
South West	12	8	21	8	39	12	8800

Notes:
1 In England and Wales the basis for these figures is the number of households accepted for rehousing by local authorities under the homelessness provisions of Part III of the Housing Act 1985, and Part VII of the Housing Act 1996. The Welsh figures also include: 1) non-priority cases, given advice and assistance; 2) intentionally homeless, priority accepted; and 3) intentionally homeless, non-priority accepted. In Scotland the basis of these figures is households assessed by the local authorities as homeless or potentially homeless and in priority need, as defined in Section 24 of the Housing (Scotland) Act 1987. In Northern Ireland, the Housing (Northern Ireland) Order 1988 (Part II) defines the basis under which households (including one-person households) are classified as homeless. The figures relate to priority cases only.
2 A large proportion of the Northern Ireland total is classified as 'Other reasons' due to differences in definitions used.

Source: DETR/National Assembly for Wales/Scottish Executive/Department of the Environment, Northern Ireland, 1999

Table A2.10 Percentage of households with selected durable goods, 1997–98

	Microwave	Washing machine	Tumble drier	Dishwasher	Deep freezer	Telephone	Video	Compact disc player	Satellite dish	Home computer
Wales	80	91	48	15	91	92	80	54	27	20
Scotland	75	93	53	19	89	93	82	63	27	24
Northern Ireland	74	91	40	23	84	92	77	48	22	21
England	75	90	50	22	91	95	82	63	27	29
North East	78	92	45	13	91	92	82	62	30	21
North West	77	90	51	19	91	94	82	61	31	24
Yorkshire and the Humber	77	90	47	16	90	93	81	57	26	24
East Midlands	77	92	55	20	92	94	82	63	28	27
West Midlands	75	91	52	19	91	95	81	60	27	27
East	75	91	52	28	93	96	84	68	27	34
London	68	85	42	21	89	96	80	61	28	31
South East	77	91	54	31	92	97	85	69	26	37
South West	75	89	52	26	92	95	81	60	21	27
United Kingdom	75	90	50	22	91	95	82	62	27	28

Source: DSS, 1998; Northern Ireland Statistics and Research Agency, 1997

Appendix 3

Social Environment

Table A3.1 Notifiable offences against individuals recorded by the police: by offence group, 1997 (rates per 100,000), and percentage change, 1996–97[1]

		Violence against the person	Sexual offences	Burglary	Robbery	Theft and handling stolen goods	Fraud and forgery	Criminal damage[2]	Other	Total
1997	England and Wales	482	64	1952	121	4163	258	1686	115	8841
	North East	355	44	2431	73	4319	185	2196	108	9713
	North West	466	64	2180	141	4210	238	2000	124	9422
	Yorkshire and the Humber	426	65	3032	91	4938	217	1961	128	10857
	East Midlands	602	64	2123	71	4188	234	1795	110	9187
	West Midlands	403	52	2362	144	4162	185	1644	104	9055
	East	380	52	1268	38	3391	180	1254	79	6643
	London	695	100	1869	362	4903	571	1860	167	10527
	South East	400	52	1386	44	3695	200	1398	101	7276
	South West	453	58	1603	56	3895	195	1152	79	7490
	England	476	64	1973	127	4195	262	1675	114	8885
	Wales	595	64	1590	28	3623	197	1883	131	8111
	Scotland[3]	287	88	1083	88	3668	420	1581	999	8212
	Northern Ireland[3]	308	86	854	99	1764	228	280	96	3715
% change 1996–97	England and Wales	4	5	–13	–15	–10	–2	–8	7	–9
	North East	–7	–9	–19	–17	–12	–1	–21	4	–16
	North West	10	17	–10	–8	–9	–1	–6	3	–7
	Yorkshire and the Humber	1	4	–13	–14	–10	–4	–6	2	–10
	East Midlands	5	3	–15	–20	–11	–8	–9	15	–10
	West Midlands	7	15	–10	–17	–11	–13	–9	24	–10
	East	5	3	–12	–14	–11	–8	–8	2	–9
	London	5	2	–15	–17	–5	9	–8	12	–7
	South East	–1	2	–14	–8	–11	–4	–9	4	–11
	South West	5	1	–14	–18	–9	–11	–8	–5	–9
	England	4	5	–13	–15	–10	–2	–9	7	–9
	Wales	10	11	–11	–6	–7	–5	4	3	–4
	Scotland[3]	–10	23	–14	–15	–9	–2	–9	14	–7
	Northern Ireland[3]	–9	–18	–12	–5	–10	–7	–4	–2	–10

Notes:

1 In England and Wales and Northern Ireland, indictable offences cover those offences which must or may be tried by jury in the Crown court and include the more serious offences. Summary offences are those for which a defendant would normally be tried at a magistrate's court and are generally less serious – the majority of motoring offences fall into this category. In general in Northern Ireland non-indictable offences are dealt with at a magistrate's court. Some indictable offences can also be dealt with there. In Scotland the term 'crimes' is generally used for the more serious criminal acts (roughly equivalent to indictable offences); the less serious are termed 'offences', although the term 'offence' is also used in relation to serious breaches of criminal law. The majority of cases are tried summarily (without a jury) or in the high court. With effect from April 1996 (the date on which the relevant section of the Criminal Procedure (Scotland) Act 1995 came into force) offending while on bail is no longer a notifiable offence.

2 The Northern Ireland figures exclude criminal damage valued at under £200 in 1996 and 1997.

3 Figures for Scotland and Northern Ireland are not comparable with those for England and Wales, nor with each other, because of differences in the legal systems, recording practices and classifications.

Source: Home Office/Scottish Executive/Royal Ulster Constabulary, 1999

Table A3.2 Crimes committed against households, 1998[1]

		Vandalism	Burglary[2]	Vehicle thefts[3]	All household offences[4]
England and Wales	Offences per 10,000 households	1345	756	2122	4914
	Percentage of households victimised at least once	8.2	5.6	15.7	27.7
North East	Offences per 10,000 households	888	1049	2158	4794
	Percentage of households victimised at least once	4.6	8.6	15.4	28.2
North West	Offences per 10,000 households	1755	977	2521	6021
	Percentage of households victimised at least once	9.6	6.8	18.6	31.7
Yorkshire and the Humber	Offences per 10,000 households	1597	1085	2704	6263
	Percentage of households victimised at least once	9.1	8.3	20	32.5
East Midlands	Offences per 10,000 households	1236	735	1961	4564
	Percentage of households victimised at least once	8.2	5.6	14.7	26.6
West Midlands	Offences per 10,000 households	1108	735	2092	4363
	Percentage of households victimised at least once	7.1	5.9	16	27
East	Offences per 10,000 households	1291	428	1911	4249
	Percentage of households victimised at least once	7.9	3.1	15.2	26.7
London	Offences per 10,000 households	1135	710	2372	4279
	Percentage of households victimised at least once	7.9	5.7	15.6	25
South East	Offences per 10,000 households	1586	649	1889	5016
	Percentage of households victimised at least once	9.6	4.3	13.8	27.6
South West	Offences per 10,000 households	1043	558	1785	4537
	Percentage of households victimised at least once	7.2	4.4	13.5	25.7
England	Offences per 10,000 households	1333	753	2137	4918
	Percentage of households victimised at least once	8.2	5.7	15.8	27.9
Wales	Offences per 10,000 households	1548	812	1869	4861
	Percentage of households victimised at least once	8.7	4.8	14.2	25
Scotland	Offences per 10,000 households	1105	386	1657	3211
	Percentage of households victimised at least once	6.4	3	12.6	18.6
Northern Ireland	Offences per 10,000 households	863	301	1163	2112
	Percentage of households victimised at least once	6.9	2.4	8.4	15.4

Notes:

1. The British Crime Survey (BCS) was conducted by the Home Office in 1982, 1984, 1988, 1992, 1994, 1996 and 1998. Each survey measured crimes experienced in the previous year, including those not reported to the police. The survey also covers other matters of Home Office interest including fear of crime, contacts with the police, and drug misuse. The 1998 survey had a nationally representative sample of 14,947 people aged 16 or over in England and Wales. The sample was drawn from the Small User Postcode Address File, a listing of all postal delivery points. The response rate was 79 per cent. Scotland participated in sweeps of the BCS in 1982 and 1988 and ran its own Scottish Crime Surveys in 1993 and 1996 based on nationally representative samples of 5000 repondents aged 16 or over interviewed in their homes. In addition 495 people aged between 12 and 15 completed questionnaires in 1993 and 353 completed questionnaires in the 1996 survey. Addresses were randomly generated from Postcode Address File.

2. The term used in Scotland is housebreaking. The figures include attempts at burglary/housebreaking.

3. Comprises theft of vehicles, thefts from vehicles and associated attempts. The vehicle theft rates are based on vehicle-owning households only.

4. Comprises the three individual categories plus thefts of bicycles and other household thefts.

Source: Home Office, 2000; Scottish Executive, 2000; Northern Ireland Office, 2000

A HUMAN DEVELOPMENT REPORT FOR THE UK

Table A3.3 Percentage of notifiable offences cleared up by the police: by offence group, 1997[1,2]

	Violence against the person	Sexual offences	Burglary	Robbery	Theft and handling stolen goods	Fraud and forgery	Criminal damage[3]	Other	Total
England and Wales	79	77	23	27	24	48	19	96	28
North East	74	80	17	34	26	49	21	99	27
North West	73	82	18	23	24	57	18	98	26
Yorkshire and the Humber	81	80	23	36	23	51	15	99	26
East Midlands	83	86	27	33	28	52	21	98	32
West Midlands	79	77	22	24	25	46	18	94	27
East	84	76	28	38	28	50	20	99	32
London	70	61	23	24	19	41	18	87	26
South East	82	78	21	36	23	50	21	98	28
South West	85	82	21	30	23	52	22	99	28
England	78	76	22	27	24	48	19	95	28
Wales	88	92	38	62	36	51	26	99	41
Scotland[4]	80	74	18	28	28	77	22	98	39
Northern Ireland[4,5]	59	86	18	16	26	56	28	86	31

Notes:

1. In England and Wales and Northern Ireland, indictable offences cover those offences which must or may be tried by jury in the Crown court and include the more serious offences. Summary offences are those for which a defendant would normally be tried at a magistrate's court and are generally less serious – the majority of motoring offences fall into this category. In general in Northern Ireland non-indictable offences are dealt with at a magistrate's court. Some indictable offences can also be dealt with there. In Scotland the term 'crimes' is generally used for the more serious criminal acts (roughly equivalent to indictable offences); the less serious are termed 'offences', although the term 'offence' is also used in relation to serious breaches of criminal law. The majority of cases are tried summarily (without a jury) or in the high court. With effect from April 1996 (the date on which the relevant section of the Criminal Procedure (Scotland) Act 1995 came into force) offending while on bail is no longer a notifiable offence.

2. Some offences cleared up in 1997 may have been initially recorded in an earlier year.

3. Figures for England and Wales exclude criminal damage valued at £20 or under. The Northern Ireland figure excludes criminal damage valued at under £200.

4. Figures for Scotland and Northern Ireland are not comparable with those for England and Wales, nor with each other, because of the differences in the legal systems, recording practices and classifications.

5. The Northern Ireland figure includes offences against the state.

Source: Home Office, 2000; Scottish Executive, 2000; Royal Ulster Constabulary, 2000

Table A3.4 *Percentage of people with feelings of insecurity: by gender, 1998*

		Males	Females
England and Wales	Percentage feeling very unsafe at night when alone at night	–	3
	Percentage feeling very unsafe at night when walking alone	3	18
North East	Percentage feeling very unsafe at night when alone at night	–	4
	Percentage feeling very unsafe at night when walking alone	5	22
North West	Percentage feeling very unsafe at night when alone at night	2	3
	Percentage feeling very unsafe at night when walking alone	4	23
Yorkshire and the Humber	Percentage feeling very unsafe at night when alone at night	1	2
	Percentage feeling very unsafe at night when walking alone	3	22
East Midlands	Percentage feeling very unsafe at night when alone at night	1	3
	Percentage feeling very unsafe at night when walking alone	3	16
West Midlands	Percentage feeling very unsafe at night when alone at night	1	3
	Percentage feeling very unsafe at night when walking alone	5	17
East	Percentage feeling very unsafe at night when alone at night	–	2
	Percentage feeling very unsafe at night when walking alone	2	17
London	Percentage feeling very unsafe at night when alone at night	–	3
	Percentage feeling very unsafe at night when walking alone	4	17
South East	Percentage feeling very unsafe at night when alone at night	–	2
	Percentage feeling very unsafe at night when walking alone	2	16
South West	Percentage feeling very unsafe at night when alone at night	1	2
	Percentage feeling very unsafe at night when walking alone	2	17
England	Percentage feeling very unsafe at night when alone at night	1	3
	Percentage feeling very unsafe at night when walking alone	3	18
Wales	Percentage feeling very unsafe at night when alone at night	–	5
	Percentage feeling very unsafe at night when walking alone	5	15
Scotland[1]	Percentage feeling very unsafe at night when alone at night	1	3
	Percentage feeling very unsafe at night when walking alone	6	23
Northern Ireland[2]	Percentage feeling very unsafe at night when alone at night	3	12
	Percentage feeling very unsafe at night when walking alone	11	34

Notes:
1 Data for Scotland relate to 1996.
2 For Northern Ireland the question relates to fear of walking in the dark (ie alone or with others); the figures also include those people who never go out.

Source: Home Office, 2000; Scottish Executive, 2000; Northern Ireland Office, 2000

Table A3.5 *Percentage of householders participating in local voluntary work, 1996–97*

	Still volunteering	No longer volunteering	Interested in volunteering	Not interested in volunteering
North East	8	1	32	59
North West	11	2	36	52
Yorkshire and the Humber	8	1	30	61
East Midlands	10	2	39	49
West Midlands	11	2	35	53
East	14	1	39	46
London	10	2	43	45
South East	14	2	40	45
South West	16	2	40	43
England	11	2	37	50

Note: Participation by householders in voluntary work to benefit their local area in the 12 months before interview. The Survey of English Housing interviews one person in each household, almost always the household head or their partner. For convenience the respondents are referred to as 'householders'.

Source: DETR, 1999

Table A3.6 *Internet access in Britain*

Adults online at home or work, January 1999: 29%

December 1999 37%

Age groups, December 1999	
18–24 years of age	60%
25–34 years of age	53%
35–64 years of age	36%
65 and over	8%
Gender	
Men	42%
Women	32%
Regional	
South	44%
Midlands	33%
North and Scotland	32%

Source: ICM/*The Guardian*, 1999

Appendix 4

Human Poverty Index for British Parliamentary Constituencies and OECD Countries

Table A4.1 *HPI-2 for British parliamentary constituencies*

Name	Party	Death	Unemp	Income	Illit	HPI-2
Glasgow Shettleston	Labour	27.2	2.3	35	26	27.1
Glasgow Springburn	Labour	25.3	2.6	34	25	26.0
Glasgow Maryhill	Labour	23.4	2.5	34	25	25.8
Birmingham Ladywood	Labour	18.6	2.9	35	27	25.7
Manchester Central	Labour	21.4	2.5	34	23	24.7
Camberwell and Peckham	Labour	17.1	2.6	34	25	24.6
Glasgow Baillieston	Labour	21.6	2.1	33	24	24.5
Liverpool Riverside	Labour	21.4	3.3	35	20	24.5
Hackney South and Shoreditch	Labour	17.0	2.3	34	23	24.0
Bethnal Green and Bow	Labour	17.8	1.6	32	24	23.6
Poplar and Canning Town	Labour	18.3	1.2	32	24	23.5
Vauxhall	Labour	18.5	3.2	33	21	23.2
Birmingham Sparkbrook and Small Heath	Labour	17.7	2.9	29	27	23.0
Tyne Bridge	Labour	19.6	3.3	31	22	22.9
Southwark North and Bermondsey	Liberal Democrat	18.7	2.6	31	22	22.9
Glasgow Pollock	Labour	22.1	2.2	29	23	22.9
Hackney North and Stoke Newington	Labour	16.6	2.4	32	20	22.3
Holborn and St Pancras	Labour	18.2	2.8	29	23	22.1
Liverpool Walton	Labour	17.2	3.0	29	23	21.6
Bootle	Labour	17.6	2.8	28	23	21.6
Glasgow Anniesland	Labour	21.5	2.0	27	22	21.6
Manchester Blackley	Labour	20.7	2.1	27	22	21.6
Liverpool West Derby	Labour	17.3	3.3	29	22	21.5
Islington South and Finsbury	Labour	15.9	3.5	30	19	21.3
Salford	Labour	20.2	1.6	28	21	21.2
Leeds Central	Labour	17.9	2.7	28	21	20.8
Tottenham	Labour	15.3	3.3	30	18	20.8
Glasgow Govan	Labour	20.9	2.2	26	20	20.6
Airdrie and Shotts	Labour	18.2	0.8	26	22	20.6
West Ham	Labour	15.9	1.2	28	21	20.6
Manchester Gorton	Labour	19.4	2.1	27	20	20.5
Islington North	Labour	15.7	3.6	29	17	20.4
Sheffield Central	Labour	15.9	3.1	29	18	20.3
Sheffield Brightside	Labour	15.6	3.0	26	22	20.1
Motherwell and Wishaw	Labour	17.7	0.8	26	21	20.1
Deptford	Labour	15.2	3.1	28	18	19.9

* For a full description of the four weighted components 'Death', 'Unemp', 'Income' and 'Illit', see David Gordon's Technical Note on page 156

A4.1 *HPI-2 for British parliamentary constituencies (continued)*

Name	Party	Death	Unemp	Income	Illit	HPI-2
Dundee West	Labour	17.1	1.1	26	21	19.8
Greenock and Inverclyde	Labour	19.8	0.8	25	20	19.8
Glasgow Cathcart	Labour	18.3	2.0	25	20	19.6
Birmingham Hodge Hill	Labour	15.5	2.8	24	23	19.6
Middlesbrough	Labour	18.0	2.6	24	21	19.5
Regents Park and Kensington North	Labour	16.0	3.1	27	17	19.5
Glasgow Kelvin	Labour	19.8	1.8	24	20	19.5
Coatbridge and Chryston	Labour	17.6	1.0	25	21	19.5
Nottingham East	Labour	16.9	1.3	26	20	19.4
Glasgow Rutherglen	Labour	18.8	1.8	24	20	19.3
Birmingham Erdington	Labour	17.6	3.5	24	21	19.3
Hamilton North and Bellshill	Labour	18.4	1.1	24	20	19.2
Wolverhampton South East	Labour	15.8	2.0	24	22	19.1
Greenwich and Woolwich	Labour	14.9	3.0	26	19	19.1
Knowsley South	Labour	15.3	2.8	25	21	19.1
Birkenhead	Labour	17.8	2.3	24	20	19.1
Bradford West	Labour	16.5	1.1	23	22	19.0
South Shields	Labour	15.7	1.3	25	20	19.0
Newcastle East and Wallsend	Labour	16.3	2.7	25	19	19.0
Paisley North	Labour	17.4	1.7	24	20	18.9
Cunninghame South	Labour	16.7	1.5	24	20	18.9
Dundee East	Labour	16.7	1.5	24	20	18.8
Brent South	Labour	14.5	2.8	26	18	18.8
Sunderland North	Labour	15.5	2.6	24	20	18.7
Hull East	Labour	15.7	0.8	24	21	18.7
Paisley South	Labour	17.2	2.2	24	20	18.7
Hamilton South	Labour	17.4	1.2	23	20	18.7
Leeds East	Labour	15.3	2.7	24	21	18.7
Sunderland South	Labour	14.9	3.0	25	19	18.6
East Ham	Labour	14.8	1.1	25	19	18.5
Barking	Labour	14.8	1.2	22	22	18.5
West Bromwich West	Speaker	15.4	3.7	23	21	18.4
Wythenshawe and Sale East	Labour	16.2	2.3	23	20	18.4
Nottingham North	Labour	15.4	1.5	24	20	18.3
Hull North	Labour	13.5	0.8	24	20	18.2
Merthyr Tydfil and Rhymney	Labour	15.3	0.9	23	20	18.1
Wolverhampton North East	Labour	14.6	2.1	22	21	18.0
Streatham	Labour	15.1	2.6	25	16	18.0
Walsall North	Labour	15.5	3.0	22	21	17.9
Bradford North	Labour	15.8	1.2	21	21	17.9
Rochdale	Labour	16.2	1.3	21	21	17.7
Easington	Labour	16.8	1.7	21	20	17.6
Hull West and Hessle	Labour	15.0	.9	23	19	17.6
Houghton and Washington East	Labour	16.0	2.0	21	20	17.6
Leicester West	Labour	15.3	1.4	22	19	17.6
Jarrow	Labour	15.8	1.1	23	18	17.6
Clydebank and Milngavie	Labour	15.6	2.2	22	19	17.5

North Tyneside	Labour	14.6	2.4	23	19	17.5
Liverpool Wavertree	Labour	15.3	3.1	23	18	17.4
Hartlepool	Labour	15.7	2.6	22	19	17.4
Liverpool Garston	Labour	15.2	3.1	23	18	17.3
Knowsley North and Sefton East	Labour	14.6	2.6	23	17	17.3
Gateshead East and Washington West	Labour	14.1	1.7	22	19	17.3
Hampstead and Highgate	Labour	13.1	3.2	23	19	17.2
West Bromwich East	Labour	15.0	1.9	21	20	17.2
Bolton South East	Labour	16.5	0.6	20	20	17.2
Falkirk West	Labour	15.5	1.4	21	19	17.2
Carrick Cumnock and Doon Valley	Labour	14.8	2.0	22	19	17.2
Acton and Shepherds Bush	Labour	15.5	3.3	24	15	17.2
Brent East	Labour	14.7	2.8	24	14	17.2
Stockton North	Labour	16.1	2.9	21	19	17.1
Kilmarnock and Loudoun	Labour	15.1	2.6	21	19	17.1
Warley	Labour	15.3	2.9	21	19	17.0
Aberdeen Central	Labour	15.9	1.3	21	19	17.0
Battersea	Labour	15.0	2.3	23	16	16.9
Rotherham	Labour	14.1	2.7	21	19	16.9
Walsall South	Labour	15.0	2.5	20	20	16.9
Leicester South	Labour	13.9	1.3	22	18	16.9
Hammersmith and Fulham	Labour	16.2	3.1	23	14	16.9
Doncaster North	Labour	14.7	2.3	20	20	16.9
Dunfermline East	Labour	14.4	0.9	21	19	16.8
Sheffield Heeley	Labour	13.2	2.7	22	18	16.8
Linlithgow	Labour	14.6	0.7	21	19	16.8
Preston	Labour	17.0	0.8	20	18	16.8
Dagenham	Labour	13.6	1.5	19	21	16.7
Nottingham South	Labour	14.7	1.4	21	18	16.7
Huddersfield	Labour	14.2	0.9	20	20	16.7
Barnsley Central	Labour	14.8	1.6	20	19	16.7
Edinburgh North and Leith	Labour	17.4	1.2	20	17	16.6
Birmingham Northfield	Labour	13.6	3.3	20	20	16.6
Blackburn	Labour	16.1	1.0	20	18	16.5
Dulwich and West Norwood	Labour	14.6	2.7	23	14	16.5
Dumbarton	Labour	16.1	1.9	20	18	16.5
Leeds West	Labour	14.2	2.2	21	18	16.5
Ashton under Lyne	Labour	15.9	1.1	19	19	16.5
Newcastle Central	Labour	15.5	3.0	22	15	16.4
Birmingham Perry Barr	Labour	13.7	2.9	19	20	16.4
Coventry North East	Labour	14.7	2.4	21	18	16.4
Stoke Central	Labour	17.1	0.9	19	18	16.4
Caithness Sutherland and Easter Ross	Liberal Democrat	15.1	2.8	20	18	16.4
Cities of London and Westminster	Conservative	12.2	1.9	24	13	16.3
Barnsley East and Mexborough	Labour	13.9	1.7	20	19	16.3
Kirkcaldy	Labour	14.6	2.5	20	18	16.3
Oldham West and Royton	Labour	15.1	1.2	19	19	16.3
Redcar	Labour	14.9	2.4	19	19	16.3
Central Fife	Labour	14.7	1.8	20	18	16.3
Pontefract and Castleford	Labour	14.5	1.2	19	19	16.3
Midlothian	Labour	15.0	0.8	20	18	16.3

A4.1 *HPI-2 for British parliamentary constituencies (continued)*

Name	Party	Death	Unemp	Income	Illit	HPI-2
Bradford South	Labour	14.7	1.2	18	20	16.2
Lewisham East	Labour	14.0	3.7	22	16	16.2
Great Grimsby	Labour	15.5	1.8	19	18	16.1
Leicester East	Labour	14.5	1.1	20	18	16.1
Edinburgh Central	Labour	16.9	1.3	19	17	16.1
Eccles	Labour	15.6	1.6	19	18	16.1
Argyll and Bute	Liberal Democrat	16.0	2.2	19	18	16.0
Cardiff South and Penarth	Labour	15.0	2.4	20	17	16.0
Halifax	Labour	15.1	2.0	18	19	16.0
Walthamstow	Labour	13.8	1.4	22	15	15.9
Blaenau Gwent	Labour	14.4	2.5	19	18	15.9
Manchester Withington	Labour	15.7	2.3	21	14	15.9
Edinburgh East and Musselburgh	Labour	15.7	0.9	19	17	15.9
Cunninghame North	Labour	15.8	1.2	19	17	15.9
Clydesdale	Labour	14.3	0.9	19	18	15.8
Birmingham Yardley	Labour	13.7	2.6	19	19	15.8
Plymouth Devonport	Labour	13.5	2.0	19	19	15.8
Halton	Labour	14.4	1.9	18	19	15.8
Leyton and Wanstead	Labour	13.0	1.6	22	15	15.8
Doncaster Central	Labour	13.6	2.6	19	18	15.8
Erith and Thamesmead	Labour	12.8	2.9	20	17	15.7
Southampton Test	Labour	14.0	2.4	18	19	15.7
Wallasey	Labour	15.8	2.5	19	17	15.7
Rhondda	Labour	15.8	1.7	19	17	15.7
Falkirk East	Labour	13.2	1.2	19	18	15.6
Lewisham West	Labour	13.0	3.4	21	15	15.6
Dewsbury	Labour	13.3	0.6	17	20	15.6
Derby South	Labour	14.0	1.3	19	18	15.6
St Helens South	Labour	14.8	1.3	18	18	15.6
Cumbernauld and Kilsyth	Labour	14.9	0.9	19	17	15.6
Hornsey and Wood Green	Labour	12.2	2.7	22	13	15.6
Wentworth	Labour	13.5	2.3	19	18	15.5
Cynon Valley	Labour	15.0	1.5	19	17	15.5
Cardiff West	Labour	14.5	2.6	19	17	15.4
Stalybridge and Hyde	Labour	14.3	1.7	18	18	15.4
Livingston	Labour	14.5	0.5	19	17	15.4
Swansea East	Labour	14.6	0.8	19	17	15.4
Dudley North	Labour	13.2	1.8	19	18	15.3
Plymouth Sutton	Labour	14.2	2.3	20	15	15.3
Birmingham Edgbaston	Labour	13.8	3.0	20	16	15.3
Bristol South	Labour	13.2	1.0	18	18	15.3
Southampton Itchen	Labour	13.8	2.1	18	18	15.3
Ochil	Labour	14.3	1.9	19	17	15.2
Lincoln	Labour	14.5	2.1	18	17	15.2
Bolton North East	Labour	15.0	0.6	18	17	15.2
Portsmouth South	Liberal Democrat	14.3	1.5	19	16	15.2
Sedgefield	Labour	14.4	1.4	17	18	15.2

Bishop Auckland	Labour	14.2	2.0	18	18	15.2
Blackpool South	Labour	16.6	0.7	18	16	15.2
Western Isles	Labour	16.0	2.4	18	16	15.2
Ross Skye and Inverness West	Liberal Democrat	14.4	1.8	18	17	15.2
Newcastle North	Labour	12.9	2.7	20	16	15.1
Wansbeck	Labour	14.1	3.0	18	17	15.1
Galloway and Upper Nithsdale	SNP	15.0	2.3	18	17	15.1
Coventry South	Labour	14.1	2.3	17	18	15.1
Darlington	Labour	14.8	2.3	18	17	15.1
Southall	Labour	14.2	2.0	19	16	15.1
North West Durham	Labour	14.6	2.1	18	17	15.1
Tooting	Labour	14.3	3.1	21	12	15.1
Heywood and Middleton	Labour	14.8	1.7	19	16	15.1
Batley and Spen	Labour	13.1	1.0	16	19	15.0
Luton South	Labour	14.4	2.7	17	18	15.0
Torfaen	Labour	14.2	1.3	18	17	14.9
Birmingham Selly Oak	Labour	14.1	2.9	19	16	14.9
Sheffield Attercliffe	Labour	12.9	2.8	18	17	14.9
Norwich South	Labour	11.8	1.7	19	17	14.9
Oxford East	Labour	12.7	2.0	18	17	14.9
Swansea West	Labour	13.5	1.0	18	17	14.8
Putney	Labour	13.3	3.1	19	15	14.8
Wigan	Labour	13.2	1.2	18	17	14.8
Oldham East and Saddleworth	Labour	14.9	1.5	17	17	14.8
North Durham	Labour	12.7	2.1	18	17	14.7
East Lothian	Labour	12.6	1.0	18	17	14.7
Hemsworth	Labour	13.3	1.6	18	17	14.7
Aberavon	Labour	14.5	0.8	17	17	14.7
Bristol North West	Labour	12.4	1.0	16	19	14.6
Burnley	Labour	15.7	0.6	17	16	14.6
Stoke North	Labour	15.2	0.6	17	16	14.6
Middlesbrough South and East Cleveland	Labour	14.1	2.5	17	17	14.6
Wolverhampton South West	Labour	13.0	2.1	17	17	14.5
Brighton Kemptown	Labour	14.5	2.4	17	16	14.5
Ayr	Labour	14.5	1.7	17	16	14.5
Leigh	Labour	14.0	1.0	17	17	14.5
Aberdeen North	Labour	14.1	1.2	17	17	14.5
Peterborough	Labour	12.3	0.8	18	17	14.5
Slough	Labour	13.9	1.6	15	18	14.5
Birmingham Hall Green	Labour	13.2	3.0	17	17	14.5
Dunfermline West	Labour	15.0	0.8	17	16	14.5
West Renfrewshire	Labour	14.8	1.0	17	16	14.4
City of York	Labour	12.8	1.6	17	17	14.4
Denton and Reddish	Labour	13.8	1.5	16	17	14.4
Stirling	Labour	14.9	1.3	17	16	14.4
Copeland	Labour	14.0	2.9	16	17	14.4
Roxburgh and Berwickshire	Liberal Democrat	12.8	0.9	17	17	14.4
Coventry North West	Labour	13.3	2.2	15	18	14.4
Banff and Buchan	SNP	13.1	0.6	17	17	14.3
Kensington and Chelsea	Conservative	11.9	3.2	20	12	14.3
Stretford and Urmston	Labour	13.6	1.7	17	16	14.3

A4.1 *HPI-2 for British parliamentary constituencies (continued)*

Name	Party	Death	Unemp	Income	Illit	HPI-2
Ogmore	Labour	14.2	1.6	17	16	14.3
Newport West	Labour	13.2	2.1	17	16	14.3
Worsley	Labour	14.2	0.7	17	16	14.3
East Kilbride	Labour	14.0	1.8	17	16	14.3
Carlisle	Labour	14.5	1.8	16	16	14.2
Blyth Valley	Labour	13.0	2.1	17	16	14.2
Bolsover	Labour	13.4	1.9	16	17	14.2
Caerphilly	Labour	13.3	1.9	17	16	14.2
Stockport	Labour	14.7	1.8	16	16	14.2
Barnsley West and Penistone	Labour	12.9	1.5	16	17	14.2
Blaydon	Labour	12.7	2.5	17	16	14.2
Perth	SNP	14.9	1.3	16	16	14.2
Edinburgh South	Labour	13.5	0.8	17	16	14.2
Harlow	Labour	11.6	1.8	17	17	14.2
Chesterfield	Labour	13.6	2.1	17	16	14.2
Thurrock	Labour	13.4	2.5	16	17	14.1
Edmonton	Labour	12.2	3.2	18	15	14.1
Eltham	Labour	11.5	3.2	18	16	14.1
St Helens North	Labour	13.4	1.2	17	16	14.1
Workington	Labour	13.4	2.9	16	17	14.0
Newport East	Labour	13.8	2.0	16	16	14.0
Morley and Rothwell	Labour	12.3	2.2	16	17	14.0
Corby	Labour	14.0	1.6	16	16	14.0
Bristol East	Labour	13.0	1.0	17	16	13.9
Angus	SNP	13.2	1.9	16	16	13.9
Feltham and Heston	Labour	13.0	1.4	17	16	13.9
Wrexham	Labour	13.3	1.9	16	16	13.9
Mitcham and Morden	Labour	12.5	2.5	18	15	13.9
Mansfield	Labour	12.9	1.4	16	16	13.9
Makerfield	Labour	13.6	0.8	16	16	13.9
Dumfries	Labour	13.5	1.7	16	16	13.9
Barrow-in-Furness	Labour	14.0	1.7	14	17	13.9
Wakefield	Labour	12.7	1.6	16	16	13.8
Stoke South	Labour	14.0	0.7	16	16	13.8
Weaver Vale	Labour	12.4	1.9	16	17	13.8
Great Yarmouth	Labour	12.7	2.3	16	16	13.8
Neath	Labour	14.3	0.8	15	16	13.8
Moray	SNP	13.3	1.2	16	16	13.7
Meriden	Conservative	11.2	2.7	16	17	13.7
Portsmouth North	Labour	12.5	1.4	15	17	13.7
Llanelli	Labour	13.5	2.1	16	16	13.7
Don Valley	Labour	12.4	2.2	16	16	13.7
Ipswich	Labour	12.2	2.3	16	16	13.6
Telford	Labour	12.2	1.2	16	16	13.6
Cardiff Central	Labour	12.1	2.2	17	15	13.6
Scunthorpe	Labour	14.1	2.0	17	14	13.6
Basildon	Labour	11.5	2.0	15	17	13.6

Rother Valley	Labour	12.7	2.2	16	16	13.6
Croydon North	Labour	13.0	3.3	18	13	13.6
Halesowen and Rowley Regis	Labour	12.4	1.3	16	16	13.5
Milton Keynes South West	Labour	12.6	1.2	16	16	13.5
Berwick upon Tweed	Liberal Democrat	12.3	2.1	16	16	13.5
Warrington North	Labour	14.5	1.2	15	15	13.5
Ashfield	Labour	12.5	2.3	16	16	13.5
Brighton Pavilion	Labour	13.2	2.1	18	13	13.5
Clwyd South	Labour	12.9	1.4	15	16	13.5
Islwyn	Labour	12.9	1.0	15	16	13.5
Enfield North	Labour	11.2	2.9	15	17	13.4
Blackpool North and Fleetwood	Labour	15.0	0.9	14	15	13.4
Rochford and Southend East	Conservative	13.1	3.3	16	15	13.4
Dudley South	Labour	12.1	1.7	16	16	13.4
City of Durham	Labour	12.0	1.5	17	15	13.4
Hastings and Rye	Labour	12.9	2.3	16	15	13.4
Luton North	Labour	12.1	2.6	14	17	13.3
Inverness East Nairn and Lochaber	Labour	13.1	1.4	16	15	13.3
North Tayside	SNP	12.4	1.6	15	16	13.3
Brentford and Isleworth	Labour	12.7	1.8	17	14	13.3
Hyndburn	Labour	14.4	0.8	15	15	13.3
Hayes and Harlington	Labour	13.2	1.7	14	16	13.3
Tynemouth	Labour	13.1	2.4	16	14	13.2
North Thanet	Conservative	13.4	2.5	15	15	13.2
Northampton North	Labour	12.3	2.0	16	15	13.2
Bassetlaw	Labour	12.9	2.2	15	15	13.2
Stevenage	Labour	10.5	1.1	16	16	13.2
Derby North	Labour	13.1	1.4	15	15	13.1
Orkney and Shetland	Liberal Democrat	12.6	1.5	14	16	13.1
Ealing North	Labour	11.4	2.5	16	15	13.1
Havant	Conservative	12.4	1.1	14	16	13.1
Ynys Mon	Plaid Cymru	13.4	3.4	15	15	13.1
Edinburgh Pentlands	Labour	12.1	0.7	16	15	13.1
Redditch	Labour	10.4	2.8	14	17	13.0
Newcastle under Lyme	Labour	13.2	0.6	15	15	13.0
Vale of Clwyd	Labour	13.8	1.9	14	15	13.0
Cambridge	Labour	10.0	1.7	17	14	13.0
West Lancashire	Labour	12.0	2.0	15	15	13.0
Boston and Skegness	Conservative	13.2	0.7	14	15	12.9
Pendle	Labour	13.6	0.5	14	15	12.9
Scarborough and Whitby	Labour	12.2	2.1	15	15	12.9
Conwy	Labour	12.4	2.1	15	15	12.9
Sittingbourne and Sheppey	Labour	12.2	2.3	14	16	12.9
Croydon Central	Labour	11.5	3.1	15	15	12.9
Cannock Chase	Labour	12.9	1.8	15	15	12.9
Bedford	Labour	12.0	2.0	15	15	12.9
Hereford	Liberal Democrat	11.1	1.0	13	17	12.9
Dover	Labour	12.8	2.3	15	15	12.9
South Thanet	Labour	12.2	2.5	15	15	12.9
Crewe and Nantwich	Labour	12.2	1.1	14	16	12.9
Hove	Labour	12.8	1.9	16	13	12.8

A4.1 *HPI-2 for British parliamentary constituencies (continued)*

Name	Party	Death	Unemp	Income	Illit	HPI-2
Bury South	Labour	13.2	1.2	14	15	12.8
Normanton	Labour	12.9	1.6	14	15	12.8
Harwich	Labour	12.6	1.9	13	16	12.8
Amber Valley	Labour	12.8	1.5	13	16	12.8
Caernarfon	Plaid Cymru	12.6	2.6	14	15	12.8
Keighley	Labour	12.1	1.3	14	16	12.8
Morecambe and Lunesdale	Labour	13.3	2.0	14	15	12.8
Erewash	Labour	12.1	0.8	13	16	12.7
Ellesmere Port and Neston	Labour	13.0	1.4	14	15	12.7
Falmouth and Camborne	Labour	12.5	1.7	14	15	12.7
Bournemouth West	Conservative	12.0	2.8	16	14	12.7
Pontypridd	Labour	12.6	1.7	14	15	12.7
St Ives	Liberal Democrat	12.0	2.0	14	15	12.6
Calder Valley	Labour	12.6	1.6	14	15	12.6
Stockton South	Labour	13.0	2.5	15	14	12.6
Cleethorpes	Labour	12.8	1.4	14	15	12.6
Tweeddale Ettrick and Lauderdale	Liberal Democrat	11.4	0.7	15	15	12.6
Sheffield Hillsborough	Labour	11.5	2.6	15	15	12.6
Brigg and Goole	Labour	13.2	2.2	13	15	12.6
Crawley	Labour	11.4	1.7	15	15	12.5
Rossendale and Darwen	Labour	13.7	0.5	14	14	12.5
Worcester	Labour	12.4	1.8	14	15	12.5
Aberdeen South	Labour	12.3	1.4	14	15	12.5
Gloucester	Labour	12.6	2.8	13	15	12.5
The Wrekin	Labour	12.3	1.0	14	15	12.5
Preseli Pembrokeshire	Labour	13.0	2.1	14	14	12.4
Exeter	Labour	12.2	2.1	15	14	12.4
Eastbourne	Conservative	11.5	1.7	14	15	12.4
Hendon	Labour	10.8	2.3	16	13	12.4
Medway	Labour	12.5	1.1	14	14	12.3
Torbay	Liberal Democrat	12.2	1.9	14	14	12.3
City of Chester	Labour	12.4	2.0	15	13	12.3
Gravesham	Labour	11.3	1.6	15	14	12.3
Ilford South	Labour	12.0	1.0	14	14	12.3
Bury North	Labour	12.3	0.2	13	15	12.3
North East Derbyshire	Labour	11.5	2.1	15	14	12.3
Newark	Labour	12.8	1.6	14	14	12.2
North East Fife	Liberal Democrat	11.9	1.8	13	15	12.2
Tamworth	Labour	12.0	1.5	14	14	12.2
Isle of Wight	Liberal Democrat	11.7	3.1	13	15	12.2
Waveney	Labour	12.4	2.7	14	14	12.2
Leeds North East	Labour	11.5	2.8	15	13	12.2
Burton	Labour	12.4	1.7	14	14	12.2
Colne Valley	Labour	12.0	0.8	13	15	12.2
Carmarthen West and South Pembrokeshire	Labour	12.3	2.3	14	14	12.2
East Yorkshire	Conservative	12.1	2.1	13	15	12.1

Cheltenham	Liberal Democrat	11.8	2.9	14	14	12.1
Wyre Forest	Labour	11.8	1.7	13	15	12.1
North East Cambridgeshire	Conservative	12.6	1.4	12	15	12.1
Aldridge-Brownhills	Conservative	11.3	2.2	13	15	12.1
Gosport	Conservative	11.4	1.7	13	15	12.1
Edinburgh West	Liberal Democrat	12.2	1.2	14	14	12.1
Colchester	Liberal Democrat	11.3	1.1	14	14	12.0
Bridgend	Labour	12.5	1.7	13	14	12.0
Folkestone and Hythe	Conservative	11.8	2.7	14	14	12.0
Carshalton and Wallington	Liberal Democrat	11.5	2.3	14	14	12.0
Swindon South	Labour	11.7	1.4	14	14	12.0
Bath	Liberal Democrat	10.7	1.2	15	13	12.0
Delyn	Labour	13.2	1.7	12	14	12.0
Carmarthen East and Dinefwr	Labour	13.6	2.2	12	14	11.9
Merionnydd nant Conwy	Plaid Cymru	12.4	2.1	13	14	11.9
North Cornwall	Liberal Democrat	11.3	1.4	12	15	11.9
Nuneaton	Labour	12.0	1.8	13	14	11.9
South Dorset	Conservative	11.8	1.7	13	14	11.9
Welwyn Hatfield	Labour	11.0	1.0	14	14	11.9
Northampton South	Labour	12.3	2.1	13	14	11.9
Vale of Glamorgan	Labour	11.7	1.6	13	14	11.8
North Devon	Liberal Democrat	11.3	1.7	12	15	11.8
North Warwickshire	Labour	11.7	1.6	13	14	11.8
Grantham and Stamford	Conservative	11.7	1.4	13	14	11.8
Warwick and Leamington	Labour	12.0	1.8	13	14	11.7
North West Norfolk	Labour	11.6	1.7	13	14	11.7
Alyn and Deeside	Labour	12.6	1.5	12	14	11.7
Finchley and Golders Green	Labour	10.2	2.5	15	12	11.7
Sherwood	Labour	11.9	1.4	13	14	11.7
Weston super Mare	Liberal Democrat	11.7	0.9	13	14	11.7
Reading West	Labour	11.4	1.2	13	14	11.7
Upminster	Labour	11.2	1.1	13	14	11.7
Norwich North	Labour	10.9	1.6	13	14	11.7
Wellingborough	Labour	11.0	1.3	13	14	11.7
High Peak	Labour	11.8	1.6	12	14	11.6
Clwyd West	Labour	12.2	2.2	12	14	11.6
Bournemouth East	Conservative	12.8	2.5	13	12	11.6
Canterbury	Conservative	10.6	2.0	13	14	11.6
Bristol West	Labour	12.0	1.3	15	11	11.6
Stourbridge	Labour	11.0	1.6	13	14	11.6
Swindon North	Labour	11.2	1.4	13	14	11.6
Leeds North West	Labour	11.1	2.2	15	12	11.6
Ceredigion	Plaid Cymru	12.2	1.7	12	14	11.6
Kingswood	Labour	10.7	1.0	12	15	11.5
Brecon and Radnorshire	Liberal Democrat	12.3	1.4	12	14	11.5
Totnes	Conservative	10.1	2.0	12	15	11.5
Montgomeryshire	Liberal Democrat	11.9	0.8	12	14	11.5
Dartford	Labour	11.7	2.3	12	14	11.5
Hemel Hempstead	Labour	10.1	1.3	13	14	11.5
Taunton	Liberal Democrat	11.2	2.1	12	14	11.5
Truro and St Austell	Liberal Democrat	11.7	1.8	12	14	11.4

A4.1 *HPI-2 for British parliamentary constituencies (continued)*

Name	Party	Death	Unemp	Income	Illit	HPI-2
Southport	Liberal Democrat	13.1	1.9	13	12	11.4
Salisbury	Conservative	11.1	1.2	12	14	11.4
Bridgwater	Conservative	10.9	2.1	12	14	11.4
Strathkelvin and Bearsden	Labour	12.5	1.3	12	13	11.4
Ashford	Conservative	10.7	2.3	13	14	11.4
North West Leicestershire	Labour	11.2	1.8	12	14	11.4
Bognor Regis and Littlehampton	Conservative	12.6	0.9	12	13	11.4
West Suffolk	Conservative	10.2	1.9	13	14	11.4
North Shropshire	Conservative	11.6	1.4	12	14	11.4
South West Norfolk	Conservative	11.2	1.4	12	14	11.4
Louth and Horncastle	Conservative	12.9	1.4	11	13	11.3
Shipley	Labour	12.0	1.0	12	13	11.3
Braintree	Labour	9.7	1.7	13	14	11.3
Shrewsbury and Atcham	Labour	11.1	1.4	12	14	11.3
South Derbyshire	Labour	11.6	1.8	11	14	11.3
Warrington South	Labour	12.7	1.2	12	13	11.3
Poole	Conservative	12.0	1.9	12	13	11.3
Hornchurch	Labour	11.5	1.1	11	14	11.3
Basingstoke	Conservative	10.7	2.0	12	14	11.3
Gordon	Liberal Democrat	11.8	2.0	11	14	11.3
Pudsey	Labour	10.6	1.3	12	14	11.3
Ilford North	Labour	11.3	1.4	13	13	11.2
Forest of Dean	Labour	11.8	2.0	11	14	11.2
Gillingham	Labour	10.7	1.2	13	13	11.2
Brent North	Labour	11.0	2.4	14	12	11.2
Devizes	Conservative	10.4	1.1	12	14	11.2
Bolton West	Labour	11.7	0.5	12	13	11.2
Torridge and West Devon	Liberal Democrat	11.6	2.3	11	14	11.2
Banbury	Conservative	10.1	0.9	12	14	11.2
Gainsborough	Conservative	12.0	1.7	12	13	11.2
North Norfolk	Conservative	11.0	1.6	12	14	11.2
Yeovil	Liberal Democrat	10.5	2.2	12	14	11.2
Bexleyheath and Crayford	Labour	10.6	2.1	12	14	11.1
Uxbridge	Conservative	11.0	2.3	13	13	11.1
South East Cornwall	Liberal Democrat	10.4	1.7	12	14	11.1
Elmet	Labour	11.1	1.8	12	13	11.1
Romford	Labour	10.5	1.0	12	14	11.1
Crosby	Labour	12.3	2.2	13	11	11.1
East Devon	Conservative	9.9	1.8	10	15	11.1
Gedling	Labour	11.3	1.3	12	13	11.1
Reading East	Labour	10.8	1.3	13	12	11.0
Watford	Labour	10.7	2.2	13	13	11.0
West Dorset	Conservative	11.1	1.6	11	14	11.0
Staffordshire Moorlands	Labour	12.3	1.0	11	13	11.0
Penrith and the Border	Conservative	11.7	1.5	10	14	11.0
Chorley	Labour	11.3	0.9	12	13	11.0
Beckenham	Conservative	10.8	3.1	13	12	11.0

Stafford	Labour	11.1	1.7	12	13	11.0
Gower	Labour	11.7	0.9	11	13	10.9
Eddisbury	Conservative	11.8	1.0	11	13	10.9
Harrow East	Labour	11.0	2.3	13	12	10.9
Hazel Grove	Liberal Democrat	11.6	1.4	11	13	10.9
Chatham and Aylesford	Labour	11.8	0.8	12	12	10.9
Kettering	Labour	11.0	2.2	12	13	10.9
Worthing West	Conservative	11.7	2.0	11	13	10.9
North West Cambridgeshire	Conservative	10.4	0.8	12	13	10.9
Billericay	Conservative	10.5	1.9	12	13	10.9
Bracknell	Conservative	9.9	0.9	11	14	10.9
Worthing East and Shoreham	Conservative	11.0	1.7	12	13	10.8
Harrogate and Knaresborough	Liberal Democrat	11.6	0.8	11	13	10.8
Fylde	Conservative	12.1	0.5	10	13	10.8
Wycombe	Conservative	10.7	1.8	12	13	10.8
Loughborough	Labour	10.4	1.5	12	13	10.8
South Holland and the Deepings	Conservative	12.2	1.1	10	13	10.8
Faversham and Mid Kent	Conservative	10.0	1.5	12	13	10.8
Southend West	Conservative	10.0	3.1	12	13	10.8
Rugby and Kenilworth	Labour	11.3	1.8	11	13	10.8
Hexham	Conservative	11.1	1.8	11	13	10.8
Wirral South	Labour	10.9	2.3	11	13	10.8
Westmorland and Lonsdale	Conservative	10.9	1.0	10	14	10.7
Lancaster and Wyre	Labour	12.0	1.3	10	13	10.7
Chingford and Woodford Green	Conservative	10.1	1.5	13	12	10.7
Wells	Conservative	11.5	1.9	11	13	10.7
Broxtowe	Labour	10.5	0.9	12	13	10.7
Wirral West	Labour	11.4	1.8	12	12	10.7
South West Bedfordshire	Conservative	10.7	1.1	11	13	10.7
Leominster	Conservative	10.4	1.3	10	14	10.7
Milton Keynes North East	Labour	9.8	1.5	12	13	10.6
Teignbridge	Conservative	11.1	2.2	11	13	10.6
Wimbledon	Labour	10.0	2.3	13	11	10.6
Chichester	Conservative	10.6	1.6	11	13	10.6
Beverley and Holderness	Conservative	10.4	0.8	11	13	10.5
Sleaford and North Hykeham	Conservative	11.0	1.6	10	13	10.5
Richmond	Conservative	10.6	1.4	11	13	10.5
North East Hertfordshire	Conservative	9.9	1.2	13	12	10.5
Monmouth	Labour	10.5	1.8	11	13	10.5
Broxbourne	Conservative	10.4	1.7	11	13	10.5
Oxford West and Abingdon	Liberal Democrat	9.7	1.7	12	13	10.5
Westbury	Conservative	10.5	2.1	11	13	10.5
Ludlow	Conservative	10.5	1.7	11	13	10.5
Kingston and Surbiton	Liberal Democrat	10.3	1.9	12	12	10.5
Selby	Labour	10.9	1.9	10	13	10.5
Skipton and Ripon	Conservative	10.9	0.9	10	13	10.4
Hertsmere	Conservative	10.4	1.9	12	12	10.4
Epping Forest	Conservative	10.7	1.5	12	12	10.4
Cardiff North	Labour	11.6	1.6	11	12	10.4
Bromsgrove	Conservative	10.4	2.0	11	13	10.4
Tiverton and Honiton	Conservative	10.4	1.7	10	13	10.4

A4.1 *HPI-2 for British parliamentary constituencies (continued)*

Name	Party	Death	Unemp	Income	Illit	HPI-2
Eastwood	Labour	11.0	1.4	11	12	10.4
Central Suffolk and North Ipswich	Conservative	10.0	2.0	11	13	10.3
Bury St Edmunds	Conservative	9.6	1.3	11	13	10.3
Aylesbury	Conservative	10.5	1.4	12	12	10.3
Somerton and Frome	Liberal Democrat	10.0	2.0	11	13	10.3
Richmond Park	Liberal Democrat	10.1	2.6	13	10	10.3
Ryedale	Conservative	10.6	1.9	10	13	10.3
West Derbyshire	Conservative	10.2	1.0	10	13	10.3
Southgate	Labour	9.7	2.5	13	11	10.3
Stratford on Avon	Conservative	10.4	2.1	10	13	10.3
Lewes	Liberal Democrat	11.0	1.6	11	12	10.3
Bexhill and Battle	Conservative	10.3	1.9	10	13	10.2
South Ribble	Labour	11.9	0.9	10	12	10.2
Stone	Conservative	12.2	0.8	9	12	10.2
Suffolk Coastal	Conservative	9.4	1.8	11	13	10.2
Aldershot	Conservative	10.7	0.9	11	12	10.2
North Wiltshire	Conservative	10.0	1.3	10	13	10.2
Christchurch	Conservative	9.6	1.7	9	14	10.2
Rutland and Melton	Conservative	10.2	1.0	10	13	10.2
Tunbridge Wells	Conservative	9.8	1.1	12	12	10.2
West Aberdeenshire and Kincardine	Liberal Democrat	10.5	1.3	10	13	10.2
Guildford	Conservative	9.5	1.7	11	13	10.2
Mid Worcestershire	Conservative	10.9	1.3	10	12	10.1
Reigate	Conservative	11.2	1.1	10	12	10.1
Altrincham and Sale West	Conservative	11.2	1.9	11	11	10.1
Macclesfield	Conservative	10.8	0.8	10	12	10.1
Wantage	Conservative	9.5	1.3	10	13	10.1
North East Bedfordshire	Conservative	11.1	1.0	10	12	10.1
Lichfield	Conservative	10.6	1.4	11	12	10.1
South Suffolk	Conservative	9.0	2.0	10	13	10.0
Bromley and Chislehurst	Conservative	10.5	2.6	12	11	10.0
Bosworth	Conservative	10.8	1.1	10	12	10.0
Cotswold	Conservative	9.9	1.4	11	12	10.0
Tonbridge and Malling	Conservative	9.4	1.3	11	12	10.0
Huntingdon	Conservative	9.8	1.1	11	12	10.0
Sutton and Cheam	Liberal Democrat	10.6	2.0	10	12	10.0
Twickenham	Liberal Democrat	10.0	2.3	12	11	10.0
Orpington	Conservative	10.1	1.8	11	12	9.9
Eastleigh	Liberal Democrat	10.7	1.6	10	12	9.9
Witney	Conservative	9.0	1.1	10	13	9.9
Harrow West	Labour	9.7	2.1	12	11	9.9
Stroud	Labour	9.9	1.7	11	12	9.9
Congleton	Conservative	11.0	1.1	9	12	9.9
North West Hampshire	Conservative	9.5	1.3	11	12	9.8
Haltemprice and Howden	Conservative	10.0	1.0	9	13	9.8
Sevenoaks	Conservative	10.2	2.1	10	12	9.8
Rushcliffe	Conservative	10.2	1.4	10	12	9.8

Chipping Barnet	Conservative	9.5	2.1	12	11	9.8
Ribble Valley	Conservative	12.4	0.6	8	11	9.8
Runnymede and Weybridge	Conservative	10.1	1.6	10	12	9.8
Castle Point	Labour	10.1	2.2	10	12	9.8
New Forest East	Conservative	10.6	1.5	9	12	9.8
Maidstone and the Weald	Conservative	10.3	1.0	11	11	9.7
Ruislip-Northwood	Conservative	10.6	2.1	10	11	9.7
Vale of York	Conservative	10.5	1.4	9	12	9.7
Tatton	Independent	11.3	2.8	10	11	9.7
Old Bexley and Sidcup	Conservative	9.5	2.4	10	12	9.7
St Albans	Labour	10.2	1.1	11	11	9.7
New Forest West	Conservative	10.3	1.7	9	12	9.7
Tewkesbury	Conservative	10.0	1.9	10	12	9.7
Daventry	Conservative	9.7	1.3	10	12	9.7
Newbury	Liberal Democrat	10.5	1.0	10	11	9.7
Maldon and East Chelmsford	Conservative	10.6	2.6	10	11	9.6
East Surrey	Conservative	10.2	1.4	9	12	9.6
Harborough	Conservative	10.1	1.0	9	12	9.6
South Staffordshire	Conservative	9.7	1.9	10	12	9.6
Mid Norfolk	Conservative	9.9	1.4	10	12	9.6
North Dorset	Conservative	9.8	1.4	10	12	9.6
South West Surrey	Conservative	9.6	1.6	10	12	9.6
Woking	Conservative	9.4	1.3	10	12	9.6
Hitchin and Harpenden	Conservative	10.0	1.8	11	11	9.5
South West Hertfordshire	Conservative	9.9	1.7	11	11	9.5
Mid Bedfordshire	Conservative	9.7	1.5	9	12	9.5
Horsham	Conservative	9.6	1.4	9	12	9.5
Winchester	Liberal Democrat	9.7	1.8	11	11	9.5
Windsor	Conservative	9.7	1.7	10	11	9.4
West Chelmsford	Conservative	9.0	2.5	11	11	9.4
Mole Valley	Conservative	9.4	1.6	9	12	9.4
Henley	Conservative	9.2	1.6	9	12	9.4
West Worcestershire	Conservative	10.0	1.8	10	11	9.3
Hertford and Stortford	Conservative	9.7	1.5	10	11	9.3
East Hampshire	Conservative	10.4	1.6	9	11	9.3
Arundel and South Downs	Conservative	9.4	1.5	9	12	9.3
South Norfolk	Conservative	8.9	1.9	9	12	9.3
Spelthorne	Conservative	10.1	1.8	9	11	9.2
North Essex	Conservative	10.0	1.3	9	11	9.2
Maidenhead	Conservative	10.0	2.3	9	11	9.1
Fareham	Conservative	10.1	1.4	9	11	9.1
Epsom and Ewell	Conservative	10.1	1.5	9	11	9.1
Sheffield Hallam	Liberal Democrat	8.6	2.1	11	10	9.1
Wansdyke	Labour	9.7	0.9	9	11	9.0
South West Devon	Conservative	9.8	1.5	9	11	9.0
Brentwood and Ongar	Conservative	10.0	1.9	10	10	9.0
Mid Sussex	Conservative	9.5	1.3	9	11	9.0
Wealden	Conservative	9.9	1.3	8	11	9.0
South East Cambridgeshire	Conservative	9.7	1.7	10	10	9.0
Blaby	Conservative	9.8	1.1	9	11	9.0
Charnwood	Conservative	10.0	1.2	8	11	9.0

A4.1 *HPI-2 for British parliamentary constituencies (continued)*

Name	Party	Death	Unemp	Income	Illit	HPI-2
Esher and Walton	Conservative	9.0	1.8	9	11	9.0
Solihull	Conservative	9.5	1.7	9	11	8.9
Croydon South	Conservative	9.6	2.0	10	10	8.9
Saffron Walden	Conservative	9.2	1.6	10	10	8.9
Surrey Heath	Conservative	9.5	0.8	8	11	8.8
Mid Dorset and North Poole	Conservative	9.7	2.1	9	10	8.8
Sutton Coldfield	Conservative	9.6	2.8	9	10	8.7
South Cambridgeshire	Conservative	8.7	1.8	10	10	8.6
Beaconsfield	Conservative	9.4	2.0	9	10	8.6
Rayleigh	Conservative	9.7	1.9	8	10	8.5
North East Hampshire	Conservative	9.2	1.2	9	10	8.4
Romsey	Liberal Democrat	8.5	1.9	9	10	8.3
Chesham and Amersham	Conservative	8.8	1.6	8	10	8.3
Buckingham	Conservative	9.2	1.8	9	9	8.2
Woodspring	Conservative	8.4	1.1	8	10	8.1
Cheadle	Conservative	9.2	1.3	8	9	7.9
Northavon	Liberal Democrat	9.1	0.9	8	9	7.9
Wokingham	Conservative	8.4	1.0	7	9	7.5

Technical Note on the Construction of the HPI-2 for Parliamentary Constituencies in Britain
By David Gordon

In the 1998 *Human Development Report*, the UNDP defined a Human Poverty Index for Industrial Countries (HPI-2). It is made up of four weighted components:

1 The percentage of people not expected to survive to age 60.
2 The functional illiteracy rate.
3 The percentage of people living below the income poverty line (50 per cent of median disposable income).
4 The long-term unemployment rate (12 months or more).

The first three components of this index focus on deprivation of longevity, knowledge and a decent standard of living, which are also measured in the Human Development Index (HDI) and the Human Poverty Index for Developing Countries (HPI-1). However, the final component, long-term unemployment, is included as an indicator of social exclusion (or lack of participation). This technical note describes how these four components of the HPI-2 were estimated at parliamentary constituency level in Britain (Table A4.1).

The percentage of people not expected to survive to age 60

The under-60 death rates were calculated by Danny Dorling for each parliamentary constituency using nationally available mortality data aggregated to current parliamentary constituency boundaries and standard methods (see Shaw et al, 1999).

The functional illiteracy rate

The functional illiteracy rate was assumed to be equivalent to the 'low' and 'very low' literacy levels recorded in 17 adult basic skills surveys of adults aged 16 to 60 who had been educated or part educated in the UK and who spoke English fluently. These surveys were carried out during 1996 and 1997 for the Adult Basic Skills Agency by Opinion Research Business (ORB).

Estimates of functional illiteracy using this definition are available on CD-ROM for each electoral ward in England. These estimates were aggregated to parliamentary constituency level using electoral ward/parliamentary constituency look-up tables created by Danny Dorling. The rates of 'low' and 'very low' literacy were estimated by ORB for each of the 17 CACI ACORN cluster groups and then rates for each electoral ward were estimated by applying the relevant ACORN cluster rates to the populations of each ward. A logistic regression model exercise was undertaken to estimate the rates for Scottish constituencies.

These estimates currently represent the official geography of literacy and numeracy which the Adult Basic Skills Agency uses for planning purposes. However, these estimates lack academic rigour. The ACORN classification is a marketing research tool designed to identify market segments, so may not be an optimal instrument for estimating functional illiteracy and innumeracy. Similarly, the questionnaire used by ORB to measure literacy is not directly comparable with those used in other countries. It should be possible to produce more internationally comparable and reliable estimates of functional illiteracy for use in the HPI-2 in Britain by using the data from the International Adult Literacy Survey (IALS) (Carey et al, 1997). The Social Survey Division of the Office for National Statistics have recently produced some best practice recommendations which ought to significantly improve the international comparability of the measurement of functional illiteracy using the IALS methodology (Carey et al, 2000).

The percentage of people living below the income poverty line (50 per cent of median disposable income)

Estimates of the number and percentage of people living in households with incomes below 50 per cent of the national median were made for each parliamentary constituency using results from a logistic regression modelling exercise. Estimates of the size of the low income population for those in the economically active population have been made from 1991 Census and New Earnings Survey data (Gordon and Forrest, 1995). More recently, Gordon and Loughran (1997) have show how Family Expenditure Survey (FES) data can be combined with 1991 Census data to produce estimates of low income at small area level.

The Department of Social Security's (DSS) Households Below Average Income (HBAI) datasets for 1989, 1990 and 1991 were linked to their respective FES datasets from which they had originally been derived. Those with incomes at or below 50 per cent of the median (using HBAI methodology) were identified from the combined data set after deflation using the retail price index (RPI). Logistic regression analysis was used to obtain weightings for the best subset of low income indicator variables that were measured in both the 1991 Census and the FES. The results from the best-fit model were then used to estimate the number and rates of people living below the income poverty line, using the methods described in Gordon (1995).

The long-term unemployment rate (12 months or more)

Estimates of the number and percentage of people unemployed for longer than six months are published at regular intervals by the House of Commons Library as research papers. The methodology used is described in two research papers (House of Commons, 1996; Twigger and Presland, 2000). Since these House of Commons estimates are based upon Claimant Count data, the following two adjustments were required:

1   The rates were adjusted from unemployed for more than six months to unemployed for more than 12 months, as required by HPI-2. This adjustment assumed that the ratio of those unemployed for more than six months to those unemployed for more than 12 months was the same in each

constituency as it is nationally.

2   The final rate for unemployed for more than 12 months was inflated to correspond with ILO definitions of unemployment as measured in the Labour Force Survey. The ILO long-term unemployment rate (more than 12 months) is slightly higher than the Claimant Count rate. This small adjustment assumed that the ratio of claimant count long-term unemployment to ILO long-term unemployment was the same in each constituency as it is nationally.

Table A4.2 *How the UK compares with other OECD countries*

Country	HPI-2 rank	HPI-2 value (%)	HDI rank
Norway	1	7.3	2
Sweden	2	7.6	6
The Netherlands	3	8.2	8
Finland	4	8.6	11
Denmark	5	9.3	15
Germany	6	10.4	14
Luxembourg	7	10.5	17
France	8	11.1	12
Japan	9	11.2	9
Spain	10	11.6	21
Canada	11	11.8	1
Italy	12	11.9	19
Australia	13	12.2	4
Belgium	14	12.4	7
New Zealand	15	12.8	20
United Kingdom	16	14.6	10
Ireland	17	15.0	18
United States	18	15.8	3

Note: The lower the index value, the less human poverty and therefore the higher the ranking achieved.

Source: UNDP, 2000

Appendix 5

Participating Organisations

Centre for Citizen Participation, Brunel University
Church Action Against Poverty
Clayton Brook Community House Project Team
Communities Against Poverty
Community Development Foundation
Community Environment Resource Unit
European Anti-Poverty Network (England)
Friends of the Earth
International Institute for Environment and Development
Lancashire Global Education Centre
London School of Hygiene and Tropical Medicine
Lower Ormeau Road Action Group
Moor Nook Estate Management Board
National Association of Citizens Advice Bureaux
New Economics Foundation
Oxfam
The Poverty Alliance
Preston Borough Council
Single Parents Action Network
Sustain
Townsend Centre for International Poverty Research, University of Bristol
United Nations Environment and Development–UK Committee
UK Coalition Against Poverty
Welsh Anti-Poverty Network

Note: Owing to the wide scope of this book, the organisations listed can only commit themselves to the policy objectives that fall within their areas of competence. However, they all support its main theme of promoting human development.

References

Chapter 1

DETR (1999) *Quality of Life Counts. Indicators for a strategy for sustainable development for the United Kingdom: A baseline assessment.* London: Department of the Environment, Transport and the Regions

EEC (1977) *The Perception of Poverty in Europe.* Brussels: Commission of the European Communities

EEC (1985) 'On Specific Community Action to Combat Poverty (Council Decision of 19 December 1984) 85/8/EEC', *Official Journal of the EEC* 2(24)

Jowell, R et al (1999) *British Social Attitudes: The 16th report: Who shares New Labour values?* Aldershot: Ashgate

Smith, G (1998) 'A very social capital: Measuring the vital signs of community life in Newham'. In: Knight, B et al (eds) *Building Civil Society: Current initiatives in voluntary action.* West Malling: Charities Aid Foundation

UNDP (1995) *Human Development Report 1995: Gender and Human Development.* New York: Oxford University Press

UNDP (1997) *Human Development Report 1997: Human Development to Eradicate Poverty.* New York: Oxford University Press

UNDP (1999) *Human Development Report 1999: Globalisation with a Human Face.* New York: Oxford University Press

UN (1995) *The Copenhagen Declaration and Programme of Action: World Summit for Social Development 6–12 March 1995.* New York: United Nations Department of Publications

WCED (1987) *Our Common Future: The Report of the World Commission on Environment and Development.* Oxford: Oxford University Press, 1987

Chapter 2

Acheson, D et al (1998) *Independent Inquiry into Inequalities in Health Report.* London: The Stationery Office

Arblaster, L, Leonardi, G et al (1999) 'Will new trade agreements damage health?' Letter, *British Medical Journal*, 10 November

Bennett, F (2000) 'Marking five-year review of the Copenhagen Summit'. *Social Watch* 4. Montevideo, Uruguay: Instituto del Tercer Mundo

Bertrand, A and Kalafatides, L (1999) 'The WTO and Public Health'. *The Ecologist* 29(6): 365–368

CBD Secretariat (2000) *Connections.* UNED-UK Quarterly Newsletter, February–April

DETR (1999) *A Better Quality of Life: A strategy for sustainable development in the United Kingdom.* London: The Stationery Office

Drager, N (1999) 'Making trade work for public health. WTO talks in Seattle offer an opportunity to get public health on the trade agenda'. *British Medical Journal* **319**: 1214

Environmental Protection Agency (1999) Cited in: Institute of Medicine, *Towards Environmental Justice.* Washington, DC, National Academy Press

Fitzgerald, E (1998) *The development implications of the Multilateral Agreement on Investment. Report for the UK Department for International Development.* Oxford: University of Oxford

Friends of the Earth maps http://www.foe.co.uk

Her Majesty's Government (1999) *Opportunity for All.* London: The Stationery Office

Lang, T (1999) 'The new GATT Round: Whose development? Whose health?' *Journal of Epidemiology and Community Health* **53**(11): 681–682

Mabey, N (2000) 'Learning from Seattle'. *Connections.* UNED-UK Quarterly Newsletter, February–April: 11

McBride, G (1999) *Scottish Applications of Environmental Justice.* Edinburgh: University of Edinburgh

McLaren, D, Bullock, S and Yousuf, N (1998) *Tomorrow's World: Britain's Share in a Sustainable Future.* London: Earthscan

McLaren, D et al (1999) *The Geographic Relation Between Household Income and Polluting Factories.* London: Friends of the Earth

Koivusalo, M (1999) *World Trade Organization and Trade-creep in Health and Social Policies.* Geneva: GASSP, STAKES

Scandrett, E, McBride, G and Dunion, K (2000) *The Campaign for Environmental Justice in Scotland.* Edinburgh: Friends of the Earth Scotland

Shrybman, S (1999) 'The World Trade Organization: The New World Constitution Laid Bare'. *The Ecologist* **29**(4): 270–275

Stephens, C, Lewin, S, Leonardi, G et al (2000) 'Health, Equity and Sustainable Development: Global trade in the brave new world', lead review article, *Global Change and Human Health* **1**(1)

Stevenson, S, Stephens, C, Landon, M, Fletcher, T, Wilkinson, P and Grundy, C (1998) 'Examining the inequality and inequity of car ownership and the effects of pollution and health outcomes such as respiratory diseases'. Paper presented at International Society of Environmental Epidemiology, Boston, MA, August

UNDP (1996) *Human Development Report 1996: Sustainability and Human Development.* New York: Oxford University Press

UNDP (1999) *Human Development Report 1999: Globalization with a Human Face.* New York: Oxford University Press

UNECE (1996) *Economic Bulletin for Europe* Volume 48. Geneva: Secretariat for the Economic Commission for Europe

UNEP (1999) *Global Environment Outlook 2000.* London: Earthscan Publications

Wilkinson, R G (1996) *Unhealthy Societies: The afflictions of inequality.* London: Routledge

Wolfe, M (1995) 'Globalization and Social Exclusion: Some paradoxes'. In: Rodgers, G, Gore, C and Figueiredo, J B (eds) *Social exclusion; rhetoric, reality, responses.* Geneva: International Labour Organization, pp81–103

World Bank (1999) *Inequality: Trends and Prospects.* Washington, DC: The World Bank Group

World Bank (2000) *Growth is Good for the Poor.* Washington, DC: The World Bank Group

WHO (1997) *Health and Environment in Sustainable Development: Five Years after the Earth Summit*. Geneva: World Health Organization

World Resources Institute (1999) *World Resources 1998–99*. Oxford: Oxford University Press

Chapter 3

Acheson, D et al (1998) *Independent Inquiry into Inequalities in Health Report*. London: The Stationery Office

Carey, S, Low, S, and Hansbro, J (1997) *Adult Literacy in Britain: A survey of adults aged 16–65 in Great Britain carried out by Social Survey Division of the Office of National Statistics*. London: The Stationery Office

Company of Parish Clerks (1604) 'London Bills of Mortality. London'. In: Brakenridge, W A, letter from the Reverend William Brakenridge, DD and FRS to George Lewis Scot, Esq, FRS, concerning the London Bills of Mortality. *Philosophical Transactions of the Royal Society*, London 1755, **48**: 788–800

DETR (1998a) *Index of Local Deprivation: Summary of results*. London: Department of the Environment, Transport and the Regions

DETR (1998b) *Modernising Local Government: Improving local services through Best Value*. London: Department of the Environment, Transport and the Regions

DETR (1999) *A Better Quality of Life: A strategy for sustainable development in the United Kingdom*. London: The Stationery Office

DHSS (1980) *Inequalities in Health: Report of a working group*. Black Report. London: Department of Health and Social Security

Department of Health (1990) *On the State of the Public Health 1990: The annual report of the Chief Medical Officer of the Department of Health for the year 1990*. London: The Stationery Office

Department of Social Security (1998) *Households Below Average Income 1979–1996/97*. London: Corporate Document Services

Department of Social Security (1999) *Opportunity for All*. London: The Stationery Office

Dobson, F/Department of Health (1997) 'Government takes action to reduce health inequalities: Frank Dobson, DoH: Press release in response to the Joseph Rowntree Publication *Death in Britain*'. London: Department of Health Press Release 97/192, 11 August

Dorling, D (2000) 'A mortality league table for Cabinet Ministers?' In: Pantazis, C and Gordon, D (eds) *Tackling Inequalities: Where are we now and what can be done?* Bristol: The Policy Press

Fletcher, J (1849) 'Moral and educational statistics of England and Wales'. *Journal of the Royal Statistical Society of London* **12**: 151–176; 189–335

Goodman, A and Webb, S (1994) *For Richer, For Poorer: the changing distribution of income in the United Kingdom 1961–91*. London: Institute of Fiscal Studies Commentary no 42

Gordon, D (2000) 'Inequalities in income, wealth and standard of living in Britain'. In: Pantazis, C and Gordon, D (eds) *Tackling Inequalities: Where are we now and what can be done?* Bristol: The Policy Press

Gordon, D et al (in press 2000) *Poverty and Social Exclusion Survey of Britain*

Healey, P (ed) (1992) *Rebuilding the City: Property-led urban regeneration*. London: E & FN Spon

Jacobson, J L (1993) 'Women's health: the price of poverty'. In: Koblinsky, M, Timyan, J and Gay, J (eds) *The Health of Women: A global perspective*. Boulder, San Francisco and Oxford: Westview Press and The National Council for International Health

Kelly, G and McCormick, J (1998) 'Private interests and public purposes: Exclusion and the private sector'. In: Oppenheim, C (ed) *An Inclusive Society: Strategies for tackling poverty*. London: IPPR

Lee, P, Murie, A and Gordon, D (1995) *Area measures of deprivation: A study of current methods and best practices in the identification of poor areas in Great Britain*. Birmingham: University of Birmingham, Centre for Urban and Regional Studies

Le Grand, J and Bartlett, W (eds) (1993) *Quasi Markets and Social Policy*. Basingstoke: Macmillan

Luxembourg Income Study 2000: http://www.zuma-mannheim.de/data/en/evs/lis.htm

Murie, A (2000) 'How can we end inequalities in housing?' In: Pantazis, C and Gordon, D (eds) *Tackling Inequalities: Where are we now and what can be done?* Bristol: The Policy Press, pp101–116

New Economics Foundation (1997) *More isn't always better: A special briefing on growth and quality of life in the UK*. London: New Economics Foundation/ Friends of the Earth

Office for National Statistics (1999) *Regional Trends*. London: The Stationery Office

PAT 3 (1999) *Enterprise and Social Exclusion*. London: The Treasury

PAT 7 (1999) *Unpopular Housing*. London: Department of the Environment, Transport and the Regions

PAT 13 (1999) *Improving Shopping Access for People Living in Deprived Areas*. London: Department of Health

PAT 14 (1999) *Access to Financial Services*. London: The Treasury

Power, A and Mumford, K (1999) *The Slow Death of Great Cities: Urban decline or urban renaissance?* York: YPS Press

Robson, B, Bradford, M, Deas, I, Hall, E, Harrison, E, Parkinson, M, Evans, R, Garside, P, Harding, A and Robinson, F (1994) *Assessing the Impact of Urban Policy*. London: Department of the Environment

Rubinstein, W D (1986) *Wealth and Inequality in Britain*. London: Faber and Faber

Saltow, L (1968) 'Long run changes in British income inequality'. *Economic History Review*, 2nd Series, 21

Shaw, M, Dorling, D, Gordon, D and Davey Smith, G (1999) *The Widening Gap: Health inequalities and policy in Britain*. Bristol: The Policy Press

Singh, S, Darroch, J E (2000) 'Adolescent Pregnancy and Childbearing: Levels and trends in developed countries'. *Family Planning Perspectives* **32**(1): 14–23

SEU (1998) *Bringing Britain Together: A national strategy for neighbourhood renewal*. London: Social Exclusion Unit

Townsend, P (1979) *Poverty in the UK: A survey of household resources and standards of living*. Berkeley, CA: University of Berkeley Press

Turok, I, Edge, N (1999) *The Jobs Gap in Britain's Cities: Employment loss and labour market consequences*. Bristol: The Policy Press

Turok, I (2000) 'Inequalities in employment: problems of spatial divergence'. In: Pantazis, C and Gordon, D (eds) *Tackling Inequalities: Where are we now and what can be done?* Bristol: The Policy Press, pp59–86

UNDP (1997) *Human Development Report 1997: Human Development to Eradicate Poverty*. New York: Oxford University Press

UNDP (1998) *Human Development Report 1998: Consumption for Human Development*. New York: Oxford University Press

UNDP (2000) *Human Development Report 2000. Human Rights and Human Development*. New York: Oxford University Press

Wedgwood, J (1929) *The Economics of Inheritance*. Harmondsworth: Penguin

Wilkinson, R G (1996) *Unhealthy Societies: The afflictions of inequality*. London: Routledge

Chapter 4

Acheson, D et al (1998) *Independent Inquiry into Inequalities in Health Report*. London: The Stationery Office

Department of Social Security (1999) *Opportunity for All*. London: The Stationery Office

Garnett, T (1999) *City Harvest: The Feasibility of Growing More Food in London*. London: Sustain

Leather, S (1996) *The Making of Modern Malnutrition*. London: The Caroline Walker Trust

Low Income Project Team for the Nutrition Task Force (1996) *Low Income, Food, Nutrition and Health: Strategies for improvement. A report by the Low Income Project Team for the Nutrition Task Force*. London: Department of Health

McGlone, P, Dobson, B, Dowler, E and Nelson, M (1999) *Food Projects and How They Work*. York: Joseph Rowntree Foundation

Orr, J (1937) 'Scotland as it might be'. In: Maclehose, A *The Scotland of Our Sons*. Edinburgh: W R Chambers

Oxfam (1995) *Food Fight: Community Action to Build Local and Global Food Security*. Canada: Oxfam

Riches, G (ed) (1997) *First World Hunger: Food Security and Welfare Politics*. Basingstoke: Macmillan Press

Ross, S, Lean, M and Anderson, A (1999) 'Review of Dietary Interventions in Finland, Norway and Sweden'. Glasgow: Department of Human Nutrition, University of Glasgow

Scottish Home and Health Department (1993) *Scotland's Health, A Challenge To Us All: The Scottish Diet. Report of a working party to the Chief Medical Officer*. Edinburgh: Scottish Home and Health Department

Webster, J and Hawkes, C (2000) *Too Much and too Little? Debates on surplus food distribution*. London: Sustain

Chapter 5

Bate, R (1999) *A Guide to Land Use and Housing*. York: Joseph Rowntree Foundation

Boardman, B, Bullock, S and McLaren, D (1999) *Equity and the Environment: Guidelines for green and socially just government*. London: Catalyst/Friends of the Earth

Department of the Environment (1996) *English House Condition Survey 1991, Energy Report*. London: HMSO

DETR (1999) *Energy Sense Information Pack*. London: Department of the Environment, Transport and the Regions

DETR (1998) Analysis of the Responses to the UK Government's Consultation Paper on Sustainable Construction. http://www.environment.detr.gov.uk/sustainable/construction/consult/response/3.htm#2.2

DETR (1999) *Fuel Poverty: The New HEES*. London: Department of the Environment, Transport and the Regions

DETR/DSS (2000) *Quality and Choice: A decent home for all. The housing green paper*. London: Department of the Environment, Transport and the Regions

Environmental Audit Committee (1999) *Environmental Audit Committee. Seventh Report: Energy Efficiency. Summary of conclusions and recommendations*. London: The Stationery Office

DETR (2000) Housing Statistics Summary No 3, 1999: 1998/99 Survey of English Housing: Preliminary Results and Definitions: http://www.housing.detr.gov.uk/research/hss/003/01.htm

Green, H, Deacon, K, Iles, N and Down, D (1997) *Housing in England 1995/6. A report of the 1995/6 Survey of English Housing carried out by the Social Survey Division of the Office of National Statistics on behalf of the Department of the Environment*. London: The Stationery Office

Gwilliam, M, Bourne, C, Swain, C, Prat, A (1998) *Sustainable Renewal of Suburban Areas*. York: Joseph Rowntree Foundation

Haungton, G and Hunter, C (1994) *Sustainable Cities*. London: Regional Studies Association

Llewelyn-Davies and University of Westminster (2000) *Conversion and Development: Process and Potential*. London: Department of the Environment, Transport and the Regions

Wilkinson, P, et al (in press) *Housing and excess winter death from cardiovascular disease in England, 1986–1996*

WCED (1987) *Our Common Future: The Report of the World Commission on Environment and Development*. Oxford: Oxford University Press, 1987

Chapter 6

Arthur, S, Corden, A, Green, A, Lewis, J, Loumidis, J, Sainsbury, R, Stafford, B, Thornton, P and Walker, R (1999) 'New Deal for Disabled People: Early Implementation'. Research Report 106, DSS Research Report Summaries

Atkinson, J (1999) 'The New Deal for Young Unemployed People: A Summary of Progress'. Institute of Employment Studies/Employment Service, ESR13, March

Barrell, R and Genre, V (1999) *Employment Strategies for Europe: Lessons from Denmark and the Netherlands*. NIESR, April

Buchele, R and Christiansen, J (1998) 'Do Employment and Income Security Cause Unemployment? A Comparative Study of the US and the E-4', *Cambridge Journal of Economics*, January

Burchell, B, Day, D, Hudson, M, Ladipo, D, Mankelow, R, Nolan, J, Reed, H, Wishert, I and Wilkinson, W (1999) *Job Insecurity and Work Intensification: Flexibility and the Changing Boundaries of Work*. York: York Publishing Services

Casey, B, Keep, E and Mayhew, K (1999) *Flexibility, Quality and Competiveness*. NIESR, April

Deve, F, Inglis, S, Moss, P and Petrie, P (1998) 'State of the Art Review on the Reconciliation of Work and Family Life for Men and Women and the Quality of Care Services'. *Research Briefs*, Research Report No 44. London: DfEE

DSS (1998) *A New Contract for Welfare: The Gateway to Work. Cm 4102*. London: DSS

The Economist (1999) 'Employment Minimum Losses', *The Economist*, April

Edwards, P and Gilman, M (1999) 'Pay Equity and the Minimum Wage: What can theories tell us?' *Human Resource Management Journal* 9(1): 20–38

Hasluck, C (1999) *Employers, Young People and the Unemployed: A review of the research*. Institute of Employment Studies/Employment Service

Kitching, J (1999) 'The National Minimum Wage: Helping small firms to cope'. *International Small Business Journal* 17(3) 91–94

Kozak, M (1998) 'Employment, Family Life and the Quality of Care Services: A review of research in the UK'. *Research Briefs*, Research Report No 54. London: DfEE

Machin, S and Manning, A (1997) 'Minimum Wages and Economic Outcomes in Europe'. *European Economic Review* 41: 3–5; 734–742

McKay, S and Middleton, S (1998) 'Characteristics of Older Workers: Secondary analysis of the family and working lives survey'. *Research Briefs*, Research Report No 45. London: DfEE

Morgan, O (2000) 'Drop-out crisis hits New Deal for jobless'. *The Observer*, April 2, p5

MORI (1998) 'The Effect of JSA on 16/17 Year Olds: Follow-up survey report'. *Research Briefs*, Research Report No 50. London: DfEE

NACAB (1997) *Flexibility Abused: A NACAB report on employment conditions in the labour market*. London: National Association of Citizens Advice Bureaux, 1997

OECD (1997) *Labour Market Policies: New Challenges: Policies for Low-Paid Workers and Unskilled Job Seekers: Meeting of the Employment, Labour and Social Affairs Committee at Ministerial Level held at the Chateau de la Muette, Paris*. OECD/GD (97) 160. Paris: Organisation for Economic Co-operation and Development

Office for National Statistics (1999) *Social Trends* 29. London: The Stationery Office

Payne, J, Payne, C, Lissenburgh, S and Range, M (1999) 'Work-based Training and Job Prospects for the Unemployed: An evaluation of training for work'. *Research Briefs*, Research Report No 96. London: DfEE/Policy Studies Institute

Rajan, A, van Eupon, P, Chapple, K and Lane, D (1999) *Employability: Bridging the Gap Between Rhetoric and Reality, First Report: Employers' Perspective*. Tonbridge, Centre for Research in Employment and Technology in Europe

Rix, A, Davies, K, Gaunt, R, Hare, A and Cobbold, S (1999) 'The Training and Development of Flexible Workers'. *Research Briefs*, Research Report No 118, DfEE August: http://www.dfee.gov.uk/research/report118.htm

Shropshire, J, Warton, R and Walker, R (1999) 'Unemployment and Jobseeking: Specific groups and their experiences'. *Research Briefs*, Research Report No 102–106. London: DfEE

Skills and Enterprise Network (1999) *Skills and Enterprise Executive*. Skills and Enterprise Network, 4 November

Stone, V, Cotton, D and Thomas, A (2000) 'Mapping Troubled Lives: Young people in education, employment or training'. *Research Briefs*, Research Report No 181. London: DfEE

TUC (1998) *New Deal: An occasional briefing*. London: TUC, April

Vickery, G and Wurtzburg, G (1996) Flexible Firms, Skills and Employment. *OECD Observer*, October/November, p202

Vincent, J (1998) 'Jobseeker's Allowance Evaluation: Qualitative Research on Disallowed and Sanctioned Claimants'. *Research Briefs*, Research Report No 86. London: Centre for Research in Social Policy/DfEE

Watson, A, Owen, G, Aubrey, J and Ellis, B (1998) 'Integrating Disabled Employees: Case studies of 40 employers'. *Research Briefs*, Research Report No 56. London: DfEE

Chapter 7

Acheson, D et al (1998) *Independent Inquiry into Inequalities in Health Report*. London: The Stationery Office

Boyle, A (1998) 'The role of international human rights law in the protection of the environment'. In: Boyle, A and Anderson, M (eds) *Human Rights Approaches to Environmental Protection*. London: Clarendon Press, Chapter 3

Carley, M and Spapens, P (1998) *Sharing the World: Sustainable Living and Global Equity in the 21st Century*. London: Earthscan

Jowell, R et al (1999) *British Social Attitudes: The 16th Report: Who shares New Labour values?* Aldershot: Ashgate

New Economics Foundation (1997) *Participation Works: 21 Techniques of Community Participation for the 21st Century*. London: New Economics Foundation

Partnerships in Participation (1999) *Participation: Warwickshire's Papers*, Issue 1, spring

Porter, S and Raistrick, P (1998) *The Impact of Out-of-centre Superstores on Local Retail Employment*. London: The National Retail Planning Forum

UNECE (1999) *Convention on Access to Information, Public Participation in Decision Making and Access to Justice in Environmental Matters*. Geneva: United Nations Economic Commission for Europe

Appendix 1

Department of Health/Welsh Office/National Health Service in Scotland/Department of Health and Social Services, Northern Ireland (1999) In: *Social Trends* 29. London: The Stationery Office

DETR (1998) *National Road Traffic Survey 1998*. London: Department of the Environment, Transport and the Regions

DETR (1999) In: *Regional Trends* 34. London: Office for National Statistics

DETR/Royal Ulster Constabulary (1999) In: *Regional Trends* 34. London: Office for National Statistics

Environment Agency (1999) 'Regional coastal bathing water compliance, 1999': http://www.environment-agency.gov.uk/s-enviro/viewpoints/3compliance/5bathing/3-5b.html

Environment Agency/Department of the Environment, Northern Ireland (1999) In: *Regional Trends* 34. London: Office for National Statistics

Environment Agency/Scottish Environment Protection Agency/Department of the Environment, Northern Ireland (1999) In: *Regional Trends* 34. London: Office for National Statistics

The Forestry Commission/Department of the Environment, Northern Ireland (1999) In: *Regional Trends* 34. London: Office for National Statistics

National Centre for Social Research (1997) *British Social Attitudes Survey 1997*. London: National Centre for Social Research

National Environmental Technology Centre (1999) In: *Regional Trends* 34. London: Office for National Statistics

Northern Ireland Statistics and Research Agency (1996) *Continuous Household Survey 1996*. Northern Ireland Statistics and Research Agency

Northern Ireland Statistics and Research Agency (1997) *Continuous Household Survey 1997.* Northern Ireland Statistics and Research Agency

ONS (1996) *1996 General Household Survey.* London: Office for National Statistics

ONS (1999) *1998 General Household Survey.* London: Office for National Statistics

Social and Community Planning Research (1997) *British Social Attitudes Survey 1997.* London: National Centre for Social Research

Appendix 2

DETR/National Assembly for Wales/Scottish Executive/Department of the Environment, Northern Ireland (1999) In: *Regional Trends* 34. London: Office for National Statistics

DSS (1998) *Family Resources Survey 1997/98.* London: Department of Social Security

Eurostat (1995) *European Community Household Panel Survey.* Eurostat

Northern Ireland Statistics and Research Agency (1997) *Continuous Household Survey 1997.* Northern Ireland Statistics and Research Agency

ONS (1999) In: *Regional Trends* 34. London: Office for National Statistics

ONS/Department of Economic Development, Northern Ireland (1999) 'Labour Force Survey 1998'. *Regional Trends* 34. London: Office for National Statistics

ONS/Northern Ireland Statistics and Research Agency (1998) *Family Expenditure Survey 1998.* London: Office for National Statistics

Appendix 3

DETR (1999) 'Survey of English Housing'. *Regional Trends* 34. London: Office for National Statistics

Home Office (2000) 'British Crime Survey'. *Regional Trends* 34. London: Office for National Statistics

Home Office/Scottish Executive/Royal Ulster Constabulary (1999) In: *Regional Trends* 34. London: Office for National Statistics

ICM/*The Guardian* (1999) poll, December

Northern Ireland Office (2000) 'Northern Ireland Crime Survey'. *Regional Trends* 34. London: Office for National Statistics

Royal Ulster Constabulary (2000) In: *Regional Trends* 34. London: Office for National Statistics

Scottish Executive (2000) 'Scottish Crime Survey'. *Regional Trends* 34. London: Office for National Statistics

Appendix 4

Carey, S, Bridgewood, A, Thomas, M and Avila, P (2000) *Measuring Adult Literacy: The international adult literacy survey in the European context.* London: Office for National Statistics

Carey, S, Low, S and Hansbro, J (1997) *Adult Literacy in Britain: A survey of adults aged 16–65 in Great Britain carried out by Social Survey Division of ONS.* London: The Stationery Office

Gordon, D (1995) 'Census Based Deprivation Indices: Their weighting and validation'. *Journal of Epidemiology and Community Health* 49(suppl 2): S39–S44

Gordon, D and Forrest, R (1995) *People and Places Volume II: Social and Economic Distinctions in England – A 1991 Census Atlas.* Bristol: SAUS/Statistical Monitoring Unit

Gordon, D and Loughran, F (1997) 'Child Poverty and Needs Based Budget Allocation'. *Research, Policy and Planning* 15(3): 28–38

House of Commons (1996) *New Unemployment Rates for Parliamentary Constituencies*, Research Paper 96/63. London: House of Commons Library

Shaw, M, Dorling, D, Gordon, D and Davey Smith, G (1999) *The Widening Gap: Health inequalities and policy in Britain.* Bristol: The Policy Press

Twigger, R and Presland, A (1996) Unemployment by Constituency: Revised rates, Research Paper 00/29, 15 March. London: House of Commons Library

UNDP (1998) *Human Development Report 1998: Consumption for Human Development.* New York: Oxford University Press

UNDP (2000) *Human Development Report 2000: Human Rights and Human Development.* New York: Oxford University Press

Index